THE WRITE

366 EXERCISES TO FULFILL YOUR DAILY WRITING LIFE

2nd Edition

By Robert Yehling
Compiled by Melissa Jenkins

Robert Yehling has written a collection of 366 writing exercises designed to help people of all ages put pen and paper into a lived experience. He guides you through various opportunities to explore aspects of yourself through daily experiences, nature, your personality, your character, and your soul. Each time you sit down to write you will be encouraged to expand your awareness of your environment and your place in it.

You will find concrete and esoteric aspects to your writing that enable you to write your way into an experience. In so doing, you will be able to connect to the world around you through reflective observation. Bob challenges you to see through your eyes what cannot often be seen with them. Here, you will find yourself deepening your respect for the life you view outside yourself and what is held sacred within you.

…If you are a writer professionally or simply love to journal, you must read and utilize this work of art in your daily contemplations.

Sam Oliver, Cleveland Book Review
Author of *The Path into Healing*

Open Books
PRESS

Published by

Bloomington, Indiana
(812) 837-9226
info@PenandPublish.com
www.PenandPublish.com

ISBN: 978-1-941799-20-8

This book is printed on acid free paper.

Printed in the USA

THE WRITE TIME: 366 EXERCISES TO FULFILL YOUR DAILY WRITING LIFE

Contents

FOREWORD

I had the absolute pleasure of meeting Robert Yehling (digitally) during my first year of teaching Advanced Placement Literature and Composition. Knowing how much of my students' test would be comprised of poetry, I felt the heavy burden of responsibility to prepare these students to face verse obstacles, to equip them with the necessary skills to meet poetry on the AP battlefield and to walk away unscathed. Most of my students had very little exposure to poetry before this class, so we set out on a journey to learn as many different forms and genres of poetry as we could when I stumbled across Mr. Yehling's poem "A Marriage Rises from the Ashes" on the *amazing* website he helped develop, *Poetry Through the Ages*.

Fascinated by his work, and equally by his vast wealth of knowledge, my AP class reached out to Mr. Yehling, and several weeks later we found ourselves face-to-face with our poet on a class-sponsored "Skype With the Author" event. An academic friendship was born that evening, but little did I know that Yehling's influence on me as a writer, reader, and teacher of poetry was just beginning.

Through ongoing discussions with Robert Yehling, I had my high school purchase copies of the first edition of the book you hold in your hands now. With the pun only slightly intended, *The Write Time* came at just the right time for me. Literally. For the first time in our school's history, we had enough students to justify one section of Poetry, a class that has always been on our curriculum roster but had never been taught until the Fall semester of 2015.

Ecstatic and completely overwhelmed by the task of building this class by myself, from the ground up, *The Write Time* arrived in the mail. I already knew the great things that Robert Yehling was capable of; what I did not know, at least not fully, was how rich this resource was going to be. I was, and still am, utterly astounded by the breadth, the scope, of this book. The subtitle promises to provide "366 exercises to fulfill your daily writing life," and that is so far from an overstatement.

What *The Write Time* does not provide, however, is an over-simplified, laundry-list of "journal prompts." It offers so much more. *The Write Time* is instructive in its daily assignments, possessing the potential to teach you *while* encouraging your pen to glide across the paper; it's engaging, offering thought-provoking opportunities to push your writing in ways you most certainly would not push your writing on your own; it's overflowing with supplemental tidbits (such as astrological signs, famous birthdays, inspiring quotes, and featured website/blog information) that spur on the inspired writer; and, most importantly, it serves as a invocation to come sit at the shore of new creativity, take up your ink-cup, drink plentifully, and be refreshed by the waters of a new day, all *intentionally* assembled by a fellow writer, reader and lover of literature.

At Yehling's invitation through *The Write Time*, my students have interpreted their dreams, learned about *and* written parallel constructions, and so much more. From "Point of View Workshops" to "Storycrafting" exercises, "Cross-training" to "Self-Cultivation," this resource truly has it all. It is multifaceted on so many levels, likening itself more to a comprehensive curriculum than just another "writing book."

Robert Yehling's love, passion, time, and effort is evinced in every single page. I saw it right away, and every time I hand the book to a student on "pick-a-prompt" days, they see it, too. It has settled into the foundation of my Creative Writing and Poetry curriculum, and I highly recommend it to anyone who finds him/herself at sea, navigating the waters of teaching writing of all kinds to young minds of equal variance.

The Write Time can be your compass, whether you are the writer or the teacher. Take the year-long journey that is plotted in these pages, give yourself over to its process, and behold the inevitable transformation. As you open this book for the first time, I am excited for you. I was once where you were, and it is a thrilling precipice.

Write on!
Andres Torres
Minooka Community High School

DEDICATION

For two schoolteachers who nurtured and fully supported (or, at times, *tolerated*) my writing, music and drawing habits: my grandmother, Gratia Stedman Bellizia (1915-1996); and my mother, Heidi Yehling (1938-2008). Their legacy of touching young lives through heart-centered teaching continues through my Aunt Janet, cousin Jennifer, daughter Jessica, and myself.

ABOUT *THE WRITE TIME*

"If we say that only certain people can write, then we're left with less."

— Sapphire, author, *Push*

A 94-year-old great-great grandmother and an 11-year-old poet started talking. The grandmother shared how she and her parents used to ride into the town nearest their Kentucky farm in a horse and buggy. The 11-year-old couldn't believe it.

"Soooo... how did you get somewhere you needed to go, like, *quickly?*"

"We didn't. You got there as fast as the horses got you there."

"No cars? TVs? *Texting?*"

The grandmother laughed, her eyes shining with compassion and a dash of mystery.

The young poet was intrigued. "What kinds of other things did you do?"

"You'll have to read my stories when I'm done writing them, honey."

This is a favorite exchange from my writing workshops. It illustrates how each of us has stories to tell, and it's never too late to get started. Or too early. Stories provide a liberating way to share our experiences, imagination and vision with others. Writing conveys our deepest feelings, greatest ideas and loftiest aspirations. We can produce them in the privacy of our hearts, souls and minds — or, if we so desire, in the public forum of publishing for countless readers to enjoy.

Our words can change our minds, hearts, communities, societies, political institutions and world. Our stories can prompt readers to explore aspects of their lives or, in the case of fiction, to find entertainment, enlightenment and fulfillment. Our works can define our views, missions and purposes to a very (Internet) connected world, while amplifying how we feel about ourselves and others, and what creates significance and fulfills purpose. Our creativity can be contagious, habit-forming. The sum of our work can (and will) reflect back to us every time someone says, "I really like what you read tonight," or "Your essay changed my life." Or, my favorite: "I want to write everything that's pouring through me."

A question often arises in my workshops: "Which forms or genres do I focus on?" If you're already a professional writer, or someone who knows your form(s) and genre(s), then seek greater depth and proficiency. If you're still searching for your ideal expression, then try to write about everything, and experiment with every form. What do you like? Dislike?

What stretches your brain to its intellectual capacity — and forces you to expand?

What gives rhythm, texture, structure and meaning to the feelings, thoughts or stories brewing in your heart and mind?

What *excites* you, causes you to hit the pillow for an adventurous night of dreaming — followed by a potentially electrifying day of writing?

What grabs you so completely that you eat-drink-think-sleep your work?

What absolutely *has to be written?* How will you write it?

I believe that we serve ourselves best by experimenting until we find our best means of communicating. You'll know when that happens, if it hasn't already; the realization feels like being catapulted into a warm cloud. It's an "a-ha!" feeling. Run with it. Many people will find that one particular genre suits them best; others will learn that they can switch back and forth seamlessly between genres. They prefer a variety of creative channels to express themselves, working in a state of perpetual diversity.

I belong to the latter club. I sway constantly between fiction, essay, poetry, and narrative non-fiction. This penchant for variety comes from constant experimentation with the written word since I was in kindergarten. To their enormous credit, my first newspaper editors did not pigeonhole me as a sportswriter. They fed my desire to write about everything. This led to a lifetime of travels, adventures, events, credits, friends and experiences I would not trade for any financial treasure. Those first editors, Bill Missett and Steve Scholfield, also taught me two cardinal rules of writing, in any form: *Get the details right.* And, *be truthful.* Even in fiction. As Stephen King says, "Fiction is a lie. Good fiction is *the truth within the lie.* (my emphasis)"

"*The minute I decided I was going to be a writer…that's how I defined myself. I was a writer. From the start. I wrote every night. And every weekend.*"

I'd love to take credit for writing this, but I can't. It comes from Peter Carey's book *Oscar and Lucinda.* However, I have lived by this mantra since the autumn day in 1964, during kindergarten at Magnolia School in Carlsbad, Calif., when our teacher, Mrs. Price, told us to write our names.

I wrote a story. It led to another story. And another. My mother's decision to read to me nightly from birth, which led to my ability to read at age four, has paid off since.

Subsequently, I spent seven years as a newspaper reporter and editor, 15 years as a magazine editorial director and associate publisher, and nearly 15 years of owning a writing services business. This includes a decade of writing and editing books, and teaching writing workshops in the United States and Europe.

In 1999, I was asked to give presentations about my career, and to share some exercises I'd developed for my own use. Soon, students grew interested. More and more teens and young adults trickled into my adult workshops, eager to write, explore and express themselves. Their ideas, voices, growing self-confidence and sheer enthusiasm to *write* electrifies every room — and I'm the first person cheering them on, because they are the future. I was once there — 16, scared about approaching adult life, a bit over my head as a reporter for a daily newspaper, but knowing that *I was a writer for life.*

Diversify…Desire…Express. This is the three-pronged departure point for *The Write Time*. We meet at the intersection of two boulevards: everything you've ever wanted to write (and have yet to think up or imagine); and every conceivable way in which you can write and communicate it. I've condensed more than 30 years of experience into 366 exercises that apply to every form and nearly every genre. Some are designed to ignite and keep your inner writing lamp aflame. Others are more advanced, pertaining to specific characters and plot situations, writing crisp transitions, or digging out the most exquisite detail that revealed itself to *you* to share through your pen.

The Write Time promotes creativity, tenacity, technique, voice, inspiration, enthusiasm, motivation, zest for learning and experimentation — the nine qualities great writers have in common. The one-a-day approach reminds us that great writers pursue their craft daily, no matter what. They write. Experiment. Explore. Discover. Create. Refine. Polish. Dig, deeply. They work until they find the ideal way to convey what they see, think and feel. "My goal every day is to produce one perfect sentence," said Ernest Hemingway, who generated enough perfect sentences to become a 20th century literary giant.

This book is interactive. Some of the daily quoted authors are still living; others are deceased. Their books will live forever. I've listed their most famous and/or more recent works. For more, I present one of the best collections of author birthdays yet committed to print. Read or explore their bodies of work as well. Always expand your reading base. *The Write Time* also lists more than 120 featured websites and blogs — one for every three days. These cover the gamut of the profession and craft. Included are prompt sites, Web-based radio shows, social networking sites with literary components, reference and research resources, tools and techniques, online writers' forums and communities, and editing, marketing and publishing services. I selected the sites based on relevance and quality — with no commercial strings attached. Visit them.

Extend your *Write Time* experience by visiting our official site, www.thewritetimecompanion.com. You'll find a calendar of upcoming events and additional exercises, along with posted examples of writing from the exercises and prompts in the book.

If you're a professional writer seeking to sharpen your craft or switch genres — from journalism to fiction, for example — this book will help you reach the next level. I have included plenty of exercises on self-editing, the importance of which cannot be overstated in this tough seller's market. Word to the wise: Polish and perfect *before* you mail or e-mail the manuscript.

Most of all (my dual personality as a track and cross-country coach is speaking now), I hope you will write daily, experiment often, create constantly, and dedicate yourself to continuous intellectual, emotional, creative and spiritual fulfillment. Use *The Write Time* as a resource to improve and master your craft and voice. Create an audience, whether family and friends or something much larger, or expand your existing audience. Share your stories, poems, books, essays and songs with them. You may achieve commercial success; you may not. You may already have books on the shelves or online.

Regardless, write every day. Give yourself this ageless gift.

Start now. If you don't already have a journal, buy one. Write your lives, feelings, circumstances and stories. Avoid the dire comment made by *Roots* author Alex Haley: "Every death is like the burning of a library."

Let's embark on a wonderful lifetime of writing.

Robert Yehling
Fall 2015

JANUARY 1
New Year's Day
MAKE EACH DAY YOUR WRITING PROCESS

Today is the day for New Year's Resolutions, so let's create one: *I will make each day part of my writing process.* Form a new series of routines. Read books, magazines and writers you wouldn't ordinarily touch. Research a subject about which you'd like to write. Take notes of experiences, events and people that strike you as fascinating, bizarre, impressive or otherwise extraordinary. Write about how your writing process works, where you would like it to proceed, and what you would accomplish if you practiced your ideal writing process.

"All our knowledge has its origin in our perceptions."
— Leonardo da Vinci, artist-scientist-author

SELF-PROMPTS:

Signs:
Capricorn • Goose • Birch
Featured Website/Blog:
http://www.writerstudio.com

SELF-PROMPTS:

Signs:
Capricorn • Goose • Birch
Birthdays:
Isaac Asimov (b. 1920)
Jimmy Santiago Baca (b. 1952)
Featured Website/Blog:
http://www.writerstudio.com

JANUARY 2
TURNING A NEW PAGE

In your journal, write a detailed answer to this question: *What will I accomplish this year with my writing?* Maybe you will write a book, play or story. Maybe you will compose a poem, song or essay for the first time. Perhaps you will take a trip to a famous literary landscape, and create a travel journal. How will the experience provide growth in your life? What type of story or book, or series of articles, could come from this trip? Revisit this page as you move through the year.

"Life hides many things until the time is right."

— Anna Lee Waldo, author, *Sacajawea*

SELF-PROMPTS:

Signs:
Capricorn • Goose • Birch
Birthdays:
J.R.R. Tolkien (b. 1892)
Carolyn Haywood (b. 1898)
Patricia Lee Gauch (b. 1934)
Featured Website/Blog:
http://www.thefirstline.com

JANUARY 3
THE FIRST LINE: Movement

The first line of a song, story, poem, essay or letter establishes direction, intent, tone and identity. It opens the door for all that follows. For many, though, it is the most difficult line to write; many great ideas never see daylight because of it.

Let's change that outcome. Start by writing a short journal entry, essay, vignette, or a short-short story. Don't worry about the first line being perfect—just write a first line. Now go through each of the paragraphs of your piece, and polish up the first line—the topic sentence. Collect all of the first lines, and bring them together. Well-written first lines often create a thumbnail of the story when combined.

"The writer's obligation is to give every character the best lines. Every character."

— Stanley Elkin, author, *The MacGuffin*

JANUARY 4
THE FIRST LINE: Polishing Act

Reach into your bookshelf and grab twenty novels or creative non-fiction books (essays, memoirs, travelogues, well-storied food books). Read the first line of each, studying and feeling the rhythm and where it leads you. Return to your work, and sharpen up your first line to convey the direction, intent, tone and identity of *your* story. Invite readers to enter.

Signs:
Capricorn • Goose • Birch
Birthdays:
Jakob Grimm (b. 1785)
Phyllis Naylor (b. 1933)
Doris Kearns Goodwin (b. 1943)
Featured Website/Blog:
http://www.thefirstline.com

"A word is the quintessential symbol. Its power comes from the fact that every member of a linguistic community uses it interchangeably in writing, speaking and understanding."
　　　　　　　　　—Stephen Pinker, author, *The Language Instinct*

JANUARY 5
SOMETHING NEW

Write a 100 to 200-word vignette about a person, event, observation or occurrence entirely new in your life. See if you can identify something that you never saw or experienced before, to the best of your memory and knowledge. When you write, feel the wonder! The discovery! Your sense of presence! Approach this moment with the eager anticipation of a child making a new discovery. Repeat whenever your writing feels stale or fallow. Take time to read your entries, and see how these experiences *renew* your life.

Signs:
Capricorn • Goose • Birch
Birthdays:
Lynn Cherry (b. 1952)
Featured Website/Blog:
http://366writing.wordpress.com

"As I write I create myself again and again."
　　　　　　　　　—Joy Harjo, poet, author, *The Native Americans*

SELF-PROMPTS:

JANUARY 6
BRAINSTORMING

Winter reminds us of the need to warm up. Our blood needs a few more minutes to circulate; perhaps we require an extra cup of coffee or tea. If we live in colder climes, we must start our cars and trucks a few minutes before driving, to avoid damaging the engine.

Likewise, good writing requires a good warm-up. For the next 20 minutes, open your journal or a notepad and mind-dump. Clear your head. Write down your most immediate thoughts, feelings and concerns (or joys). If an idea pops up in your mind, or the memory of a recent museum exhibit or music concert, write about it. Find precise words to capture the energy of the experience.

When you're finished with this *timed* writing, proceed directly to the work you plan to do today. Use the clearing power of brainstorming to move with authority into your day. Don't forget the hidden benefit of this exercise: within a good brainstorm often lies the nugget for a future piece of writing!

"Use self-exploration as a way to pay attention to the world, within and outside your self, and dive into writing to learn what you truly think and who you truly are."

— Allen Ginsberg, poet, author, *Howl*

Signs:
Capricorn • Goose • Birch
Birthdays:
Carl Sandburg (b. 1878)
Kahlil Gibran (b. 1883)
Wright Morris (b. 1910)
E.L. Doctorow (b. 1931)
Featured Website/Blog:
http://366writing.wordpress.com

SELF-PROMPTS:

JANUARY 7
THE SPIRIT OF ME

What is your spirit like? What feeds you, motivates you, seizes you and propels you to reach higher, dive deeper and stretch for the sun and stars? What touches every cell and fiber of your being?

Identify these objects, feelings and qualities—they clothe your essential self. Describe and embrace your spirit by dialoguing with it, or writing a letter to it. If necessary, give your spirit a name. Ask what it needs from you. See how it influences your movements, and identify where it is taking you within your creative, spiritual, emotional or intellectual self. Write the journey into which you and your spirit are walking, hand-in-hand.

"The heart of the atom, the heart of the word, blazes with pure spirit. It's all material and it's all spiritual."

— George Leonard, educator, author, *The Silent Pulse*

Signs:
Capricorn • Goose • Birch
Birthdays:
Eleanor Clymer (b. 1906)
Robert Duncan (b. 1919)
Featured Website/Blog:
http://www.absolutewrite.com

JANUARY 8
MOMENTS IN MONTAGE: First Movement

Montage ties together many perspectives, angles and views of the same subject, sometimes within the same moment. A prime example is the shower scene of *Psycho,* in which editor George Tomasini and director Alfred Hitchcock created 45 seconds of cinematic legend by piecing together 70 separate shots.

If we can write montage, we can maneuver through any scene we conceive. Think of a recent experience that involved a number of people, such as shopping in a busy boutique or skiing down a crowded slope. Visualize the scene, and then imagine it from another's eyes. Go to another person, and another. Why were they there? What was their motivation? How did they act? What did they do?

Take four sentences or less—a short paragraph—to answer these questions for each person. Capture their moment, and move on. See if you follow this thread with eight or ten people. Add a conclusive observation.

"We make our lives bigger or smaller, more expansive or more limited, according to the interpretation of life that is our story."

— Christina Baldwin, author, *Storycatcher*

Signs:
Capricorn • Goose • Birch
Birthdays:
Peter M.H. Taylor (b. 1917)
Stephen Manes (b. 1949)
Featured Website/Blog:
http://www.absolutewrite.com

JANUARY 9
MOMENTS IN MONTAGE: Second Movement

For a more advanced variation of montage writing, review the vignettes you wrote yesterday. As you move from one vignette to the next, see if you can insert a sentence or phrase that ties one person to another by action, gesture, comment, relation or motive. Create further inter-relationship between the people in your scene. Mix up your presentation: make obvious connections in some montages, more subtle ties in others. When you're finished, edit your piece to a fine shine.

"The real voyage of discovery is not in seeking new places, but in seeing with new eyes."

— Marcel Proust, author, *Swann's Way*

Signs:
Capricorn • Goose • Birch
Birthdays:
Clyde Robert Bulla (b. 1914)
Joan Baez (b. 1941)
Featured Website/Blog:
http://www.stonethread.com

SELF-PROMPTS:

JANUARY 10
MAGIC, INNOCENCE AND WONDER

Richard Paul Evans, author of *The Christmas Box,* speaks often about magic, innocence and wonder, the three prevalent qualities of a child's soul. If we combine magic, innocence and wonder, our works will resonate with readers—because they, too, crave these qualities, consciously or subconsciously. It is never too late to find the magic in a moment of observation, the innocence in a smile or flick of the eye, or the wonderment in a painting or witnessing of a great feat.

Write a story or vignette that focuses on magic, innocence and/or wonder—whether in an experience you had, one you'd like to have, or a character you created. Feel the *openness* and *power* rising from within. Try to compose a piece so imbued with these qualities that it carries you away. See if you can include magic, innocence and/or wonder in everything you write.

Signs:
Capricorn • Goose • Birch
Birthdays:
Remy Charlip (b. 1929)
Featured Website/Blog:
http://www.stonethread.com

"Creativity is a shapechanger. One moment it takes this form, the next that. It is like a dazzling spirit who appears to us all, yet is hard to describe for no one agrees on what they saw in that brilliant flash."
— Clarissa Pinkola Estes, author, *Women Who Run with the Wolves*

SELF-PROMPTS:

JANUARY 11
PICTURE YOUR MEMORY... IN WORDS

When we turn back to a childhood or adolescent memory—or even something that happened five or ten years ago—rarely does it flow as a smooth stream. Rather, our mind flashes it together in pieces, images… visual ellipses. For example, take an early childhood memory, its connective tissue eroded by more than forty years: *Kids dance on TV… dance-along, hop along … dance through the living room… hand crashes through glass door… blood squirting from my thumb in the sink.*

Take an event in your life from long enough ago that you don't remember every detail. Use ellipses to string together the images. Portray the event exactly as your mind feeds it to you. Write a story from the images you have recalled. See if you can fill in more blanks while writing the narrative.

Signs:
Capricorn • Goose • Birch
Birthdays:
Robert C. O'Brien (b. 1918)
Mary Rodgers (b. 1931)
Featured Website/Blog:
http://www.writingitreal.com

"To be nobody but yourself—in a world which is doing its best, night and day, to make you everybody else—means to fight the hardest battle which any human being can fight; and never stop fighting."
— e.e. cummings, poet, author, *The Enormous Room*

JANUARY 12
UNFORGETTABLE EXPERIENCES

SELF-PROMPTS:

Make a list of the 10 most unforgettable experiences in your life—positive or negative. Re-live each experience by going into the middle of the moment, and use dialogue, narrative, observation and characterization to write through the moment. Tell your story. When finished, note how (or if) your perspective has changed since the experience first occurred.

"There is only one history of importance and it is the history of what you once believed and the history of what you came to believe in."
— Kay Boyle, educator- author, *Generation Without Farewell*

Signs:
Capricorn • Goose • Birch
Birthdays:
Charles Perrault (b. 1628)
Jack London (b. 1876)
Featured Website/Blog:
http://www.writingitreal.com

JANUARY 13
WRITING THE HEART

SELF-PROMPTS:

Nothing connects readers to your words faster than showing how you and/or your characters feel, emotionally act and respond. Heartfelt emotions are present, immediate, and a portal through which the reader can relate the story to her/his own feelings. They are universal.

Look inside your heart, and call upon every emotion you're feeling *right now*. What caused/is causing the emotion? How is it affecting your feelings? Does it trigger deeper feelings, unresolved issues, or greater hopes?

Take one emotion and write it out; follow the string to its end. When you're finished, grab the next emotion and do the same. Master the writing of your own heart—then transfer it to your characters and subjects. Writing the heart enlivens characters. It makes stories.

"The way for me is the middle path, the organic, the heart, the hinge that all hinges on."
— Mary Caroline Richards, sculptor-poet-author, *Centering*

Signs:
Capricorn • Goose • Birch
Birthdays:
Horatio Alger (b. 1832)
Igor Gouzenko (b.1919)
Micheal Bond (b. 1926)
Featured Website/Blog:
http://www.writing.com

Signs:
Capricorn • Goose • Birch
Birthdays:
John dos Passos (b. 1896)
Featured Website/Blog:
http://www.writing.com

SELF-PROMPTS:

JANUARY 14
THE DIRECTOR'S CHAIR I: Storyboarding

For the next seven days, let's sit in the film director's chair and develop a piece of writing as though we're shooting a film. Taking our work through a director's process enables us to see how stories grow, and provides a fun and challenging series of exercises.

Come up with a topic or story idea — a slice of life, piece of fiction, or something you observed between two people. Write out the idea in a couple of sentences. Next, "storyboard" the idea. Sketch how you see the piece progressing (you'll have the opportunity to change it later). Identify scenes, moments. Jot down your vision for this story or essay. Dabble with your idea off and on for the rest of the day.

"The basis of all good writing comes from deep compassion for the people you co-exist with."

— Jimmy Santiago Baca, National Book Award-winning poet, author, *Healing Earthquakes*

Signs:
Capricorn • Goose • Birch
Birthdays:
Lynn Cherry (b. 1952)
Featured Website/Blog:
http://www.zoetrope.com

SELF-PROMPTS:

JANUARY 15
THE DIRECTOR'S CHAIR II: Casting/Dialogue

Your piece is storyboarded. Who are your characters? Picture their faces and facial expressions, mannerisms and habits, what makes them happy or angry, how they walk, what they like and dislike. How do they talk? With accents? Dialects? Are they from New York? The South? Or California?

Practice writing dialogue between two or more characters that will be in your story or slice-of-life "documentary." Listen to how the characters "speak." Let them do the "talking." But remember: In literature, unlike film, you have the space and time to allow characters long, deep, meaningful conversations that define them and your story. Practice writing long conversations, as well as short exchanges. They all count.

"Movies can only show glimpses of a character's inner life. A movie cannot portray the sustained, nuanced, mutable, and gradual inner workings of a character's mind and heart. Only literature can do that."

—Nancy L. Sullivan, author, *Treasury of American Poetry*

JANUARY 16
THE DIRECTOR'S CHAIR III: Atmospherics

SELF-PROMPTS:

Four-time Academy Award-winning cinematographer Leon Shamroy (*The Robe, The King and I, South Pacific*) termed the feeling and setting of a movie "Atmospherics"; specifically, how setting affects and/or defines the characters and plot. Working in the large color formats of the 1950s and 1960s, Shamroy produced exquisite, legendary camerawork. So great was his work that older film buffs can close their eyes and imagine themselves in one of his settings.

Let's do the same. Take the storyboard of your piece, and fill it in. Where does the story take place? Can you picture it? What natural features define and surround the location? What is the air like? How clear is the water? What do sunrises, sunsets and full moons look like? What moods and feelings do the surroundings convey in your characters? How does the setting affect their physical appearance? Write out the atmospherics of your story.

"You're grabbing through the veil, layers of language, you reach out and then pull back into yourself to render into words with landscape. You have the space that ordinary life doesn't give you."

— Lois-Ann Yamanaka, author, *Blu's Hangin'*

Signs:
Capricorn • Goose • Birch
Birthdays:
Anthony Kennedy (b. 1928)
Susan Sontag (b. 1933)
Robert Liposyte (b. 1938)
Featured Website/Blog:
http://www.zoetrope.com

JANUARY 17
THE DIRECTOR'S CHAIR IV: Staging

SELF-PROMPTS:

Now that we've fleshed out the atmospherics of our piece, let's develop staging. In what rooms, outside locations or buildings will the action of your story take place? Write descriptions. What pieces of furniture, clothing, keepsakes, curtains or mementos are in the rooms? Are there doors, or other exits, to move your characters "on" and "off" stage?

Fill in your "stage" by furnishing it. Try to make the furnishings, knick-knacks, adornments and other objects *specific and unique* to the characters — visual extensions of their personalities and tendencies. Make your stage a living embodiment of your characters.

"No one can imitate when you write of the particular, because no others have experienced exactly the same thing."

— Johann Wolfgang Goethe, scientist, poet, author, *Faust*

Signs:
Capricorn • Goose • Birch
Birthdays:
Robert Cormier (b. 1925)
John C. Bellars (b. 1938)
Featured Website/Blog:
http://www.writerspace.com

SELF-PROMPTS:

JANUARY 18
THE DIRECTOR'S CHAIR V: Shooting—Camera Angles

It's time to roll. We've storyboarded our idea into scenes, identified the characters and how they move, act and speak, developed our atmospherics and created a stage on which the story will unfold. Now, let's shoot!

Write out a "scene" in one take. Create interaction between your characters, and bring in the external (atmospherics) and internal (stage) environments. Use "the camera"—your inner vision and imagination. When describing the overall setting, use a wide-angle or long lens, to see the entire picture. When diving into dramatic moments or intense conversation between characters, give us close-ups so we can "see" the tension on their faces, the way their eyes blink or lips purse. When the conversation is over, give us a chance to catch our breath by "zooming" the "camera" to a mid-range shot, where we can follow the characters to their next moves.

Practice writing in close-up, mid-range, long-range, wide-angle, zooming and panning— all vital positions for the reader's eye.

Signs:
Capricorn • Goose • Birch
Birthdays:
A.A. Milne (b. 1882)
Arthur Ransome (b. 1884)
Featured Website/Blog:
http://www.writerspace.com

"My process is best where I don't know where's it going to take me. If I have a rough idea of the direction I'm going, I can wander and meander and write fragments and not worry where they're going, then sift into phrases that eventually organize themselves."

— Mei-Mei Bersenbrugge, poet,
author, *I Love Artists: New and Selected Poems*

SELF-PROMPTS:

JANUARY 19
THE DIRECTOR'S CHAIR VI: Re-Takes

What happens when a scene doesn't come out the way you intended? This can be difficult, especially if we become so attached to our writing that changing anything becomes a painful event. Yet, re-takes (re-writes) are common and necessary. Some movie scenes require upwards of 80 takes. Likewise, most great authors have re-written pages, scenes or entire books 10 or more times to get them right. By writing a scene from different angles, we can gain a broader perspective of the moment, and deliver much stronger work.

Take the scene you wrote, and re-write it from another angle— perhaps another character's point-of-view. Or, write from an intimate, close-up, "fish eye" view rather than a detached, "long lens" view. See what you can add to your original scene with a "re-take."

Signs:
Capricorn • Goose • Birch
Birthdays:
Edgar Allen Poe (b. 1809)
Patricia Highsmith (b. 1921)
Nina Bawden (b. 1925)
Featured Website/Blog:
http://www.writerswrite.com

"The beautiful part of writing is that you don't have to get it right the first time, unlike, say, a brain surgeon."

— Robert Cormier, author, *The Rag and Bone Shop*

JANUARY 20
THE DIRECTOR'S CHAIR VII: Editing and Final Cut

SELF-PROMPTS:

We've come to the final stage: editing. In movie making, editing is a two-step process—the initial edit, and the final cut. On the initial edit, the director will pare thousands of hours of raw footage to shape the polished story. (Before digitization, some directors rolled 1 *million* feet of film to craft a two-hour movie—which uses 10,000 feet of film.) Ideally, the director's final cut will appear on screen. Often, however, the studio makes further changes on its own. This is the same experience we often have when we submit books to publishers.

Take your scene and cut away all "excess" baggage—extra scene description, dialogue that doesn't move, and other extraneous or redundant phrases, sentences or side stories. Check for consistency of character and setting. Finally, pull out your sharpest pen and remove, add or change individual words or phrases to create the most polished presentation of the piece—in its proper mood, tone, and voice. A tip: Don't become too attached to anything you write until final edit (final cut). It makes the editing and polishing process less painful.

"Always make sure you get the moon in the right part of the sky."
— Eudora Welty, novelist, author, *Golden Apples*

Signs:
Capricorn • Goose • Birch
Birthdays:
Joy Adamson (b. 1910)
Featured Website/Blog:
http://www.writerswrite.com

JANUARY 21
TO BE CONTINUED...

SELF-PROMPTS:

How often do you watch a movie, and say to yourself as the credits roll, "I can see them going on and doing…"?

Indulge your imagined next scene! Write the next step in the lives of the characters on which you are focusing. Write it as a short story, with conflict, resolution, dialogue, and subtle shifts in character. When finished, if you feel so inclined, break it out into script form, stripping away the emotional descriptions and all but basic setting descriptions, and roll out the dialogue. Then read it aloud — and breathe new life into the characters into whom you've breathed new life.

This is an outstanding way to develop fiction- and story-writing skills, and playing with characters you may not have created yourself. Something else: This process is one way serial novelists and franchise film screenwriters tee up their next installments.

"Writing is a tricky business. It's the engagement of a soul, and you can't rush your psychological development, your experience."
— Rosellen Brown, author, *Civil Wars: A Novel*

Signs:
Aquarius • Otter • Rowan
Featured Website/Blog:
http://www.youwriteon.com

SELF-PROMPTS:

JANUARY 22
WRITE THE SILENCE, Part I

Silence is a state of sound, or lack of sound, for which most people yearn in this noisy world. Silence provides its own tone and character, the rhythm between two sounds, as mysterious as darkness. In writing, silence creates the same "negative space" an artist experiences with open canvas. When used properly, it is an extremely effective space-holder between two scenes, build-up to a dramatic moment, or reflection of mood between characters. How do you work with this negative space?

Today, write in a place where silence is assured. Close your eyes. Listen intently. Plumb the silence, move within it. What do you see? Feel? *Hear?* Describe the silence and its qualities. Try to create as many similes, metaphors and analogies to silence as you can.

Signs:
Aquarius • Otter • Rowan
Birthdays:
Sir Francis Bacon (b. 1561)
Lord Byron (b. 1788)
Blair Lent (b. 1930)
Brian Wildsmith (b. 1930)
Featured Website/Blog:
http://www.youwriteon.com

"Listening to the silence immediately creates stillness within you. Only the stillness in you can perceive the silence outside."

— Eckhart Tolle, author, *The Power of Now*

SELF-PROMPTS:

JANUARY 23
WRITE THE SILENCE, Part II

Visit the sacred, silent space you frequented yesterday. Sit until you feel a place of stillness. *Write the silence* in a vignette, story or scene. Describe your (or a character's) place in the silence, how the stillness amplifies your feelings and thoughts, and where they are leading you. Turn silence into a journey.

Signs:
Aquarius • Otter • Rowan
Birthday:
Derek Alton Walcott (b. 1930)
Featured Website/Blog:
http://www.ourecho.com

"Solitude is a state in which a wide variety of feelings come to inform us about our lives and those of others we are concerned about. You can explore, take in, give out, breathe freely."

— Sheila Bender, author, *Keeping A Journal You Love*

JANUARY 24
A MULTIMEDIA DAY: Switching Media

Let's spend the next two days expanding our definition of "writing" to include anything created with a pen or pencil. Start by writing a vignette of 100 to 150 words on any subject that fascinates you. When finished, draw pictures or symbols of your subject, either illustrating your vignette or—better yet—portraying the next movement. Don't worry about drawing ability. If words or phrases pop up while you're drawing, add them.

"You can't depend on your judgment when your imagination is out of focus."

— Mark Twain, author, *The Adventures of Huckleberry Finn*

Signs:
Aquarius • Otter • Rowan
Birthdays:
Russell Hoban (b. 1925)
Featured Website/Blog:
http://www.ourecho.com

JANUARY 25
A MULTIMEDIA DAY: Many Expressions

Read yesterday's vignette, and edit or change as you'd like. Grab a magazine and pair of scissors, and find a photograph or two that relates to the story. Cut out the picture(s) and glue them to the page. Give the piece a title, and study it. Imagine how you would script a video or short movie of your subject. Write it out. Repeat this two-day exercise every time you feel blocked.

"I think of narrative not as a path, but as three-dimensional space, or landscape, through which (by words) we can take a path."

— Bob Hughes, author, *Dust or Magic*

Signs:
Aquarius • Otter • Rowan
Birthdays:
Robert Burns (b. 1759)
W. Somerset Maugham (b. 1874)
Virginia Woolf (b. 1882)
James Gordon Farrell (b. 1935)
Featured Website/Blog:
http://www.writingtime.net

SELF-PROMPTS:

JANUARY 26
IMMEDIATE EXPERIENCE

We often talk about "presence," "in the moment," the "eternal now," "the point of power is in the present" and other terms synonymous with *right this second*. This very moment is our fulcrum between creations past and future. It is the dawn of the rest of our lives. Everything that transpired before this moment can only inform and season us for what lies ahead.

Take your journal with you today, no matter where you go. Something will happen about which to write. Capture the experience *instantly* — preferably as you're having it. Record the emotional joy, upheaval or physical intensity of the experience. Use only live, active verbs — show it happening now! See if you can convey the details, feelings, highlights or lowlights, what is said…what is *unsaid*.

A few hours later, go back to your journal and read…rich, isn't it? Writing immediate experience creates the fluency we need to write about anything, at any time.

Signs:
Aquarius • Otter • Rowan
Featured Website/Blog:
http://www.writingtime.net

"When you do something, you should burn yourself completely, like a good bonfire, leaving no trace of yourself."

— Shunryu Suzuki, Zen priest

SELF-PROMPTS:

JANUARY 27
BEAUTIFUL DIVERSIONS

To lead healthy lives, we often have to let go of our schedules and embrace the diversions that come our way. This also holds true for our writing practice. Today, for the next 30 minutes to an hour — or longer — follow the diversions of your mind and heart. Be the hiker without a map. As a new idea, observation, fantasy, intuition or glimpse into a loved one or friend grabs you, write it out. Go where the journey takes you. Repeat whenever you feel stagnant in your daily writing or journaling.

Signs:
Aquarius • Otter • Rowan
Birthdays:
Charles Dickens (b. 1812)
Lewis Carroll (b. 1832)
Fred Gipson (b. 1908)
Featured Website/Blog:
http://www.mediabistro.com

"Ten times a day something happens to me like this — some strengthening throb of amazement — some good sweet and empathic ping and swell. This is the first, the wildest and the wisest thing I know: that the soul exists and is built entirely out of attentiveness."

— Mary Oliver, poet, author, *What Do We Know*

JANUARY 28
WRITING IMPERFECTION

SELF-PROMPTS:

We live in a society that seeks escape from its imperfections by idealizing looks, weight, abundance, food, status, stardom, possessions and more. Good writers know, however, that *imperfection* creates the character and personality of life. What experiences do the wrinkles on an old sailor's face reveal? Which ancestor, or past-century resident, made the smudges on an antique chest? Is there anything more heart-wrenching, or more beautiful, than the final smile on the face of an ailing loved one about to pass away? When we write about imperfections, we dig into the grist of lives—the stuff of great writing. There we find hidden perfection.

Think of a person or object whose imperfections you've noticed. Or, identify one of your imperfections. Describe, and then ask, "What caused those imperfections?" Write as deeply and completely as you can. Seek to find the *perfect* rhythm lodged within the imperfection—then write about how the imperfection *enhances* the beauty and realism of the person or object. Write an edge; make it raw. See where it leads.

"If you see a whole thing—it seems that it's always beautiful. Planets, lives... But close up, a world's all dirt and rocks."
— Ursula K. LeGuin, author, *The Earthsea Books*

Signs:
Aquarius • Otter • Rowan
Birthdays:
Jules Verne (b. 1828)
Collette (b. 1873)
Susan Sontag (b. 1933)
Anne Rockwell (b. 1934)
Featured Website/Blog:
http://www.mediabistro.com

JANUARY 29
INTENSIFY THE ENCOUNTER, Part I

SELF-PROMPTS:

Writers regularly hold back their "best material" when writing dramatic dialogue, to save it all for one "knockout" moment. Unless we're surrounded 24/7 by people with no ability to express what they feel, this approach does not reflect reality. To produce compelling writing, we must intensify the encounter. This is different than *over-dramatizing* an encounter.

Write out a quick scene between two people who disagree about something. Let their dialogue drive the scene. Make it conversational. Use narrative only to set up scenes and describe body language or facial expressions. Review what you wrote, and omit dialogue that circles around what the people are trying to say.

"The only real strength is confrontation of yourself. The only real weakness is being unable to confront yourself."
— William S. Burroughs, author, *Naked Lunch*

Signs:
Aquarius • Otter • Rowan
Birthdays:
Anton Chekhov (b. 1860)
Edward Abbey (b. 1927)
Featured Website/Blog:
http://www.dailywriting.net

SELF-PROMPTS:

JANUARY 30
INTENSIFY THE ENCOUNTER, Part II

Polish and amplify the vignette, story or scene you wrote yesterday. Change all passive verbs to active verbs — creating more immediacy and movement. Insert a few brief descriptions of specific facial or bodily expressions by your character(s) — especially the movements of their eyes and tones of their voices. Strike all superfluous words (especially adverbs) that slow down the action. See if you can *feel* an increased intensity from your original draft.

Signs:
Aquarius • Otter • Rowan
Birthdays:
Lloyd Alexander (b. 1924)
Shirley Hazzard (b. 1931)
Michael Dorris (b. 1945)
Featured Website/Blog:
http://www.dailywriting.net

"After you've taken your chair and have written a while — perhaps an hour or so — it comes along, and you start to move ahead strongly. It appears to be a very deep order of energy. It's like the prizefighter who crosses himself before a fight. It isn't he who will win, it's something else through him. Same goes for writing."

— William Saroyan, author, *The Human Comedy*

SELF-PROMPTS:

JANUARY 31
JOY AND SADNESS

What brings you joy? What brings you deep sadness?

Recall five specific sources of joy, and five specific sources of deep sadness. As you jot each source down, sit for a few minutes to embrace and absorb their energy. Try to feel the way they're connected with your body, how they have contributed to the person you are today. Then write about the joy or sadness that stems from each source, and why each causes you to feel exalted or despondent. See if you can discover new threads about yourself. This exercise is recommended for developing and determining the emotional range of your characters.

Signs:
Aquarius • Otter • Rowan
Birthdays:
Zane Grey (b. 1872)
John O'Hara (b. 1905)
Norman Mailer (b. 1923)
Featured Website/Blog:
http://www.webforauthors.com

"Our job is to be an awake people...utterly conscious, to attend to our world."

— Louis Owens, author, *Nightland*

February

FEBRUARY 1
WRITE THE ETERNAL, NOW

The point of power is in the present. What you write in this moment is the freshest, newest material in your life. It can also be the most powerful. Write about what strikes you this very moment, using active verbs and a pace that reflects your feelings. What does your emotion, activity or surroundings sound, feel, taste, look or smell like? Who is sharing this moment with you? Write the eternal moment, now.

"Words are infinitely reverential, about being present — words impart presence."

— Li-Young Lee, poet, author, *Rose*

SELF-PROMPTS:

Signs:
Aquarius • Otter • Rowan
Birthdays:
Langston Hughes (b. 1902)
Featured Website/Blog:
http://www.webforauthors.net

SELF-PROMPTS:

Signs:
Aquarius • Otter • Rowan
Birthdays:
Ayn Rand (b. 1905)
Judith Viorst (b. 1931)
Featured Website/Blog:
http://www.webforauthors.net

FEBRUARY 2
AFFECTIONS

What brings you affection? What makes you feel affectionate? What inspires you to share affection with others? Create a scenario in which someone or something brings you affection. Describe the people (or things) and the actions taken, but dive a level deeper and write this piece through your heart. Describe how you were touched by the affection, and how your affection touched others — then show it through "feeling" verbs. Step out to a day influenced by the affection you wove with your pen and your heart.

"It never occurred to me that what I wrote was something to define. I am governed by the pull of the sentence as the pull of a fabric is governed by gravity."

— Marianne Moore, author, *Tell Me, Tell Me*

SELF-PROMPTS:

Signs:
Aquarius • Otter • Rowan
Birthdays:
Horace Greeley (b. 1811)
James A. Michener (b. 1907)
Walt Morey (b. 1907)
Joan Lowery Nixon (b. 1927)
Featured Website/Blog:
http://www.aaww.org

FEBRUARY 3
POTTER'S WHEEL: ONE PIECE, MANY FORMS

Given today's online world, and the prevalence of writer self-promotion (completely necessary), smart writers take their creative content and reshape it into different forms— blogs, social media posts, articles, blurbs, excerpts, etc. Our proficiency at this will lead to opportunities to sell stories or books, drum up additional reviews, and draw more readers — whether or not we're professional writers.

Let's spin the potter's wheel. Locate a piece you have written, or the chapter of a book. Or, write something new. Take this material and reshape into these forms:
• A 500-word press release or article on the material.
• A 400-word blog, describing the story and including excerpts.
• A 150-word description of your piece that would serve as book jacket copy.
• A story or book trailer, a 60-second script (about 100 spoken words) that combines brief excerpts with information about the story or book.

"Remember your roots, your history, and the forbears' shoulders on which you stand. And pass these roots onto your children and to other children."
— Marian Edelman, children's activist, author, *I Can Make a Difference*

FEBRUARY 4
A MOST DELICIOUS SECRET

What is the most delicious secret you've ever personally experienced and kept? What lies within you that is so tantalizing, scrumptious, dangerous or wild that, revealed, would blow the doors off everyone you know? *Why* is the secret so delicious that you return to it over and over? Write out your most delicious secret, and try to use food metaphors when describing it, so you can taste it, eat it or drink from it over and over again. Keep adding to the story of your secret, drawing it fully out of the sanctum of your heart, spreading some of its magic and wonder into the other areas of your life.

"Wildness is the state of complete awareness. That's why we need it."
— Gary Snyder, author, *Turtle Island*

Signs:
Aquarius • Otter • Rowan
Birthdays:
MacKinlay Kantor (b. 1904)
Russell Hoban (b. 1925)
Featured Website/Blog:
http://www.aaww.org

FEBRUARY 5
SHARING SECRETS

Secrets are truths driven into exile by potential embarrassment, humiliation, betrayal, discovery or danger. While secrets can create moral dilemmas in everyday life, they provide endless material for writers. A well-kept, well-crafted, well-revealed secret often becomes the most memorable part of a book. It is a sure way to increase a reader's attention level.

Create a dialogue scenario between you and one other character. Reveal one of your deepest secrets in a back-and-forth exchange. Give the other character the license to ask leading questions. Keep the dialogue moving. Turn the sharing of your secret into a page-turning story that rolls out one tantalizing detail at a time. *Show* the difficulty of conveying this truth, but convey the *entire truth*. When finished, examine how you feel by releasing this secret—then add this technique to your fiction or creative non-fiction writing.

"I am the only one who can tell the story of my life and say what it means."
— Dorothy Allison, author, *Bastard Out of Carolina*

Signs:
Aquarius • Otter • Rowan
Birthdays:
Patricia Lauber (b. 1924)
David Wallechinsky (b. 1948)
Featured Website/Blog:
http://www.aaww.org

SELF-PROMPTS:

Signs:
Aquarius • Otter • Rowan
Featured Website/Blog:
http://www.writers.net

FEBRUARY 6
MAGNETIC POETRY: Word Play

Playing with the magnetic poetry on our refrigerators or in our offices provides a great way to stimulate writing. Let's play some magnetic poetry—with our own words. Choose 30 words—15 nouns, 10 verbs and 5 adjectives. Select nouns that are particularly powerful or meaningful. Pick verbs that describe how you move and feel. If a verb doesn't exactly match a movement or feeling, take a page from Anne Lamott (*Bird By Bird*) and make up a verb! Find adjectives that spice up your life—favorite colors, descriptions, etc.

Move your 30 words around in various combinations. Don't write at first; just play. After a few minutes, put combinations together that form strong images, write them down, and let them grow in your mind.

"I have learned to watch the relation to language among the young ones."
— Thornton Wilder, author, *The Bridge of San Luis Rey*

SELF-PROMPTS:

Signs:
Aquarius • Otter • Rowan
Birthdays:
Charles Dickens (b. 1812)
Laura Ingalls Wilder (b. 1867)
Sinclair Lewis (b. 1885)
Gay Talese (b. 1932)
Featured Website/Blog:
http://www.writers.net

FEBRUARY 7
MAGNETIC POETRY: Creating Powerful Images

Take the 30 words you generated yesterday, put them on index cards or slips of paper, and shuffle them like a deck of cards. Spend the next 30 minutes creating two sets of images: One set from four words drawn at random; and one set of at least four words chosen by you. Create at least a dozen images. Write at least a couple sentences about the images that move you most. See if you can identify seven images of particular meaning, power and resonance to you. In your journal, discover ways to make these images work together in your prose or poetry.

"Poetry to me is lightning of the moment. Writing fiction is more like sitting in a clearing and waiting to see if the deer will come."
— Tess Gallagher, author, *At the Owl Woman Saloon*

FEBRUARY 8
MAGNETIC POETRY: Sing Me The Creation

Now that you've practiced writing from magnetic poetry words you strung together, let's take the final, delicious step—writing vignettes, poems or stories from your creations.

Bring together your seven strongest images. They can interweave with each other or bear no resemblance; it doesn't matter. Use each image within a paragraph, poetic stanza, mini-vignette, or verse of a song. Create seven paragraphs, stanzas, mini-vignettes or verses. While it is easiest to use each image as the topic sentence, you can also stitch image strings at the middle or end of your piece. You can further spice it up by creating other images from your 30 original words, but see how far you can expand with your seven strongest images. See how far your vision and imagination stretch by utilizing unfamiliar combinations of familiar words. Have fun! Creation has never felt so easy.

"They say of vision that it is a deliberate gift, the revelation of a dancer who for my eyes only flings away her seven veils."

— Annie Dillard, author, *Pilgrim at Tinker Creek*

Signs:
Aquarius • Otter • Rowan
Birthdays:
Emanuel Swedenborg (b. 1688)
Jules Verne (b. 1828)
Elizabeth Bishop (b. 1911)
Featured Website/Blog:
http://www.writers.net

FEBRUARY 9
TALES OF MY WAYSIDE INN: Part One

Literature is replete with memorable roadside or wandering tales. Three examples most of us remember from school are Longfellow's *Tales of the Wayside Inn,* Chaucer's *The Canterbury Tales* and Jack Kerouac's *On the Road* (for those who had especially open-minded teachers!). Another legendary collection is Boccaccio's *The Decameron,* 100 stories shared by wandering medieval travelers. For the next week, let's go "on the road" to write within skins and personas that might not be familiar to us, but will touch ancient nomadic memories. Today, write about how you feel when traveling. Heightened senses? Curious about everything? Eager to embark on adventures you'd never try at home? Interested in meeting the people? Listening to their languages? Eating your way through a destination? Put yourself in the traveling mood by filling your "bags" with your road shoes—and senses.

"Not I, not anyone else, can travel that road for you. You must travel it for yourself."

— Walt Whitman, author, *Leaves of Grass*

Signs:
Aquarius • Otter • Rowan
Birthdays:
Hilda Van Stockum (b. 1908)
J.M. Coetzee (b. 1940)
Alice Walker (b. 1944)
Featured Website/Blog:
http://www.thestorystarter.com

SELF-PROMPTS:

Signs:
Aquarius • Otter • Rowan
Birthdays:
Charles Lamb (b. 1775)
Elaine Konigsburg (b. 1930)
Featured Website/Blog:
http://www.thestorystarter.com

FEBRUARY 10
TALES OF MY WAYSIDE INN: Part Two

Now that your mind, heart and pen have "embarked," let's plunge into our travels. Become a wandering scholar who has taken a year's sabbatical from a professorship or other position. You're sensing new streams of learning on the planet, and within yourself. What are those streams? Where do you find them? What does each discovery trigger within you? What does each discovery, and how you study it, reveal about yourself? Any lost collections of books, pottery, artifacts or archaeological digs waiting for your discovery? Write about any or all of these subjects in first person, with *you* as the wandering scholar.

"You can write about anything, and if you write well enough, even the reader with no intrinsic interest in the subject will become involved."
— Tracy Kidder, author, *Mountains Beyond Mountains*

SELF-PROMPTS:

Signs:
Aquarius • Otter • Rowan
Birthdays:
Sidney Sheldon (b. 1917)
Jane Yolen (b. 1939)
Featured Website/Blog:
http://www.thestorystarter.com

FEBRUARY 11
TALES OF MY WAYSIDE INN: Part Three

Today, you're homeless—by choice. You've chosen to rent out the house for a while, and roam the streets and countryside, drinking in life without ready accommodations, conveniences or a car. You've made this choice to achieve deeper contact with another side of humanity. How does it feel to be homeless? Are you frightened? Alarmed? Surprised by the freedom from obligation? Do you spend your time trying to survive? Or trying to experience every moment for what it brings you?

"Every writer must articulate from the specific. They must reach down where they stand, because there is nothing else from which to draw."
— Gloria Naylor, author, *The Women of Brewster Place*

FEBRUARY 12
Lincoln's Birthday
TALES OF MY WAYSIDE INN: Part Four

Pick up your lyre, pennywhistle, drum and mandolin. You're a modern-day troubadour, a wandering minstrel, playing for folks in every town and village you visit, just as minstrels did in Spain, France and Italy in the later Middle Ages. What songs are you playing? What inspires or delights you about the people and the villages? Why does playing music for complete strangers thrill you so much? How does the music move through your body as you play and walk at the same time?

Play and celebrate with the villages you visit today. Try to write lyrically, from the joy of the day.

"I write these novels in order to try to understand the world a little better for my own self. And if I help my fans and my readers to go along on the journey, that's great."

— T.C. Boyle, author, *Drop City*

SELF-PROMPTS:

Signs:
Aquarius • Otter • Rowan
Birthdays:
Judy Blume (b. 1938)
Featured Website/Blog:
http://www.writestreet.com

FEBRUARY 13
TALES OF MY WAYSIDE INN: Part Five

Now that you're halfway around the world and out of money, but intent on staying on the road, what will you do for work? Find the jobs that fit your skills; choose from everyday jobs native to that area. Write about using your hands, brain and wiles to work in faraway places that feed your sense of adventure, presence and interaction with others. Imagine being a miner in Australia, a tour guide in Hawaii, or a gondolier in Venice…whatever job gives you the best possible experience.

"I have a notebook filled with characters who I think could be really interesting to get to know in another adult novel. Just filled with their names and…"

— Judy Blume, author, *Forever*

SELF-PROMPTS:

Signs:
Aquarius • Otter • Rowan
Birthdays:
Eleanor Farjeon (b. 1881)
Georges Simenon (b. 1903)
William Sleator (b. 1945)
Featured Website/Blog:
http://www.writestreet.com

SELF-PROMPTS:

FEBRUARY 14
Valentine's Day
TALES OF MY WAYSIDE INN: Part Six

You're cutting loose today, no matter where your wandering has taken you. Pick a place and think of the adventures awaiting you there—adventures you've dreamed and fantasized about but never had. It might be mountaineering in Nepal, spelunking in South African caves, midnight spear fishing in Hawaii, or spending an evening on a Greek island during a port-of-call. Write as though you're living the adventure—now. Share your thrill, your experience, your voyage into this unknown, what that feels and looks like—and what you find on the other side. Load this piece with incisive, captivating details that titillate our senses and imaginations.

"Passion is the key. You must choose subjects you truly care about. Take time to dig deep, find out what really matters to you."

—Lois Rosenthal, author, *Living Better*

Signs:
Aquarius • Otter • Rowan
Birthdays:
Jane Highwater (b. 1942)
Carl Bernstein (b. 1944)
George Shannon (b. 1952)
Featured Website/Blog:
http://www.writestreet.com

SELF-PROMPTS:

FEBRUARY 15
TALES OF MY WAYSIDE INN: Part Seven

It's time to come home…

Assemble the previous six pieces you wrote, and read them with your heart, feeling and sensing the sights, sounds, smells, tastes and textures of the experiences. What insights or hidden talents did you find while writing "Tales of My Wayside Inn?"

Write an essay that reflects on the past week or a short-short story in which you tell your tale to one or two other characters—or embark on an entirely new adventure with them, starting another travelogue!

"This is you, a lively, directed writer in the thick of her forest and her body, using all of her powers to get what she is after."

— Sheila Bender, author, *Writing in a Convertible with the Top Down*

Signs:
Aquarius • Otter • Rowan
Birthdays:
Norman Bridell (b. 1928)
Doris Orgel (b. 1929)
Featured Website/Blog:
http://www.writingitreal.com

FEBRUARY 16
WRAPPED IN COLORS

For today, you've become Scherezade, the exotic face of the Persian epic, *A Thousand And One Nights.* You find yourself draped in nothing but scarves. What colors are the scarves? What designs? What fabrics? Do you swaddle yourself in all the scarves? Wrap them around your waist and chest—or head and shoulders? Immerse completely into the colors and designs, and write about the colors that match your emotions, feelings, sensitivities and views of the world—and how you wear them.

"To love is to transform; to be a poet."
> —Norman O. Brown, author, *Love's Body*

SELF-PROMPTS:

Signs:
Aquarius • Otter • Rowan
Birthdays:
Richard Ford (b. 1944)
Eckhart Tolle (b. 1948)
Featured Website/Blog:
http://www.writingitreal.com

FEBRUARY 17
LISTENING AT THE COFFEE SHOP

My dear friend, Pulitzer Prize and National Book Award nominee Harvey Stanbrough (*Beyond the Masks, Writing Realistic Dialogue & Flash Fiction),* commented on how to make dialogue sound more realistic: "Go into a Denny's at 2 a.m., sit at a booth, and just listen. You'll hear the real human condition all around you."

I tried his suggestion at Park City Diner in Manhattan late one night. I sat near four co-eds in their early 20s. I didn't listen so much to their words as to their accents and the cadences of their voices. I listened, absorbed, listened some more. Sure enough, from this night and a subsequent day of listening on a bench at Union Square, I developed the voice of the female protagonist, Christine, for my novel *The Voice.*

Want to write better dialogue? Then write dialogue! Go into a public place such as a park, coffee shop, beach, playground, gym or campus. Subtly eavesdrop on conversations, listening very carefully to the words and phrases the parties use, and how they speak—speed, accent, emphasis. Write down only the dialogue—no explanations, lead-ins or other qualifying statements. Only the spoken words. Develop your natural ear for dialogue by actively listening and observing others—and writing.

"The knowledge of characters who are utterly not yourself is vital; other people, people who aren't you."
> — John Irving, author, *The World According to Garp*

SELF-PROMPTS:

Signs:
Aquarius • Otter • Rowan
Birthdays:
Dorothy Canfield Fisher (b. 1879)
Andre Norton (b. 1912)
Margaret Truman Daniels (b. 1924)
Robert Newton Peck (b. 1928)
Susan Beth Pfeffer (b. 1948)
Featured Website/Blog:
http://www.writingitreal.com

FEBRUARY 18
WRITING THE COFFEE SHOP

Review the dialogue you jotted at the coffee shop or public place — or wrote down later. Picture the faces of the men, women or youth who spoke these words. Write a 500-word vignette or short story — truth or fiction, doesn't matter — that features their dialogue. Imagine a circumstance that brought them together in this public place, at this time. Keep writing, but allow the dialogue to drive the story.

"There's something about the form of a story that's just beyond what people do."

— Francine Prose, author, *The Peaceable Kingdom*

Signs:
Aquarius • Otter • Ash
Birthdays:
Wallace Stegner (b. 1909)
Toni Morrison (b. 1931)
Featured Website/Blog:
http://www.youwriteon.com

FEBRUARY 19
DIALOGUING WHAT AILS

How many times have you said about an ailment or ache, "I just wish it would go away?" Have you thought about asking why it *stays around*? Enter into a dialogue with the ailment or ache. Let it "speak" to you. Set it up like two characters talking — you and the affliction. Write a short story or vignette as if the affliction were a person. See what discoveries you make — and act upon them.

"To conjure up specific incidents and write about them well, you have to relive them and that can be painful."

— Julia Scheeres, author, *Jesusland*

Signs:
Aquarius • Otter • Ash
Birthdays:
Louis Slobodkin (b. 1903)
Featured Website/Blog:
http://www.youwriteon.com

FEBRUARY 20
PARDON THE INTERRUPTION

We tend to interrupt one another when speaking. It is human nature. However, we don't use interrupting moments enough in fiction and non-fiction writing. However, it creates scenes so vivid that readers immerse within them, their eyes and ears shifting from side to side as though they were part of the conversation.

Today, dialogue a conversation between two or more people. As you do, have the characters interrupt each other. Use long dashes at the point of interruption to show a sudden break in speech flow. Have the other person blurt out their comment. Return to the person who was speaking before. *Show* the interruption by putting ellipses before the person resumes speaking.

While being interrupted is no fun at all, writing the dialogue of interruption is a blast. It's also a powerful, but underused writing technique.

"If I transpose it for some reason, I am in danger of losing the freshness of first contact, and will have difficulty recapturing its attractiveness."

— Igor Stravinsky, composer

Signs:
Aquarius • Otter • Ash
Featured Website/Blog:
http://www.youwriteon.com

FEBRUARY 21
CRAZY NOTEPADS

When I'm writing a novel, creative non-fiction book or poetry collection, my desk and house transform into constellations of notepads, index cards, Post-its®, journals and a computer with files scattered across the screen like chicken pox. My Muse wants everything, from every source, and will flood my mind with material—much of it additional to what I need for that particular book.

What to do when your creativity is bursting in all directions? Write the ideas on any surface you can find. Set notepads, or index cards, and pens everywhere—your desk, living or reading room, bedroom night table, bathroom and kitchen. Capture the idea or inspiration, write a few sentences to preserve its seed on paper and in mind, and move back to your work-in-progress. Never let the idea consume your designated writing time, but never let it slip past you, either. At the end of each day, put your collected ideas in your journal. In your next "warm up" writing session, expand on these ideas. Within them may be your next essay, article, vignette, story, poem—or book!

"This sense of urgency, this sense of things spinning out of control—this is where the creativity is coming in."

— Jack Heffron, author, *The Writer's Idea Book*

Signs:
Aquarius • Otter • Ash
Birthdays:
Anais Nin (b. 1903)
Ha Jin (b. 1956)
David Foster Wallace (b. 1962)
Featured Website/Blog:
http://www.awaionline.com

FEBRUARY 22
Washington's Birthday
MISBEHAVE!

SELF-PROMPTS:

Signs:
Aquarius • Otter • Ash

Birthdays:
Edna St. Vincent Millay (b. 1892)
Morley Callaghan (b. 1903)

Featured Website/Blog:
http://www.awaionline.com

Yep, you read it right—misbehave (on paper)! Think of all the rebellious, shocking behavior your mischievous inner child has always wanted to express, were it not for your sensibilities, social conventions, embarrassment to self or others, or potential consequences. Write about yourself practicing one of those behaviors. Take it all the way! Cut loose! What are you like when you behave like this? Do you like yourself more? Less? Throw it all out there—and see how you feel about it. Integrate more *attitude* into your writing, and perhaps your life. Be wild! Go for it!

"We are filled with a longing for the wild."
— Clarissa Pinkola Estes, author, *The Dangerous Old Woman*

FEBRUARY 23
I AM FREE!

SELF-PROMPTS:

Signs:
Pisces • Wolf • Ash

Birthdays:
Paul West (b. 1930)
C.S. Adler (b. 1932)

Featured Website/Blog:
http://www.awaionline.com

Once in awhile, we need to excuse ourselves from our busy, duty-filled, minutely scheduled lives to remind ourselves that we are FREE! As writers, this feeling carries greater intensity—and importance—since we tend to *really* practice freedom of expression. As author-artist Henry Miller said, "Writers and artists are the antennae of the race."

Today, write out sentences that begin with the three words, "I Am Free…" What are you free to do? How does freedom feel today? To what animal would you compare your sense of freedom—bird, wildcat, dog, wild mustang, fish or other?

See how many sentences (expressions) you can create in 20 minutes, and then write vignettes with your three best opening sentences. Turn this into an essay or short story.

"Where have they got the rules of the house posted for writers? Well, the beauty of it is, there are no rules."
— Sheila Bosworth, author, *Almost Innocent*

FEBRUARY 24
EVERYTHING IS INCLUSIVE

During the day, write down some of your thoughts. Or, write down something catchy, provocative or strange that a person said. Just glimpses: nothing more. Take those random thoughts and sayings and connect them. Use the glue of your spirit and the guidance of your Muse to lead you. Write transitional sentences between the thoughts and sayings. Write a story or poem, or do a composite-character sketch. Watch what happens.

"We want people to believe it when they're reading it — we want them to enter our world fully."

— Tobias Wolff, author, *The Night in Question*

Signs:
Pisces • Wolf • Ash
Birthdays:
Wilhelm Grimm (b. 1786)
Howard Nemerov (b. 1920)
Featured Website/Blog:
http://www.forwriters.com

FEBRUARY 25
FIRE IN THE BELLY

What was your most emotional moment during the past 72 hours? What electrified you, provoked you, heightened your awareness, saddened you, angered you, and brought great happiness to you? Pinpoint that singular moment, dive back into the feelings and emotions, and write your way to clarity. Start from the tunnel-vision viewpoint of the moment-in-progress, and capture everything that led you into the moment — and carried you out of it. Often, our best stories and poems arise from these "fire in the belly" moments.

"The thrill of writing is what emerges from the process. When I sit down at my writing desk, time seems to vanish. I think it's a wonderful way to spend one's life."

— Erica Jong, author, *Sappho's Leap*

Signs:
Pisces • Wolf • Ash
Birthdays:
Helen Brodie Bannerman (b. 1862)
Frank G. Slaughter (b. 1908)
Anthony Burgess (b. 1917)
Cynthia Voigt (b. 1942)
Featured Website/Blog:
http://www.forwriters.com

SELF-PROMPTS:

FEBRUARY 26
ENLARGE THE FIRE

Canassatego, the 18th-century chief of the Onondaga people so admired by Benjamin Franklin, and whose Haudenosaunee principles of governance helped create the framework for the U.S. Constitution, said, "You said you would enlarge the fire…add more fuel to make it brighter."

Let's enlarge our passion and fire for writing by adding fuel. Look around and find something in your home, office, study or yard that you have never described in writing. If that doesn't work, grab a book off your bookshelf and read a few pages, prompting your mind beforehand to be ready to jump at the first idea, insight or experience that grabs it. For the next hour, enlarge the fire. Use your life experience as the fuel to breathe expression, substance and perspective into the journal entry, story or essay. Build and build until your piece has the energy of a bonfire.

"Never think of the effect of what you're doing while you're doing it. Don't project to a possible audience while you are writing."

— May Sarton, author, *Journal of a Solitude*

Signs:
Pisces • Wolf • Ash

Birthdays:
Christopher Marlowe (b. 1564)
Victor Hugo (b. 1802)
Miriam Young (b. 1913)

Featured Website/Blog:
http://www.forwriters.com

SELF-PROMPTS:

FEBRUARY 27
BESTSELLING PROMPTS

While reading a good book, have you ever asked yourself, "Why didn't I come up with this?" or "What would have happened if *I'd* written that next scene or paragraph?"

After more than 30 years of professional writing, I still indulge on this Rocky Road ice cream of vicarious experiences. Either a writer's voice will grab me, or a catchy line from a story … off to the journal I go, story weaving every moment of the way.

Now it's your turn. Go to a bookstore or library, and grab a novel or non-fiction work by a writer whose work and voice have deeply impressed you. Read the first paragraph of the book, and then close it. For the next 45 to 60 minutes, write your take on what follows, keying off the first paragraph but making the story your own. It could lead you to a story idea, or a further exploration into how the author triggered your voice. It will certainly provide lively entertainment and writing.

"The question is not what you look at, but what you see."

—Henry David Thoreau, author, *Walden*

Signs:
Pisces • Wolf • Ash

Birthdays:
Henry Wadsworth Longfellow (b. 1882)
John Steinbeck (b. 1902)
Florence Perry Heide (b. 1919)
N. Scott Momaday (b. 1934)
Edmund Morris (b. 1940)

Featured Website/Blog:
http://www.
fifteenminutesoffiction.com

FEBRUARY 28
INTERVIEW: MY CREATIVE WINTER

Finally, the days grow longer. The months of cold snaps near their end. It is a perfect time to reflect on your winter of creativity. Let's utilize a great technique for building characters and their stories: the planned interview. Write down 10 to 20 questions to ask yourself about your creative pursuits over the winter. Take time to answer each completely. Ask a couple of simple questions, but try to delve deeper into your motivations and passions. Try to convert the question-and-answer format into a conversation with self. A few examples:

- What type of writing, or story subject, involved me most deeply?
- What new images, metaphors or similes energized or moved me when they spilled from my pen?
- To which authors, artists or musicians (new or classic) was I introduced — and how did their works affect me?
- How have I grown as a writer and creative force this winter?
- How have I *received* intuition, inspiration and new ideas?

Review what you have accomplished, and how you have changed over the winter—because you have. Save the interview, first for posterity, but also because you can send off some of the responses on that magical day when your editor or publisher calls and requests publicity material for you!

"Evening comes bringing all the bright things which the dawn has scattered."

—Sappho, Ancient Greek poet

Signs:
Pisces • Wolf • Ash
Birthdays:
Sir John Tenniel (b. 1820)
Featured Website/Blog:
http://www.fifteenminutesoffiction.com

March

MARCH 1
MOVE AND REST

We constantly fluctuate between expansion and contraction. They flip-flop constantly. We either expand to embrace a new concept, or contract to hold our step or protect what belongs to us. Writing exposes and utilizes the relationship between these two rhythms.

Practice the back-and-forth rhythms. Start off vigorously, moving forward with the first subject that comes to mind. After 10 or 15 minutes of furious writing, slow down and let your mind and pen breathe. Become reflective, contemplative. Dive deeper into the subject. When it feels right to intensify and move faster, do so. This exercise establishes pace and also reflects our human rhythms—producing writing that every reader will feel.

"We move and live and die in the midst of miracles."

— Napoleon Bonaparte

SELF-PROMPTS:

Signs:
Pisces • Wolfe • Ash
Birthdays:
Frederic Chopin (b. 1810)
Ralph Ellison (b.1914)
Robert Lowell (b. 1917)
Tom Wolfe (b. 1931)
Featured Website/Blog:
http://www.
fifteenminutesoffiction.com

SELF-PROMPTS:

MARCH 2
ABSENCE OF SPACE

When we discuss anything that involves growing and improving our lives, we promote the use of space: *Find more space. Get some space. Expand. Breathe space.*

What happens when we employ the opposite? What if we write an essay, scene, play or poem that constricts or consumes space? We create intensity, a breaking point…an explosive moment.

Write a vignette about an encounter with another person (real or imagined) that left you (or a character) feeling claustrophobic, paralyzed, devoid of space. Squeeze every part of your vignette—your word choices, the dialogue, and your observations. Show your facial expressions, inflexible postures, the way you wring your hands.

When finished, take a deep breath, and write the most expansive paragraph of words you can string together, even if nonsensical. Feel the difference? So will your readers.

Signs:
Pisces • Wolfe • Ash
Birthdays:
Theodor Geisel (Dr. Seuss) (b. 1904)
John Irving (b. 1942)
Featured Website/Blog:
http://www.writersdigest.com/blogs

"You have to surrender to the act of writing, give up to it, and trust that if you have anything, it will discover it for you."

— E.L. Doctorow, author, *Ragtime*

SELF-PROMPTS:

MARCH 3
ASSEMBLE YOUR FRAGMENTS

Have you tried to collect fragments of your life for a single piece of writing? If not, here's a new experience. Identify a peak moment in your life, one that culminated a substantial period of build-up, training or preparation. Roll out the memories. Get into the rhythm of the experience, the sights and sounds, the flow. Recall every fragment that pinwheels into your mind. Write down whatever you receive—a sentence, word, image, or entire memory. Do this for 30 minutes, and see how much you gather. Let your words meet the memories in your body.

Signs:
Pisces • Wolfe • Ash
Featured Website/Blog:
http://www.writersdigest.com/blogs

"You choose what you're going to include. You can't lie about something, but you can choose … the people you invite on an expedition with you."

— Diane Ackerman, author, *A Natural History of the Senses*

MARCH 4
MY PROCESS OF DISCOVERY

SELF-PROMPTS:

What is your process of discovery? How do you unearth, uncover, survey, investigate, peruse, comb through, plumb and mine a tip, or lead, that unveils a new wrinkle, a new adventure? By understanding our discovery process, we can enliven our stories, characters and narrative voice by *showing* a journey, rather than explaining it.

Write about your individual *process* of discovery. Ask yourself: *What triggers me to seek out something new, to explore? What do I do when I've made the discovery? Do I share it with others — or hold it inside?* Write 400 to 500 words. Retain the power of this exercise for those inevitable days when ideas, words and life feel gray.

"My process is best where I don't know where's it going to take me. If I have a rough idea of the direction I'm going, I can wander and meander and write fragments and not worry where they're going, then sift into phrases that eventually organize themselves. I want rigor to my process, but also spontaneity and discovery."

— Mei-Mei Bersenbrugge, author, *I Love Artists: New and Selected Poems*

Signs:
Pisces • Wolf • Ash
Birthdays:
Khaled Hosseini (b. 1965)
Featured Website/Blog:
http://www.writersdigest.com/blogs

MARCH 5
USE YOUR HANDS

SELF-PROMPTS:

We use our hands on a regular basis. They are tremendous workhorses and roadmaps of our lives. Hands communicate to a degree exceeded only by the eyes; they are vital instruments for expression, and important to watch when we talk with someone.

For the next 30 to 60 minutes, be mindful of how your hands work, rest, fidget, gesture, grasp, open. Notice how they look, feel, what veins and palm lines you see, how long or short your fingers are, what the condition of your hands infer about your day and life.

Describe a familiar pair of hands in detail. They can belong to you, someone close to you, or the protagonist of your next story. Uncover the stories housed by your hands, how they express (or don't express) your mind, heart and soul. What would your hands (or the familiar person's hands) like to create? What would they like to touch? Create a "tale of two hands."

"No bird soars too high if he soars with his own wings."
—William Blake, poet, author, *Songs of Innocence and Experience*

Signs:
Pisces • Wolf • Ash
Featured Website/Blog:
http://www.articlewritingtips.com

SELF-PROMPTS:

MARCH 6
LIVE IN A HEADLINE

Look at a newspaper or magazine. What headline jumps at you? Jump *into* the headline. Imagine the place you've read about, and where you stand in the course of the event. What do you see? How do you feel? How do you move through the moment? What actions must you take? What attracts you? What repels you? Write an eyewitness account—then see how your perception of the event has changed from the experience of "being" in it.

Signs:
Pisces • Wolf • Ash
Birthdays:
Elizabeth Barrett Browning (b. 1806)
Gabriel Garcia Marquez (b. 1927)
Featured Website/Blog:
http://www.articlewritingtips.com

"I've always felt that a person's intelligence is directly reflected by the number of conflicting points of view he can entertain simultaneously on the same topic."

— Laura Alther, author, *Kinflicks*

SELF-PROMPTS:

MARCH 7
WALK IN THE DARK

Whether we're writing deeply, or searching for the next step forward, we must encounter and move through the dark. Darkness is simply the shadow side of light, giving us better appreciation for life and vision. It's also a necessary component of authentic writing and heart-centered living. "If a man wants to be sure of his road, he must close his eyes and walk in the dark," St. John of the Cross wrote.

Let's walk in the dark today, gently. Write a story about one of your scariest or most traumatic moments. Take a few paragraphs (or pages) to get centered within the sadness, despair, uncertainty and hopelessness you felt. Write from that dark, sensitive place, recalling the questions you asked, the conclusions at which you arrived (valid or not), how you felt (or feel), what you realized about yourself, and what led to you moving from that space. As you write about moving out of the darkness, *show* the moment, comment or action that led you into a brighter place.

Signs:
Pisces • Wolf • Ash
Featured Website/Blog:
http://www.articlewritingtips.com

"In a dark time, the eye begins to see."

—Theodore Roethke, poet, author, *Words for the Wind*

MARCH 8
GUEST STARS: OUR OTHER NAMES

Let's throw off the cloak and mantle and escape into fun, fanciful writing. Let's give our characters and ourselves some of the names that enrapture us with their beauty, allure, mystery.

Think of five names you like. Write down each name, then write a short story or vignette about who you are as that name, that alter-ego. Who would make the most perfect companions? Cut loose; be wild; do the things you've wanted to do but never could (or would); hold nothing back. Fantasize, idealize and dream to the max!

After writing each story, see if there are any new mannerisms, activities or passions you'd like to integrate. See if you can adopt any of these names for your characters—or for a series of ongoing stories and dialogues.

"The thing is to not follow another's pattern. Follow your own pattern of feeling and thought. Accept your own life and try not to live someone else's."
— Katherine Anne Porter, author, *Ship of Fools*

SELF-PROMPTS:

Signs:
Pisces • Wolf • Ash
Birthdays:
John McPhee (b. 1931)
Trina Schart Hyman (b. 1939)
Jeffrey Eugenides (b. 1960)
Featured Website/Blog:
http://www.ourecho.com

MARCH 9
STREET SCAPING

Typically, we think of nature when mentioning "scape," as in "landscape," "mindscape," "bodyscape." Land, mind and body give us physical symbols by which to compare or explain physical features, moods, feelings, adventures, occurrences, circumstances and more.

Let's move our "scaping" operation to the streets. Take your journal with you. Walk down a street, slowly. Choose one with character—either a well-traveled thoroughfare, a street that shows its brick or cobblestone origin, a road of local or historical renown, or one that means a lot to you. Allow your body and mind to flood you with sensory experiences and thoughts. Write them down. Capture everything you can.

Later, sit at a park, café or coffee house, and write. Compare elements of the street to aspects of nature. Maybe the sun hitting the dark pavement reminded you of a lava field, or shadows in the corners felt like caves. Perhaps a brick wall took you back to the classic stone walls that dot the New England countryside. Write a streetscape that will give your street immediate character.

"So much of what I do is unconscious. I choose not to direct why certain images appear when I'm writing. I just let them lead and take me where they will, and then I proceed to craft the language around it the best I know."
— Gloria Naylor, author, *The Men of Brewster Place*

SELF-PROMPTS:

Signs:
Pisces • Wolf • Ash
Birthdays:
Mickey Spillane (b. 1918)
Keri Hulme (b. 1947)
Featured Website/Blog:
http://www.ourecho.com

MARCH 10
PASSION FOOD

Nine centuries ago, Rumi wrote of poetry and passion:

I want
to say words that flame
as I say them

Passion is to writing what energy is to the body. We write best about that which impassions us the most. It may be a boyfriend, girlfriend, partner or spouse. It may be a sport, hobby or spicy dish you just created. It may be your new house, the garden, swimming in the ocean, hanging out with close friends, ministering to the elderly or dancing to your favorite music. It may be the act of creating. Or loving. Or dreaming.

What impassions you? What ignites you so deeply that the words *ignite* when you say them? Write a Declaration of Passion, owning and honoring the creative aspect of passion in your heart, what triggers it, and what your world *looks like* when you're impassioned. Explore your internal dialogue, your internal world. When finished, make a list of "passion trigger items," and refer to it during fallow times.

"I think that to write well and convincingly, one must be somewhat poisoned by passion."

— Edna Ferber, author, *Showboat*

SELF-PROMPTS:

Signs:
Pisces • Wolf • Ash
Birthdays:
Jack Kent (b. 1920)
Featured Website/Blog:
http://www.ourecho.com

MARCH 11
DREAMWRITING: Transformation

Some dreams transform us, literally changing our direction in daily life. As writers, we always hope for the dream that transforms or enriches a story. When we come back, we feel a new energy, state of clarity, purpose and/or desire to change ourselves in some way.

Think of a transformative dream you experienced. Write about the transformation, how it colored your perceptions of people, places, events and the world. How much more bountiful would your personal and creative life be if you carried this new way within you? Write an essay or letter, exploring the answers as deeply as you can.

"I really feel as though, not only am I creating or chronicling that person's life in the daytime while I'm writing the book, but I almost seem to be dreaming that character's dreams."

— Reynolds Price, author, *Kate Vaiden*

SELF-PROMPTS:

Signs:
Pisces • Wolf • Ash
Birthdays:
Wanda Gag (b. 1893)
Douglas Adams (b. 1952)
Featured Website/Blog:
http://www.dreamquestone.com

MARCH 12
DREAMWRITING: Interpretation

Countless books address dream symbols and interpretations. While these books are often helpful and insightful, and certainly entertaining, they cannot chronicle the absolute truth about *our* dream experiences. It is up to us to interpret the messages we receive and events we experience in the dreamtime.

Today, start a process of jotting down any dream fragments or scenarios you remember. Even a phrase or a sentence will call up the dream, or its central message. Write what the dream means to you. Focus on central concrete images within the dream, and follow them with your pen until the words stop. See if you can associate the dream with a current event in your life. Write an essay about the correlation, and how the dream expanded or enhanced your perspective about the current event.

"The central message in all mythology and all dreaming is that there are ways to tap into the wild side of us, which is where all the richness and all the healing and all the creativity comes from."

— Anne Rivers Siddons, author, *Outer Banks*

Signs:
Pisces • Wolf • Ash
Birthdays:
Edward Albee (b. 1928)
Virginia Hamilton (b. 1936)
Dave Eggers (b. 1970)
Featured Website/Blog:
http://www.dreamquestone.com

MARCH 13
DREAMWRITING: Experience

Three forms of consciousness define our lives: waking consciousness, super (or spiritual) consciousness, and the dream world. Dreams provide opportunities to experience life without the fences and borders of the waking world. As writers, we owe it to ourselves to acknowledge dreams as repositories of messages, ideas and symbols.

Write about the most recent dream that significantly impacted your life. What came true? What scared you? What direction did the dream take you? How much of it did you follow? What invigorated or titillated you? What aspects of dreamtime freedom would you bring into your daily life if possible? What would you leave behind?

Open up and receive the boundless treasures offered by your dreams.

"When an inner situation is not made conscious, it appears outside as fate."

— Carl Jung, psychoanalyst, author, *Man and His Symbols*

Signs:
Pisces • Wolf • Ash
Birthdays:
Ellen Raskin (b. 1928)
Diane Dillon (b. 1933)
Thomas Rockwell (b. 1933)
Featured Website/Blog:
http://www.dreamquestone.com

SELF-PROMPTS:

MARCH 14
DREAMWRITING: Journey

Dreamwriting recalls the previous night's journey. We crawl back into the dream, or summon it forth, and relive the oft-magical walk, run, flight or ride that enraptured us while sleeping.

To do this, get quiet, close your eyes, and invite the dream to return to your body. Recall a specific part of the journey, and "jump into it" with your pen. Write what you see and feel: an idea, a message for life, insight into a friend or spouse, or a portal into your childhood or ancestral roots.

Write until the last wisp of the dream dissipates. See if you can use the material you "bring back" in an essay or story, painting, drawing, music or other art or craft.

Signs:
Pisces • Wolf • Ash
Birthdays:
Marguerite DeAngeli (b. 1889)
Featured Website/Blog:
http://www.bellaonline.com

"Man can learn nothing except by going from the known to the unknown."
— Claude Bernard, physiologist

SELF-PROMPTS:

MARCH 15
DREAMWRITING: Applications

We can apply dreamwriting to our work by heeding the advice of three great writers. *Vampire Chronicles* creator Anne Rice likens the process of original writing to daydreaming. The late novelist John Gardner called writing "the creative dream." Eminent professor and novelist John Barth (*Giles Goat-Boy*) compared the structural flow of a novel to a good dream.

Take one of the dreams you've recalled this week, and write a 500- to 1,000-word story, letter or long poem. Use your imagination to stretch beyond the dream, into places, feelings or encounters it suggested, but did not include. Experiment. Test. Mold.

Signs:
Pisces • Wolf • Ash
Birthdays:
Ben Okri (b. 1959)
Featured Website/Blog:
http://www.bellaonline.com

"It is often amazing to see the cleverness with which a dream communicates."
— Naomi Epel, author, *Writers Dreaming*

MARCH 16
LISTEN LIKE A MARINER

Before radios, radar and GPS came along, mariners sailed the seas with oft-incomplete maps, the stars and a compass. They "listened" to the sea, following its lulls and currents, seeking bits of broken branch, terns flying overhead, or breezes with the scent of land. Likewise, when we embark on writing excursions, it is vital that we "listen" to where our pen leads us. By following the "sea," the core of what we're writing, we discover something new.

Write about something entirely new and unfamiliar to you. Don't worry about accuracy, direction or form. Just sail along with every creative impulse or phrase that "flies" into view. Try this for about 30 minutes, and read what you've discovered. Then take the adventure again.

"You say what you want to say when you don't care who's listening. It's a matter of listening to yourself as you sound when you're talking about something that's intensely important."
— Allen Ginsberg, poet, author, *Kaddish and Other Poems*

Signs:
Pisces • Wolf • Ash
Featured Website/Blog:
http://www.bellaonline.com

MARCH 17
OBSERVING LIKE A HUNTER

Author Thom Hartmann, an expert on Attention Deficit Disorder, made a startling comment that would revolutionize the educational system if implemented: Kids with ADD utilize "hunter's mind," the *natural* mind. This mind is holistic, establishing relationships between everything it senses and observes. Likewise, hunters are entirely aware of their surroundings. All senses work together. Eye glances are quick, focused; every sound, footprint or broken twig is instantly analyzed. Every muscle and fiber is relaxed, but poised for action. Nothing slips past. The hunter walks in a state of complete presence, the greatest point of power he/she possesses. By observing like hunters, we can produce our best storytelling, and our best and most descriptive prose.

Look to your immediate surroundings. Imagine yourself hunting for something. Write about everything you see and sense. Make each step purposeful. Illustrate the big picture, and your place in it.

"If a writer doesn't have continuous curiosity, he will wither."
— Ezra Pound, poet, author, *The Cantos of Ezra Pound*

Signs:
Pisces • Wolf • Ash
Birthdays:
Kate Greenway (b. 1846)
Penelope Lively (b. 1933)
Featured Website/Blog:
http://www.wordjourneys.com

SELF-PROMPTS:

MARCH 18
YOUR HOME...ORIGINALLY

Where does your home sit? In a city or town? A hillside or valley? A crowded neighborhood or rustic setting? Imagine what the site of your home looked like five or six centuries ago. If you know the history of your area, bring that knowledge into your vision.

Once you have a feel for your homesite's original appearance, write about it. Describe the land and its surroundings. Include indigenous wildlife that was plentiful during that era. Refine your piece with concrete images and crisp details. Come back to this essay and tweak it, add to it. Constantly seek finer details. See if it gives you a stronger sense of home...and a key to someone else's magic kingdom when they read about this setting in your future book or story.

"Where I am, I build my house; and where I build my house, all things come to it."

— Osage Indian proverb

Signs:
Pisces • Wolf • Alder
Birthdays:
John Updike (b. 1932)
Featured Website/Blog:
http://www.wordjourneys.com

SELF-PROMPTS:

MARCH 19
DIGGING DITCHES

Pulitzer Prize-winning novelist Edna Ferber (*So Big, Cimarron*) said that, for her, writing combined ditch-digging, mountain climbing, walking a treadmill and giving birth. The road is long and tough, but also full of discoveries and the grand reward — birthing a new story.

Where will you dig ditches to lay pipes of plot, motive and conflict? What mountains of character, challenge, and discovery — or real mountains — will your characters climb? When will you slow down, pace your narrative? Where will you dig down to extract the deepest truths? Write a story in which you address and answer these questions. Take your writing deeper.

"I have to determine whether or not I can understand this person, whether I can realize his values, live through his experiences, his failures, weaknesses, his faults as well as his successes."

— Irving Stone, author, *The Agony and the Ecstasy*

Signs:
Pisces • Wolf • Alder
Birthdays:
Irving Wallace (b. 1916)
Phillip Roth (b. 1933)
Featured Website/Blog:
http://www.wordjourneys.com

MARCH 20
WALKING FROM WINTER

We've made it through winter. Lakes and earth begin to thaw. Birds chirp again in the morning. The sun rises higher in the sky, and no longer sets so early. The biting north winds start to abate. Summer's promise of warmth and growth appears on the horizon.

How did you spend winter? By taking advantage of the extra indoor time to write, create and learn? By living or spending time in a warmer climate? By skiing, snowboarding or ice skating? What was your greatest moment in wintry nature?

Honor the passing of the season. Write an epic (historical) poem about your experience, highlighting the events of the past 90 days. Include high and low points, particular events or occurrences and your feelings. Use multiple stanzas to convey your walk through winter.

"The sun, the darkness, the winds, are all listening to what we now say."
— Geronimo, Mescalero Apache chief

Signs:
Pisces • Wolf • Alder
Birthdays:
Henrik Ibsen (b. 1828)
Hugh MacLennan (b.1907)
Anno Mitsumasa (b. 1926)
Lois Lowry (b. 1937)
Ellen Conford (b. 1942)
Featured Website/Blog:
http://www.absolutewrite.com

MARCH 21
PLANTING SEEDS

When spring arrives, my green thumb activates. I cruise nearby nurseries, lawn & garden centers and seed catalogs, searching for seeds to plant in my garden. It will forever amaze me that these tiny grains and kernels grow to provide sweeping visual beauty and plenty of food.

How do great stories, novels, movies, paintings and pieces of music begin? With little seeds, soil and sustenance. So plant your seeds. Starting today, create a habit of writing down *all* of your ideas for stories, poems, essays, articles, blog subjects or songs. No matter how outlandish an idea may seem, write it down. Write a sentence or paragraph—or more—to ground the seed, give it initial sustenance. It may take 10 seconds, or 10 minutes. Write it down.

Keep planting seeds in your journal, and review them occasionally. Chances are, many will germinate in your creative mind if given the chance.

"You write because it's an adventure to watch it come out of your hands."
— Ray Bradbury, author, *The Martian Chronicles*

Signs:
Aries • Falcon • Alder
Birthdays:
Johann Sebastian Bach (b. 1685)
Phyllis McGinley (b. 1905)
Featured Website/Blog:
http://www.absolutewrite.com

SELF-PROMPTS:

MARCH 22
SPRING FORTH!

Walk outside. Take very deep breaths of the crisp, fresh air. Look for trees that may be budding. Listen for the songs of birds, or the rustling of squirrels. See if any tulips or daffodils have started blooming. Sense the new season of growth in the wind, earth and sky. Think of all the possibilities, dreams and initiatives that await your simple "Yes!" to come to fruition. Take a digital photo; blow it up on your computer screen.

Go into your office, studio or desk, and spring forth! Begin a major new essay or story today, developing your topic and outlining your narrative until it matches the picture in your mind. Feed the energy of the day into your work; give your newest creation all of your attention. Then set your piece aside, "water" it with thoughts during the day, and set a daily schedule to complete your major project.

"Listen to all the teachers in the woods. Watch the trees, the animals and all living things."

— Joe Coyhis, Stockbridge-Munsee tribe

Signs:
Aries • Falcon • Alder
Birthdays:
Gabrielle Roy (b. 1909)
Billy Collins (b. 1941)
James Patterson (b. 1947)
Andrew Lloyd Webber (b. 1948)
Featured Website/Blog:
http://www.absolutewrite.com

SELF-PROMPTS:

MARCH 23
DEEP CLUSTERING

Identify a core issue in your forthcoming memoir, story or essay. Write three to five words that describe that issue in the center of a piece of paper. Draw a circle around them. What are five or six facts, experiences or images that support this core issue? Write those around the core issue; draw circles around them. Take one of the circles and write 100 to 150 words about it—what it evokes in you, what it represents. GO DEEP.

When finished, return to the circles and see if you missed something. Draw more circles, pick one, and write 100 to 150 words about it. Repeat five to eight times—or more—to dig up the essential material for your writing.

"Every novel, every narrator can't help offering the promise of a relationship."
— Jane Smiley, author, *A Thousand Acres*

Signs:
Aries • Falcon • Alder
Birthdays:
Eleanor Cameron (b.1912)
Featured Website/Blog:
http://www.constant-comment.com

MARCH 24
WORD STRINGS: The Lists

Time to switch gears and create a puzzle. Think of a word that automatically triggers an association. For example: Ocean:::Wave. Build a string of associated words. Key off the most recent word you wrote. Don't be concerned with the direction of the word string; simply let it happen. Example: Ocean-Wave-Breeze-Surf-Board-Tree-Banana-Fall-Ground-Grass. See if you can create a string of 50 words or more today.

"Follow an image as far as you can, no matter how useless you think it is. Push yourself."
                    — Nikki Giovanni, poet, author, *Grand Mothers*

SELF-PROMPTS:

Signs:
Aries • Falcon • Alder
Birthdays:
Lawrence Ferlinghetti (b. 1919)
Featured Website/Blog:
http://www.constant-comment.com

MARCH 25
WORD STRINGS: The Stories

Write out your word string. Either put yourself in the story, or create a character. If you'd like, place another person in the story as well. Focus on your word string for a moment. If you created your string more from impulse and play than careful thinking, it will resemble a winding, dreamy road. Write your journey, pulling trigger images from the word combinations within your string. When you're finished, consider the outer limits of your creative expression. This is the natural state of your writer's mind—exercise it daily!

"Some days you just get into a relationship with language that's a bit off-skew yet perfect….language has to exist in an exalted state to awaken wonder."
                    — Tom Robbins, author, *Even Cowgirls Get the Blues*

SELF-PROMPTS:

Signs:
Aries • Falcon • Alder
Birthdays:
Paul Scott (b. 1920)
Flannery O'Connor (b. 1925)
Featured Website/Blog:
http://www.constant-comment.com

MARCH 26
CHASE YOUR IDEA ALL THE WAY

Signs:
Aries • Falcon • Alder
Birthdays:
Robert Frost (b. 1874)
Joseph Campbell (b. 1904)
Erica Jong (b. 1942)
Bob Woodward (b. 1943)
Featured Website/Blog:
http://www.dailywriting.net

American statesman Oliver Wendell Holmes wrote, "A mind that is stretched to a new idea never returns to its original destination." Take an idea and write your way to its outer limit. What does the world look like from there? What does *your* world look like? What does it feel like in your heart? Your body? Your senses?

Return to the beginning. Do you see the idea in the same way? What has changed?

"A short story must have a single mood and every sentence must build towards it."

— Edgar Allan Poe, author, *The Raven*

MARCH 27
THE LIGHTNING ROUND

Think of a subject about which you're burning to write. Got it? Sit down, and for the next 20 minutes, write as fast as you can. Write until your pen hand or your typing fingers ache. If you come to a place that stops or slows you down, jump to the next thought and burn, baby, burn. You're a sprinter rushing down the homestretch in fifth gear. Don't let up for a moment. Make your writing *sizzle*.

Take a breath. Rub your hands. Observe how much you wrote in 20 minutes, and how much *authenticity* you poured into the content. Fill in any missing pieces. Know that when you need to write an emotionally charged or breakneck chase scene, you now have the technique for doing so.

Signs:
Aries • Falcon • Alder
Featured Website/Blog:
http://www.dailywriting.net

"Any life will provide the material for writing, if it is attended to."
— Wallace Stegner, author, *The Big Rock Candy Mountain*

MARCH 28
TURNING MOODS INTO SURROUNDINGS: Part One

A great writing technique is to link the moods of your characters, or non-fiction subjects, with their immediate surroundings. *Vampire Chronicles* author Anne Rice is masterful at this. The streets, weather, storefronts, quality of light and looming dangers of dark, purple New Orleans are enlivened by her characters. The environments feel like moving, breathing entities.

Imagine a setting that perfectly suits your mood — light or intense, happy or angry, reflective or outgoing. Maybe it's the spot in which you sit right now. Write a direct reflection of your mood, as though *you're* the setting — but without anyone there. Make it a long metaphor if you'd like. Write the setting in 200 to 500 words. When finished, go over the work, polish and detail it. See how it reflects your mood.

"Were you thinking that those were the words, those upright lines, those curves, angles, dots! No, those are not the words. The substantial words are in the ground and sea, they are in the sea, they are in you."

— Walt Whitman, poet-author, *Leaves of Grass*

Signs:
Aries • Falcon • Alder
Birthdays:
Nelson Algren (b. 1909)
Mary Stolz (b. 1920)
Maria Vargas Llosa (b. 1936)
Featured Website/Blog:
http://www.dailywriting.net

MARCH 29
TURNING MOODS INTO SURROUNDINGS: Part Two

Think of two close friends or family members, people you know very well and whose mannerisms and behaviors you've studied for years. Describe surroundings that reflect the moods in which you've seen your chosen subjects. Use weather conditions, quality of light, shadows, angles, foliage, buildings, animals or other characteristics to paint your scene.

Next, write a transitional paragraph in which you move the people from the surroundings and into a conversation or action. *Show* them emerging from the environment, and how the environment might influence their next action.

"There are significant moments in everyone's day that can make literature. That's what you ought to write about."

— Raymond Carver, author,
What We Talk About When We Talk About Love

Signs:
Aries • Falcon • Alder
Birthdays:
Sir William Turner Walton (b. 1902)
Featured Website/Blog:
http://www.fictionfactor.com

SELF-PROMPTS:

MARCH 30
FIND MAGIC IN ORDINARY MOMENTS

The packed street crackled like downed power lines. Fifty thousand fans cheered as Marty Balin and Jefferson Starship performed in a way reminiscent of the late 1960s—on a flatbed truck on San Francisco's Haight Street. When the band opened "Miracles," Marty's iconic hit, a man standing alongside the stage opened his cell phone and dialed. "This song was playing when I asked her to marry me," he said. "She won't believe this."

She still may not believe what happened next. Marty noticed the man, walked over, smiled slyly, grabbed the phone, returned to center stage and belted out his famous ballad—serenading both woman and audience. Of everything I've seen at 300 concerts, this moment was the most magical. Imagine how it felt to the serenaded woman.

Magic hides like a mysterious, demure woman within ordinary moments, one eye shrouded in silk, the other observant. It appears without notice, daring you to recognize the moment and any accompanying message. When you see life deeply, you'll lift her veil.

What stroke of magic descended upon your ordinary moments? Paint the scene, and show how your day—and perspective—changed from the magical interlude. Import magic into your work, often. You will ingratiate yourself with readers quickly.

"To be real is to be surrounded by mystery."

— James Joyce, author, *Finnegan's Wake*

Signs:
Aries • Falcon • Alder

Birthdays:
Anna Sewell (b. 1820)

Featured Website/Blog:
http://www.fictionfactor.com

MARCH 31
SCRUMPTIOUS SOUL STORIES

The language of imagery reflects our souls. Well-crafted images draw and hook the readers' attention because they are felt and perceived so deeply. They also trigger journeys into hearts and souls. The result: lyrical writing few will soon forget. Or stop feeling.

Practice writing scrumptious soul stories. Take one, two or all five prompts below, close your eyes and envision the image moving, then write a 300- to 500-word story or poem:

- Elaborate pink shadow of language
- Magical honeycomb of sound
- Music of two words joining hands
- Lovers engulfed in wild ivy gardens
- Two waves colliding at sunrise

"What writers do is workmanlike: tenacious, skilled labor. But it is also mysterious. And the mystery involved in the act of creating a narrative is attached to the mysteries of life itself."

— Lorrie Moore, author, *The Agony and the Ego*

Signs:
Aries • Falcon • Alder
Birthdays:
Franz Joseph Haydn (b. 1732)
Andrew Lang (b. 1844)
Octavio Paz (b. 1914)
John Jakes (b. 1932)
Marge Piercy (b. 1936)
Al Gore (b. 1948)
Featured Website/Blog:
http://www.fictionfactor.com

April
National Poetry Month

APRIL 1
April Fool's Day
HUMOROUS TWISTS

We associate April 1 with jokes, humor and fun—all of which serve writers well. Humorous comments lighten the mood after an intense scene, or convey the follies of life. An example from my book, *Shades of Green:*

> *We stand in an ancient courtyard and yell for help. Clouds eclipse the moon. A gnarled oak moans, chasing a white owl away. Whooooosh! Fire spits from a second-story window. A dragon. "Let's go," she pleads.*
> *Two young women walk outside. I ask, "You live here? Did you see that flame?"*
> *"Oh, we were bored and were lighting hair spray on fire," she said.*

Write a humorous twist within a slice-of-life vignette in which a character, or you, causes someone to laugh during an otherwise serious moment. It could mean cracking a joke, making a gesture or clowning around. Make the moment sudden, a truly humorous twist that changes the mood—and sheds greater light on the character (or you).

"Truth is funnier than most things you can make up."
— Margo Kaufman, author,
This Damn House: My Subcontract with America

Signs:
Aries • Falcon • Alder
Birthdays:
Anne McCaffrey (b. 1926)
Jan Wahl (b. 1933)
Featured Website/Blog:
http://www.poetsandwriters.com

SELF-PROMPTS:

APRIL 2
SURPRISE! WRITE A TWIST ENDING

Yesterday, we worked with humorous twists. Today, let's try one of the most effective literary devices—twist endings. A twist ending hits the reader by complete surprise. It is used for dramatic effect, to show a hidden aspect of a character, and to keep the reader in suspense. Mysteries and thrillers live on twist endings.

Pick a journal entry, essay or story you've written, or write something new. Lead the principal character(s) through an action, comment, conclusion, and observation or gesture that surprises everyone—including you. Try it again with another story. Work to master the twist ending, and you will find readers clamoring to see what you come up with next!

"The sense of humor organically comes through and carries the reader through tough scenes."

— Michelle Tea, author, *Valencia*

Signs:
Aries • Falcon • Alder
Birthdays:
Washington Irving (b. 1783)
Hans Christian Anderson (b. 1805)
Anne Waldman (b. 1945)
Camille Paglia (b. 1947)
Featured Website/Blog:
http://www.poetsandwriters.com

SELF-PROMPTS:

APRIL 3
CIRCLE BACK

Sometimes, we encounter a moment too difficult to write. Maybe it's a personal tragedy or suffering, an emotional upheaval so severe that the memory can stir you, or a character's suffering that you're informing with your own experience. When you try to write deeply, to get to the core truth, it just hurts or upsets you too much … and you pull up short.

What to do? Approach it differently. Think of a skyward eagle spotting his prey and circling the sky 5, 10, even 20 or more times before swooping down for the kill. Circle the subject. Write the details, including what happened before and what will happen next. Next, write from an outsider's point of view—someone not in the final draft. Convey the emotional power or upset, the causes and the effects, through this outsider. Write as truthfully and intimately as possible.

Take that "outsider's" account and make it your own. Add details that pertained to you, and import the emotionally rich writing. Hang in there; don't bail emotionally. Write your way through the moment, constantly visualizing the light at the end of this scene.

"You must push yourself beyond the limits, all the time."

— Carlos Castaneda, author, *Tales of Power*

Signs:
Aries • Falcon • Alder
Birthdays:
Herb Caen (b. 1916)
Featured Website/Blog:
http://www.poetsandwriters.com

APRIL 4
SOUL OF THE BUILDING

We don't often associate buildings with souls (unless the buildings are churches); after all, buildings might *house* souls, but are otherwise inanimate. Still, many writers fall in love with architecture and design, and use buildings in their journalistic or fictional forays. Four examples are Anne Rice's haunting New Orleans in *The Vampire Chronicles*, Ayn Rand's epic *The Fountainhead*, Marlena de Blasi's alluring depictions of Venice's storied structures in *A Thousand Days Nights in Venice*, and the surgeon's precision Tom Wolfe (*Bonfire of the Vanities, A Man in Full*) lends to any building he describes. Since buildings house people, it behooves us to ably describe them and their relationship to those people.

Find a familiar building that intrigues you. Write about its dimensions, angles, corners, hallways, atrium or foyer, ceiling, nooks and crannies, main rooms, side rooms... *hidden* rooms (what's inside?). What is your relationship to that building? Make it as vivid as a photograph. Show the soul of the building.

"I focus on a specific image, and that image takes me into a scene. Then I begin to see the scene and I ask myself, 'What's to your right? What's to your left?' and I open up into this world."
— Amy Tan, author, *The Joy Luck Club*

Signs:
Aries • Falcon • Alder
Birthdays:
Maya Angelou (b. 1928)
Elizabeth Levy (b. 1942)
Featured Website/Blog:
http://www.booktv.org

APRIL 5
SECRET LANGUAGE OF LOVERS: Part One

Virtually every lengthy, intimate relationship contains a secret language. It could be merely endearing terms or a complex series of phrases. Typically, the deeper and more communicative a relationship, the more developed its secret language. Through it, we peek into the most intimate corners of subjects' hearts, and see how those hearts interweave. Creating and writing a secret language for lovers in your book or story is a most effective, powerful way to deliver narrative.

Take your journal and write some terms and phrases of your secret language, or, if you're not presently in relationship, the secret language you once shared or would like to share. What triggers those words? What evokes such sumptuous language? What can/does it add to your relationship? What can it add to a character's relationship? Write a short-short story, a slice-of-life vignette or dialogue, and take that secret language to a place you haven't yet attained... but want to.

"Whenever you go outside yourself — whether you're writing or reading — there's a point at which you get pushed back inside at the very deepest level."
— Melanie Rae Thon, author, *Meteors in August*

Signs:
Aries • Falcon • Alder
Birthday:
Arthur Hailey (b. 1920)
Marilyn Ferguson (b. 1938)
Featured Website/Blog:
http://www.booktv.org

SELF-PROMPTS:

APRIL 6
SECRET LANGUAGE OF LOVERS: Part Two

Here's a fun take on the Secret Language of Lovers exercise that serves any work containing deeply felt and expressed love scenes:

Think of a couple you know that enjoy a particularly loving, expressive relationship. Maybe you're half of it! Imagine how they talk with each other when it's just them and candles, soft moonlight reflecting off two wine glasses, a piece of music, and silk curtains billowing over a tray of Godiva chocolates. Do they speak sensually? Do they talk to each other's hearts — or souls? How do their *eyes* and *hands* speak the language?

Write the secret language of lovers.

Signs:
Aries • Falcon • Alder
Featured Website/Blog:
http://www.booktv.org

"All writers — all artists — may be classified as romantics, for the very act of creating, and of caring passionately enough to create, is a romantic gesture."
— Joyce Carol Oates, author, *Blonde*

SELF-PROMPTS:

APRIL 7
SHE WROTE ME A LETTER

Pick up several letters you've received from the same person, whether by mail or e-mail. Study the other person's perceptions of not only his/her life, but also yours from a distance. What narrative arc, or forward movement, do you see? Changes in perception? The way feelings, situations and environment are described? Write about these changes, and what you see in yourself through the other person's writing.

Next, write a letter to that person, fueling a new correspondence by passing along these revelations. Letter writing is not only a tremendous way for us to practice our craft from our hearts, but also a great literary device for novels, memoirs, essays and biographies.

Signs:
Aries • Falcon • Alder
Birthdays:
Donald Carrick (b. 1929)
Featured Website/Blog:
http://www.pubrants.blogspot.com

"I never write more fluidly, more excitedly, more directly and more honestly than in my love letters. Then I try to do the same in my other writing."
— Pam Houston, author, *Sight Hound*

APRIL 8
CHARACTER Q&A: Know Your Characters

Without well-developed, intriguing and believable characters, we will find it difficult to keep readers enmeshed in our stories. *People love to read about people.*

Take the five questions presented for each of the next six days, and answer them as completely as possible. If your answers spin into vignettes or mini-stories, write them — because it will likely reveal more. If more questions form, answer those as well. Set a goal to develop the most complete characters possible. First questions:

- Does the character you envision fit into your story?
- Will he/she play an integral part in the plot?
- Is he/she the protagonist (main character)?
- What will be your character's name? From where does that name descend?
- What does your character look like? (Facial features, birthmarks, body type, hair color and style, hands [soft or leathered?], skin complexion, muscular/athletic or not, height, weight.)

"I liked the idea of becoming many people when I wrote a novel, and I always enjoyed the fact that when I wore out one set, I could create another."
— Jim Harrison, author, *Legends of the Fall*

Signs:
Aries • Falcon • Alder
Birthdays:
Barbara Kingsolver (b. 1955)
Featured Website/Blog:
http://www.pubrants.blogspot.com

APRIL 9
CHARACTER Q&A: Family Ties

- What is your character's immediate family like? Who is closest to your character? Who was closest to your character as a child (if the character is an adult)?
- What is your character's ethnic background — and how far back does that go?
- What was your character's *ancestral* culture?
- What was your character's childhood like? Who was president when he/she was born?
- How interested is your character in the past, present or future of his/her community?

"A central character wants something, goes after it despite opposition (perhaps including his own doubts), and so arrives at a win, lose, or draw."
— John Gardner, author, *The Sunlight Dialogues*

Signs:
Aries • Falcon • Alder
Birthdays:
Leonard Wibberly (b. 1915)
Featured Website/Blog:
http://www.pubrants.blogspot.com

SELF-PROMPTS:

APRIL 10
CHARACTER Q&A: Brains and Movement

- What aspect of education shapes your character's choices, career and life?
- How does your character *move?* Slow or fast? Loping or short strides? Hurried, or cruising? Tilted to one side, or erect? Comfortably, or anxiously? Flowing or jagged?
- What is your character's body language like? Shoulders up or slumped? Use of hand gestures when speaking? Open or closed body positioning? Folded arms or not? Projecting himself/herself, or holding in, contracting?
- How does your character dress himself/herself? Be specific—types of clothes, label names, colors, fabrics, types of logos on t-shirts, frumpy or meticulous?
- How does your character respond to good news? Bad news?

"I feel at times that I'm making up these little people and I've lost my mind. But if that's what it takes…"
— Carolyn Chute, author, *The Beans of Egypt, Maine*

Signs:
Aries • Falcon • Alder
Birthdays:
Clare Newberry (b. 1903)
David Halberstam (b. 1934)
Anne Lamott (b. 1954)
Featured Website/Blog:
http://www.writerspace.com

SELF-PROMPTS:

APRIL 11
CHARACTER Q&A: Favorite Things

- How does your character take care of himself/herself? Exercise (and type)? Healthy eating? Dieting? Long walks? Or is it not a priority?
- What are your character's hobbies? Interests? Make a lifelong list.
- What are your character's most passionate likes and dislikes?
- What are your character's realized dreams? Unfulfilled dreams? Dreams that he or she holds when your story opens?
- Who are your character's favorite authors, artists, composers, athletes, TV shows, movie stars?

"It's motive alone that gives character to the actions of men."
— Jean de la Bruyere, author, *Caracteres*

Signs:
Aries • Falcon • Alder
Birthdays:
Dorothy Allison (b. 1949)
Featured Website/Blog:
http://www.writerspace.com

APRIL 12
CHARACTER Q&A: Preferred Foods and More

- What are your character's most and least favorite foods? What does your character like to cook?
- What are the social, political and/or religious views your character holds? Passionately? What does he/she find most intolerable?
- What love interest does your character have (if any)? What is your character's past relationship history?
- How does your character's relationship history influence him/her now?
- What past relationship(s) may creep in to haunt or help your character during the time frame of the story?

"This thing happens, where the characters take over and you almost want to look behind you to see who's writing the story."

— Joseph Wambaugh, author, *The Onion Field*

SELF-PROMPTS:

Signs:
Aries • Falcon • Alder
Birthdays:
Barbara Corcoran (b. 1911)
Beverly Cleary (b. 1916)
Scott Turow (b. 1949)
Featured Website/Blog:
http://www.writerspace.com

APRIL 13
CHARACTER Q&A: The 5-to-10 List

Let's conclude our character study by using the 5-to-10 list—a list of questions which we, if asked, we could answer in 5 to 10 minutes. Make lists for the following as they pertain to your character:
- Most dangerous acts
- Greatest gifts given or received
- Toughest decisions made; toughest decisions postponed
- Life decisions that changed a direction or opinion
- Greatest trips taken (do they impact your story?)
- Most outrageous dreams or fantasies (do they impact your story?)
- People that changed character's life — and how

"Depth of character is achieved through a subtle, gradual accumulation of insights and perceptions. It is an extension of the character's original concept."

— Leonard Bishop, author, *Dare to be a Great Writer*

SELF-PROMPTS:

Signs:
Aries • Falcon • Alder
Birthdays:
Genevieve Foster (b. 1893)
Marguerite Henry (b. 1902)
Featured Website/Blog:
http//www.wildpoetryforum.com

SELF-PROMPTS:

Signs:
Aries • Falcon • Willow
Birthdays:
Arnold Toynbee (b. 1889)
Featured Website/Blog:
http//www.wildpoetryforum.com

APRIL 14
ACT YOUR CHARACTERS—THEN WRITE

Want your essay subjects and story characters to move fluidly and naturally? Act them out first! Take a page from legendary actor-director Charlie Chaplin, who acted out each scene—in *every* actor's role—before shooting. Literally walk, run, cry, laugh, dance or weave in your character's "skin," then write the movement. Act through the entire scene as it runs through your mind and back—and write it down.

"Poets and writers have to come up with the vision and they have to turn it on so it sparks and catches hold."
— Ken Kesey, author, *One Flew Over the Cuckoo's Nest*

SELF-PROMPTS:

Signs:
Aries • Falcon • Alder
Birthdays:
Albert Goldman (b. 1927)
Jeffrey Archer (b. 1940)
Featured Website/Blog:
http//www.wildpoetryforum.com

APRIL 15
LIVE READ: VOICING YOUR CHARACTERS

Let's explore a crucial aspect of theatre—the live read. Before theatrical performances, actors read to connect with the character, while the playwright and director listen intently for tone, rhythm and how the spoken dialogue moves the plot.

The stars of today's live read? Your voice and/or your characters. Take the characters you developed during the past week—or a story you wrote—and read each character's part aloud. Read from that character's skin. Don't worry about movement—just read your characters' voices into being. How does each character sound? How does each voice feel as it rolls through you? Use this self-feedback to further refine your characters' voices.

"It's an astonishing thing to have created a person alone in your room. It's an enormous privilege."
— Allan Garganus, author, *The Oldest Living Confederate Widow Tells All*

APRIL 16
GIVING ADVICE

Think of a subject, life experience or area of expertise in which you can help others. Write down all bits of advice you can give. Ask yourself, "Would I do that for myself? Did I do that for myself?" Write an essay, article or letter that spells out your advice, how to apply it into one's life and how the advice will benefit others.

"Every man has within himself the entire human condition."
— Michel de Montaigne, author, *The Essayes*

SELF-PROMPTS:

Signs:
Aries • Falcon • Willow
Birthdays:
John Christopher (b. 1922)
Featured Website/Blog:
http://www.bookpage.com

APRIL 17
READ ALOUD: Part One

Oral storytelling lies as deeply in our bones and blood as our furthest ancestral roots. Cavemen told stories of the hunt to ensure survival; this began an oral tradition that brought us such great works as the Persian bazaar and travel tales, the Vedas and Native American literature. It continues with indigenous peoples today.

Take lessons from our ancestral past to read a piece of your daily writing out loud, either to yourself or another person. Make editing changes that suit your ear. See if the resulting work reflects an added resonance and more concise structure and choice of words.

"Punch the reader. 'Look what I did to you.' Make their knees weak; that's a good thing."
— Harvey Stanbrough, author, *Beyond the Masks*

SELF-PROMPTS:

Signs:
Aries • Falcon • Willow
Birthdays:
Thornton Wilder (b. 1897)
Cynthia Ozick (b. 1928)
Featured Website/Blog:
http://www.bookpage.com

SELF-PROMPTS:

APRIL 18
READ ALOUD: Part Two

Practice three or four poems, an essay or a story that you'd like to read in public. Listen for the rhythm of your words, the *music* of your story, the way in which language serves you.

Then switch modes: Reading live is about performing, to an extent. Practice making eye contact in the mirror. Use body language and hand gestures as needed. Create the clearest possible delivery of your work; after all, the listener's ear is your audience. Then find an open mic reading, or a gathering of friends, and read aloud. Watch your audience to see how you're connecting, how they're receiving the work.

Reading live offers a great way to build an audience—and your confidence. When your books sell, you will likely hold readings at libraries, bookstores, book fairs, coffee houses and other locations. Read live when you can.

Signs:
Aries • Falcon • Willow
Featured Website/Blog:
http://www.bookpage.com

"I have a song to sing and I will sing it, although I am alone in an empty house and must sing to my own ears."
— Friedrich Nietzsche, philosopher, author, *Thus Spoke Zarathustra*

SELF-PROMPTS:

APRIL 19
MY SIX-WORD MEMOIR

Larry Smith and Rachel Fershleiser compiled an intriguing book, *Not Quite What I Was Planning: Six-Word Memoirs By Famous Authors.* The content matches the title—a series of six-word memoirs, some funny, some serious, all compelling. Even the title is six words! A memoir from yours truly: *My Home Became Pen and Road.*

See if you can capture your life's journey in six words. Make your micro memoir declarative and definitive. Create a statement that invites readers to know more about you and your life. If summarizing your life journey is difficult, then write a six-word memoir on one aspect of your life.

Signs:
Aries • Falcon • Willow
Birthdays:
Jean Lee Latham (b. 1902)
Featured Website/Blog:
http://www.literacycaferadioshow.com

"It is not because things are difficult that we do not dare; it is because we do not dare that they are difficult."
— Seneca, Onondaga chief

APRIL 20
CROSS-POLLINATION

SELF-PROMPTS:

In nature, cross-pollination occurs when seeds of different strains, or species, unite. In writing, cross-pollination combines reading, note-taking, and deep contemplation to arrive at ideas or realizations that spur growth, movement and the next paragraph. By reading several books simultaneously, we cultivate our intuitive and subconscious minds to draw instantaneous connections when we're writing.

Next time you sit down to read, grab three books on separate subjects, and read bits of them at the same time. Seek connections, points in common, among the information. Also listen to your gut, which often will make the connections for you.

Grab your journal and write about the connections. Produce a new writing that you have cross-pollinated.

"Cross-connection with other arts is crucial, in the way it feeds you. It helps you develop sound, color, rhythm to your writing; it helps create the music of your writing."

— Arthur Sze, poet, author, *Silk Dragon*

Signs:
Aries • Beaver • Willow
Featured Website/Blog:
http://www.
literacycaferadioshow.com

APRIL 21
CULTIVATE YOUR (WRITING) TOPSOIL

SELF-PROMPTS:

Eminent poet, novelist and essayist Wendell Berry writes in *The Art of the Commonplace*, "(Topsoil) is enriched by all things that die and enter into it. It keeps the past, not as history or as memory, but as richness, new possibility."

Topsoil grows our food and sustains all ground-borne plant life. When wind, floods, environmental disasters or the hands of man erode topsoil, our sustenance is threatened. Likewise, we tend to reference only the outer layer of our life experiences when writing—especially when we are freelancers with a number of concurrent assignments.

How do you feed your topsoil? Cross-read? Cross-pollinate? Go to readings? Absorb past lessons and experiences into the present? Meet other authors? Listen to music? Study art or architecture? Visit museums? Observe people with interests other than your own?

Write an essay that describes the actions you take to cultivate and nourish your writing, and explore the areas that provide richness and new possibility—and those that need to be fed.

"Approach the moment with the idea that you're in the fight to the finish."
— Mataemon Iso, martial arts master

Signs:
Taurus • Beaver • Willow
Birthdays:
Barbara Park (b. 1947)
Featured Website/Blog:
http://www.literacycaferadioshow.com

SELF-PROMPTS:

APRIL 22
Earth Day
PROVOKED BY READING

The next time you read a book that provokes your mind and heart, keep your journal next to you. Write down your thoughts and feelings the moment they occur. What line, quote or passage in the book triggered you? Why? While the passage fills you, write. Give it all you've got for the next few minutes, and see where this inspiration leads. Use the words you just read as a vehicle, and drive them as far as they will take you.

Signs:
Taurus • Beaver • Willow
Birthdays:
Paula Fox (b. 1923)
Janet Evanovich (b. 1943)
Featured Website/Blog:
http://www.poets.org

"Read, read, read. Read everything — trash, classics, good and bad, and see how they do it. Read! You'll absorb it. Then write."

— William Faulkner, author, *As I Lay Dying*

SELF-PROMPTS:

APRIL 23
LANDSCAPE LIKE THE ESKIMOS

Eskimos employ more than 70 different words for properties and uses of snow. Venetians use a dozen words to describe types of boats and textures of water — the two items that sustain their lives. Everywhere, native peoples have created rich vernaculars to describe their most immediate resource and environment.

Look around at the natural landscape where you live. What synonyms can you use to describe the hills, valleys, mountains, cliffs, seas, ponds, deserts or forests around you? Definitely include the local colloquialisms that "old-timers" and lifelong residents of the area use. Write the words, and then use them in an essay that explores your home landscape.

Signs:
Taurus • Beaver • Willow
Featured Website/Blog:
http://www.poets.org

"I saw it all for the first time as if it were happening for the first time — the poetry and the real world were inextricably merged in my perception."

— Diana O'Hehir, poet, author, *Home Free*

APRIL 24
BODY AS LANDSCAPE

SELF-PROMPTS:

Describe a landscape in terms of the human body. What do the undulating hills and valleys remind you of? Where do the rivers, creeks, streams, lakes and waterfalls take you in the body? Do high meadow grasses remind you of long hair blowing in the wind? Whether it's your home landscape, a favorite travel destination or a setting you just can't forget, give it human form and see how the landscape interacts with you in the flesh.

"If we align ourselves with that grain, we can sometimes feel a deep sense of being in the right place and doing the right thing. Such moments are rare and brief. When they come, they're so powerful that I end up reflecting on them – and often writing about them – long afterwards."

— Scott Russell Sanders, author, *Hunting for Hope*

Signs:
Taurus • Beaver • Willow
Birthdays:
Anthony Trollope (b. 1815)
Lynn Hall (b. 1914)
Featured Website/Blog:
http://www.poets.org

APRIL 25
STROKE THE SCULPTRESS

SELF-PROMPTS:

Some writers and editors compare literary writing to sculpting. The metaphor is easy to follow: a first draft "chisels" marble into a rough shape, the revision draft reveals a finer form, and the polished draft brings out the finest features of every word, working together. We spend this time sculpting our work — what about ourselves?

Today, write about the ways in which you would create a sculpture or bust of yourself. What features would stand out? Where would you polish? What would you leave rough, edgy? Would you use marble, glass, clay or another material? How can you add light or shadow to portray your view of the world?

"In every block of marble I see a statue as plain as though it stood before me, shaped and perfect in attitude and action."

— Michelangelo, sculptor-poet

Signs:
Taurus • Beaver • Willow
Featured Website/Blog:
http://www.poetry.com

SELF-PROMPTS:

Signs:
Taurus • Beaver • Willow
Birthdays:
William Shakespeare (b. 1564)
Ruth Beebe Hill (b. 1913)
Bernard Malamud (b. 1914)
Patricia Reilly Giff (b. 1935)
Lee Bennett Hopkins (b. 1938)
Featured Website/Blog:
http://www.poetry.com

APRIL 26
MOST AT HOME

Where have you felt most at home during your life? Was it the place or places where you were raised? A vacation getaway your family always frequented? Another country? On the road? Or in the home where you now reside?

Write about the place where you felt most at home. Describe the setting, then dive deep and write about how it provided you with the comfort and security to explore yourself and the world around you. Write this piece to read as deliciously as your favorite comfort food. Remember this feeling every time you center a story or character in a home.

"The everyday…is not merely ennui, pointlessness, repetition, triviality; it is beauty as well."

— Milan Kundera, author, *The Unbearable Lightness of Being*

SELF-PROMPTS:

Signs:
Taurus • Beaver • Willow
Birthdays:
John Burningham (b. 1936)
Featured Website/Blog:
http://www.poetry.com

APRIL 27
A BOW TO THE TINIEST DETAIL

All details are vital. We populate our writing with major details, so let's give a bow to the tiniest detail. When I read a subject in which I already hold some personal knowledge, I always dig for something new. In particular, I seek incisive, titillating details. Why else would biographies of Abraham Lincoln still roll off the presses more than 140 years after his death, if not for the emergence of new details or re-ordering of known facts? Unearthing these "tiny" details involve a lot of sleuthing, but they create the biggest buzz with the reader.

Write a story or essay with crisp, original details. Identify the tiniest detail—the insight that could create a sense of wonder—and exaggerate its importance. Write a vignette specifically about the detail—how you came up with it, what it symbolizes or shows, why it is significant. If you'd like, use the detail in another story to see if it resonates the same way.

"First light and a dark bird wings away – it's a poem."

— Lawrence Ferlinghetti, poet, author, *A Coney Island of the Mind*

APRIL 28
OPEN THE WINDOW

It's spring: budding trees, fresh sounds, crisp air, new growth, summer right around the corner. Open the window! Grab your journal and write down every image, observation or sensation that comes to you in the next 30 minutes. Just write images or short sentences. Feel the moment as you write it. When finished, assemble your images and short sentences into a poem. Don't worry about meter, rhyming or other structure. Just bring the images together in a natural way. Polish your piece by making sure the words reflect how you feel, what you see, how this open window sheds light on your day.

"Poetry has an interesting function. It helps people be where they are."
— Gary Snyder, author, *No Nature*

SELF-PROMPTS:

Signs:
Taurus • Beaver • Willow
Birthdays:
Alistair McLean (b. 1922)
Lois Duncan (b. 1934)
Featured Website/Blog:
http://www.webexhibits.org/poetry

APRIL 29
ANCIENT FORMS

A website exhibit I wrote, *Poetry Through The Ages*, surveys 4,500 years of western poetry. Among other things, the exhibit re-introduces obsolete, ancient poetic forms and brings them to light in the 21st century. Ancient poetry forms not only create a fun challenge, but they reflect the culture, setting, thinking, history and sentiment of the times in which they were created.

Click onto Poetry Through The Ages (http://www.webexhibits.org/poetry). Find a form that you like, and try to write a poem in that form. Don't just copy the line, syllable or rhyme pattern, but also seek the feeling of what it must have been like to sit on a hillside in Ancient Greece, pay homage in Sumeria, or recite a poem in a medieval France court or village. Experience one of the great privileges of being a writer—transporting yourself to another place and time through words.

"Because it creates autonomous structures that are imbued with life and which stir the life of those who experience them — poetry is, in process and in being, intrinsically affirmative."

— Denise Levertov, poet, author, *The Poet in the World*

SELF-PROMPTS:

Signs:
Taurus • Beaver • Willow
Birthdays:
Jill Paton Walsh (b. 1937)
Nicole Ruben (b. 1953)
Featured Website/Blog:
http//www.webexhibits.org/poetry

SELF-PROMPTS:

APRIL 30
THE ELOQUENT SPOKEN LINE

Poetry requires as much polish as creativity, and as much silent observation as bird watching. The finer art of poetry lies in its precision, in the ability to make a spoken line as eloquent and true to your soul or heart as possible.

Take a poem or a small series of poetic images you've written during the week or during National Poetry Month. Look at the words you wrote. Read them aloud. Read them softly. Mouth them in silence. *Feel* them leaving your mouth, projecting onto the world. Do they convey the moment as you intended? Read, polish, and read again until your line or lines are as eloquent and ripe as an orchard at harvest time. Create a stanza of spoken-word poetry that sends shivers in your heart, spine and skin—just as it will your audience.

Signs:
Taurus • Beaver • Willow
Birthdays:
Harriet Sobol (b. 1936)
Featured Website/Blog:
http://www.webexhibits.org/poetry

"The purpose of poetry is to take over a life and make it generate incandescent language, which moves them to awaken a glow in other lives, to rouse in them feelings so deep and daring that no return to ignorant sleep is possible."
— Will Baker, author, *Tony and the Cows: A True Story of the Range Wars*

MAY 1
WRITE NOW

What (or who) are you thinking about?

What are you feeling?

What has inspired, surprised, or delighted you the most today?

What activities touched you most in the last 24 hours?

How does all of this make you see the world in front of you right this second?

For the next 20 to 30 minutes, write it all down, like a running stream — no interruptions, no pauses except to collect the next sentence. Commit this moment right now to paper or computer — a moment you will never experience again.

"The artist needs only this: a special world to which he alone has the key."
— Andre Gide, author, *Notebooks*

Signs:
Taurus • Beaver • Willow
Birthdays:
Hugo Alfven (b. 1872)
Featured Website/Blog:
http://www.owl.english.purdue.edu/owl

SELF-PROMPTS:

MAY 2
COLLIDING METEORS: BRINGING OPPOSITES TOGETHER

The clash (or collaboration) between opposites provides one of writing's most dramatic and engaging platforms. The subject can be two lovers, political foes, enemies or people with opposing beliefs or styles. Doesn't matter. When two opposites come together, we take notice. When we see it in print, we can't turn the pages fast enough.

Write a quick sketch of two opposite characters—or recall the last time you talked with someone whose views differed sharply from your own. Point out the opposites and how far apart the subjects are, and have the subjects identify a common point and *pull closer* through it.

Master this approach—especially the art of bringing opposites together, either as allies or lovers. You will win many readers' hearts and imaginations.

Signs:
Taurus • Beaver • Willow

Featured Website/Blog:
http://www.owl.english.purdue.edu/owl

"Writers have to cultivate the habit early in life of listening to people other than themselves."

— Russell Baker, author, *On Growing Up*

SELF-PROMPTS:

MAY 3
YOUR BEST SENTENCE

When do you write your most compelling sentence or dialogue? Answer: with every sentence or piece of dialogue! Often, inexperienced authors build up for the big, dramatic moment, and then unleash their creative wiles—after most readers have checked out. Avoid that trap by letting your story or piece of writing dictate its rhythms.

Write an essay, poem, vignette or short-short story after affirming, "Every sentence is my best sentence." Be aware of your word choices and combinations, how they move the piece forward, and how they provide character, color, texture, tone and rhythm to your work. Make every sentence your best sentence.

Signs:
Taurus • Beaver • Willow

Birthdays:
May Sarton (b. 1912)
Mavis Jukes (b. 1947)

Featured Website/Blog:
http://www.owl.english.purdue.edu/owl

"Once you have the beginning and the end fixed, you can construct the most direct route between the two."

— Marsha Norman, playwright, author, *Getting Out: A Play in Two Acts*

MAY 4
STRANGERS IN THE NIGHT: Part One

Write a series of 300-word vignettes about experiences that happened at far different times and places in your life. Write about your thoughts and feelings, how you acted or reacted, and what you sensed. Why does each experience remain close to you today? Look for points in common between your pieces. Underline them.

"Let's just say I have been on many journeys into my own psyche."
— Lois Ann Yamanaka, author, *Behold the Many*

SELF-PROMPTS:

Signs:
Taurus • Beaver • Willow
Birthdays:
Beverly Butler (b. 1932)
George Will (b. 1941)
Graham Swift (b. 1949)
David Guterson (b. 1956)
Featured Website/Blog:
http://www.answers.com

MAY 5
Cinco de Mayo
STRANGERS IN THE NIGHT: Part Two

Identify the points in common from the separate life experiences you wrote out. See what motivations, ways of acting and reacting, types of interactions and views of the world match up—or differ. Write out the common traits that unite your younger and older self, and write out the traits that have changed during the subsequent years. Also use this exercise to develop characters and story subjects.

"The business of a writer is to dust away the layers of prejudice and presumption and get down to that raw, vulnerable level where you might be able to tell the truth about yourself."

— Jeanette Winterson, author, *Written on the Body*

SELF-PROMPTS:

Signs:
Taurus • Beaver • Willow
Featured Website/Blog:
http://www.answers.com

SELF-PROMPTS:

MAY 6
STRANGERS IN THE NIGHT: Part Three

Take the common and separate traits you've written out, and compose two different short pieces: The first, a memoir-type vignette that describes the enhancement of your common traits. The second, a tribute—or good riddance! — to an aspect of your old self that you've shed. See how the pieces differ in rhythm, tone, style, word choice and content.

Signs:
Taurus • Beaver • Willow
Birthdays:
Randall Jarell (b. 1914)
Judy Delton (b. 1931)
Featured Website/Blog:
http://www.answers.com

"The sense of a book is organic, it comes from within. My way of doing it is through accretion, piecing together, overlapping."
— Timothy Liu, poet, author, *Hard Evidence*

SELF-PROMPTS:

MAY 7
THE DAWN OF CONSTANT CREATION

Isn't it exciting to learn something for the first time? To feel the exhilaration of discovering something or figuring it out? I don't know about you, but I feel like the dawn of creation has visited every time I learn or write something new. Right now, I eagerly await the next moment.

When was the most recent time you learned something new about a world event or personality, a friend, an historic period, a discovery or your own potential? How did your world feel at that moment? Did the doors swing wide open and remind you that anything is possible? Did you feel wiser, more powerful, more inclined to explore further? What did you integrate into your life? What did you gain?

Sate your thirst for knowledge and wisdom by learning something new today. Continually touch the dawn of creation with the same intent as the centerpiece of Michelangelo's Sistine Chapel painting—when God and Adam touch fingertips.

Signs:
Taurus • Beaver • Willow
Birthdays:
Ruth Prawer Jhabvala (b. 1927)
Peter Carey (b. 1943)
Rabindranath Tagore (b. 1861)
Featured Website/Blog:
http://www.authorsociety.org

"It seems increasingly certain that healing and creativity are different parts of a single picture."
— Elmer Green, biopsychologist

MAY 8
WRITE YOUR BRIDGES

SELF-PROMPTS:

Bridges are among the most utilized architectural creations in human history. They cross rivers, bays, creeks and lakes. Some bridges float; others span mouths of huge bodies of water. Rope bridges allow Himalayan villagers to cross deep river gorges; draw bridges enable cars to pass over intracoastal shipping lanes. Bridges have as many designs as they do purposes. The bridges of our lives are much the same way.

What are your bridges? What do they look like? How do they serve you? Where do they lead you? Take a contemplative day in your journal to write your bridges. Give them physical features, designs. "Walk" on them, and see how they feel—whether or not you're actually utilizing one or more in your life. Explore the places they take you, or reflect on the places from which you embarked. Import bridges into your work as a literary device.

"To be nobody but yourself—in a world which is doing its best, night and day, to make you everybody else—means to fight the hardest battle which any human being can fight; and never stop fighting."
— e.e. cummings, poet, author, *Complete Poems of e.e. cummings*

Signs:
Taurus • Beaver • Willow
Birthdays:
Gary Snyder (b. 1930)
Nonny Hogrogian (b. 1932)
Thomas Pynchon (b. 1937)
Pat Barker (b. 1943)
Featured Website/Blog:
http://www.authorsociety.org

MAY 9
THE LONG SHOWER

SELF-PROMPTS:

Take a long shower today. Give yourself an extra five or ten minutes. During your shower, think and free associate. Join your thoughts and the streaming water to explore every nook and cranny, every "current" that comes along.
When finished, dry off, slip on some clothes and find your journal or computer. Write down everything that came to mind in the shower—and where it took you. If a story or essay prompt develops, or a missing piece to your work-in-progress appears, write it to completion while the thoughts are large and clear.

"We work in the dark—we do what we can—we give what we have. Our doubt is our passion, and our passion is our risk. The rest is the madness of art."
—Henry James, author, *The Ambassadors*

Signs:
Taurus • Beaver • Willow
Birthdays:
Sir James M. Barrie (b. 1860)
Richard Adams (b. 1920)
Joy Harjo (b. 1951)
Featured Website/Blog:
http://www.authorsociety.org

SELF-PROMPTS:

MAY 10
BUILD A SCRAPBOOK

Build a writer's scrapbook today. Collect magazine photos, blog items, headlines, personal photos, flyers, poems and lyrics that inspire you creatively, or that relate to a subject about which you're writing. Add comments you hear on the radio or TV, or in a favorite movie. Place the visuals onto four to eight scrapbook pages, and then surround them with the written items. Write captions or short vignettes to connect the items, or to trigger your imagination forward. Perhaps invite a creative friend over, and ask them to hand-write an impression or two.

Add to this scrapbook regularly. Turn it into an extension of your creative mind. Refer to it often for story ideas, or for reminders of your writing direction.

"Rest not! Life is sweeping by; go and dare before you die. Something mighty and sublime, leave behind to conquer time."
— Johann Wolfgang Goethe, author, *The Sorrows of Young Werther*

Signs:
Taurus • Beaver • Willow
Birthdays:
John Rowe Townsend (b. 1922)
Featured Website/Blog:
http://www.firstwriter.com

SELF-PROMPTS:

MAY 11
RANDOM ROAD TRIP

Grab an atlas—ideally, a world atlas. A thorough road atlas of the U.S. can serve as a back up. Turn to a random page. Study the features of the map and names of places. Imagine yourself visiting the area with wide eyes and endless ambition to explore and experience every waking moment. Write out the adventures you would pursue, the cities or geographic features (mountains, rivers, bays, valleys) you would visit and the people you would meet. Don't be afraid to crawl into the back alleys, walk the dusty paths or dive into restaurants or cafes off the beaten path. Create an adventure entirely your own. If you're a fiction writer, take this exercise a step further and give it to one of your characters.

"The world cannot give you what you seek, for what you seek you have brought with you from beyond the world."
— Marshall Summers, special education teacher

Signs:
Taurus • Beaver • Willow
Birthdays:
Sheila Burnford (b. 1918)
Richard Meltzer (b. 1945)
Featured Website/Blog:
http://www.firstwriter.com

MAY 12
HAND WRITE TO A LONG-LOST FRIEND

What was commonplace for centuries — the handwritten letter — has become rare in today's era of e-mailing, blogging and texting. The handwritten letter is such an organic communion between heart, mind and pen, that it should be a regular part of every writer's life.

Today, compose a hand-written letter to a long-lost friend — an old schoolmate, a friend in the service, a next-door neighbor from childhood, even a former lover for whom you hold fond (or angry) memories. Write the twists and turns of your life, places in yourself you've explored, the most compelling memories of your friendship, dreams you have realized or left behind. Be daring. Be intimate. Fill your letter with your heart. See if you notice a difference between handwriting your letter and typing it out on your computer.

When finished, put the letter in your journal, or integrate it into a story, memoir or novel. Better yet, if circumstances permit, mail it to your long-lost friend.

"The artist tells the audience, at the risk of their own displeasure, the secrets of their hearts."

— Robin Collingwood, author, *An Essay on Philosophical Method*

Signs:
Taurus • Beaver • Willow
Birthdays:
Edward Lear (b. 1812)
Dante Gabriel Rossetti (b. 1828)
Lornie Niedecker (b. 1903)
Featured Website/Blog:
http://www.firstwriter.com

MAY 13
EMBRACE CONFLICT

The driving force of story is conflict. No getting around it. Conflict motivates us in our everyday lives, as we would never grow through the experience of resolution unless we had conflict. Likewise, conflict is essential to the story, whether written or oral. Rather than seeing conflict as a negative, embrace it as the necessary first step to a positive outcome. For the writer, a good conflict creates a good plot — and a good plot results in a good story.

Write down five sources of conflict. They can stem from your life, observations you've made of others, or types of conflict that fascinate or abhor you. Pick one of those sources, and write the conflict to its resolution. Dive into the root of the conflict. Write in first person, third person, or through dialoguing between two or more people. Sense how the progression toward resolution drives the story, gives it dramatic value.

"Conflict is both king of all and father of all."

— Heraclitus

Signs:
Taurus • Beaver • Hawthorn
Birthdays:
Norma Klein (b. 1938)
Francine Pascal (b. 1938)
Bruce Chatwin (b. 1940)
Featured Website/Blog:
http://infoplease.com

SELF-PROMPTS:

MAY 14
MY DREAM COMMUNITY

I still dream of residing in a hamlet of 15 to 20 cottages filled with creative types—writers, musicians, oral storytellers, poets, potters, a minister or shaman, artists and teachers. I'd throw in a potter, organic gardener and master chef for good measure. Our inspired group would create new works, then reach out to touch minds and hearts.

What is your dream community? Who would live in it? How would you interact? What would your dwellings look like? How would you sustain yourselves? What would you create? How would you involve the world beyond your community? What sources of entertainment and education would fill you?

Cut loose. Have fun with this one. Become a community creator. Don't be surprised if this exercise creates the setting for a story or novel.

Signs:
Taurus • Beaver • Hawthorn
Birthdays:
George Selden (b. 1929)
Featured Website/Blog:
http://infoplease.com

"Since most creative nonfiction deals with men and women, the writers pay particular attention to how these people live, not in the abstract, but in the everyday world."

— Theodore A. Rees Cheney, *Writing Creative Nonfiction*

SELF-PROMPTS:

MAY 15
WRITE YOURSELF IN SILK

If you're having trouble diving into a love scene in your novel, memoir or short story, try this: Imagine yourself wrapped in the most sumptuous, form-fitting silk. How does it feel? What emotions or sensations does it provoke in you? What movements? What does its color activate in your imagination? Who do you see yourself as? Write as though you're wrapped in silk—and luxuriate in the moment.

Signs:
Taurus • Beaver • Hawthorn
Birthdays:
L. Frank Baum (b. 1856)
Katherine Ann Porter (b. 1890)
Ellen MacGregor (b. 1906)
Norma Fox Mazer (b. 1931)
Featured Website/Blog:
http://infoplease.com

"Construction on a purely spiritual basis is a slow business…the artist must not train only his eye, but also his soul."

— Wassily Kandinsky, artist

MAY 16
COMPOSING THE RAIN

The next time it rains, fully immerse with your pen. Write the face, character, movement and voice of the rain. What scents does it release? What memories does it provoke? What types of sounds do the raindrops make on rooftops, plants, and cars? Windowsills? Is the rain soft or hard? *Show* us. How do your immediate surroundings, moods and plans change from the rain? Compose the rain.

"One time when I was giving a reading in a prison, the guys convicted of heroin possession and the guys convicted of cocaine possession got into a fight — over the dialogue in one of my books. Both said it described them perfectly. I took it as a compliment."
— Elmore Leonard, author, *Killshot*

SELF-PROMPTS:

Signs:
Taurus • Beaver • Hawthorn
Birthdays:
Betty Miles (b. 1928)
Adrienne Rich (b. 1929)
Featured Website/Blog:
http://www.mostlybrightideas.com

MAY 17
FISH OUT OF WATER

What recent experience made you feel like a fish out of water? What made you feel so out of place and uncomfortable that you wanted to scurry home and crawl into bed? Or otherwise remove yourself from the moment?

Crawl into your deepest discomfort, sit with the feeling for a minute, then write. Try to be as personal and subjective as possible. If you start to disengage and write objectively, force yourself back into the "fish out of water" state. *Show* that gasping sensation, that desperation to return to what is normal, comfortable, routine.

Writing from discomfort and verbalizing the feeling is progressive: the more you do it, the longer you can sustain it. Many of literature's most memorable characters arose from the discomfort of their authors. Give it a try, and see what happens.

"There is no separation between writing, life and the mind."
— Natalie Goldberg, author, *Writing Down the Bones*

SELF-PROMPTS:

Signs:
Taurus • Beaver • Hawthorn
Birthdays:
Gary Paulson (b. 1939)
Featured Website/Blog:
http://www.mostlybrightideas.com

MAY 18
SYMBOLize YOURSELF!

My personal symbols are eagle, roadrunner, the "Om" symbol, heart, ocean and seed. Sometimes, I write about them; I also sprinkle them in my fiction and creative non-fiction work, because they seem to draw more creativity and power to my writing. Plus, they make interesting additions to my characters' lives.

What man-made or natural objects or creatures — or celestial bodies — best symbolize who and what you are today?

Write down your personal symbols. After creating your list, write 100 words (or more) about each symbol, and how you embody it and strive to reach what it represents. Try to use more personal symbols in your writing.

"Don't put yourself on the couch. Resist the urge to psychologize everything. Just write the story."
— Rachel Howard, author, *The Lost Night: A Memoir*

Signs:
Taurus • Beaver • Hawthorn
Birthdays:
Omar Khayyam (b. 1048)
Bertrand Russell (b. 1872)
Irene Hunt (b. 1907)
Lillian Hoban (b. 1925)
Featured Website/Blog:
http://www.mostlybrightideas.com

MAY 19
DELIVER THE NEXT PARAGRAPH

Sometimes, the final sentence of a paragraph carries that hurried "get it over with" feeling, like the end of a letter you're only too happy to finish and seal. In our zeal to get to the next paragraph, we might have the tendency to rush a paragraph to its conclusion, instead of allowing the moment to play itself out.

Resist that temptation at all costs. The final sentences of paragraphs in stories, essays and creative writing serve two vital purposes: They deliver the paragraph to its completion: and they establish a launching pad from which the next paragraph can take flight.

Pull your final sentences from the paragraphs of your most recent piece together. If they resonate, if your eye naturally wants to move on, you've produced a strong end sentence. If not, work hard to write a powerful, no-holds-barred closing sentence. See that every story or essay you write includes strong closing sentences in every paragraph.

"Never think of revising as fixing something that is wrong … think of it as an opportunity to improve something you already love."
— Marion Dane Bauer, author, *A Taste of Smoke*

Signs:
Taurus • Beaver • Hawthorn
Birthdays:
Pauline Clarke (b. 1921)
Peter J. Lippman (b. 1936)
Nora Ephron (b. 1941)
Featured Website/Blog:
http://www.organizedwriter.com

MAY 20
EXTREME HAIKU

Words open up a universe of associations for us—especially when packed in short, mighty punches. The Japanese poetry form of haiku distills observed moments into a 5-7-5 syllable format in its three lines. Those seventeen syllables can contain the world. That's the power of haiku.

Let's take haiku to the extreme today. Write a haiku. Read it three times, diving deeply into each word and how it relates to the next word and the next line. Now, circle the first line, draw seven lines outward, and write words or images you associate with the line. Do the same for the second and third lines. The original haiku should visually resemble the eye of a creative storm. See if you can write a short vignette or essay with the new images you've spun from your haiku—or a cluster of new haiku.

"More a way of being than a way of writing, haiku sees without ego."
— Dr. Don Eulert, author, *Field: A Haiku Circle*

Signs:
Taurus • Beaver • Hawthorn
Birthdays:
Carol Carrick (b. 1935)
Featured Website/Blog:
http://www.organizedwriter.com

MAY 21
SENTENCE PLAY: SHORTEN IT UP!

Short sentences punctuate stories. They connote fast action, dramatic moments and quick, decisive thinking—whether right or wrong. They hook the reader into the moment, and don't let go. Short, succinct sentences require clarity, solid word choice. Intent. Presence. Directness. It is no coincidence that four great action writers of the past century—Ernest Hemingway, James McElroy, Louis L'Amour and Elmore Leonard — built a combined total of nearly 200 books on short sentences.

Write an entire page in which every sentence is seven words or less in length. One- or two-sentence are permitted. Focus on the presence, drama, decision-making and action of your subject. When finished, read the piece aloud, and see if it conveys the same energy that accompanied your visualization of the scene.

"There is something about words. In expert hands, manipulated deftly, they take you prisoner. Wind themselves around your limbs like spider silk and when you are so enthralled you cannot move, they pierce your skin, enter your blood, numb your thoughts. Inside you they work their magic."
— Diane Setterfield, author, *The Thirteenth Tale*

Signs:
Taurus • Deer • Hawthorn
Birthdays:
Al Franken (b. 1951)
Featured Website/Blog:
http://www.organizedwriter.com

SELF-PROMPTS:

Signs:
Gemini • Deer • Hawthorn
Birthdays:
Richard Wagner (b. 1813)
Sir Arthur Conan Doyle (b. 1859)
Featured Website/Blog:
http://www.suite101.com

MAY 22
SENTENCE PLAY: PUNCTUATE TO ILLUSTRATE

Create a narrative scene that uses punctuation rather than lengthy description to illustrate the moment. If a lion charges you, let it charge with exclamation points!!! If something forces you to ponder deeply … let us see your thinking process … through ellipses. If you're on another planet and aliens pursue you — keep running — turn — hide — describe what happens. When someone insists on making a point and holding you in check with lengggthy, drawwwn-out enunciationnnnn...show it. Make punctuation a visual aid in your future writing. If you want to see memorable examples, review the non-fiction and fiction of the master of creative punctuation, Tom Wolfe.

"Avoid the passive voice whenever possible."

— Rita Mae Brown, author, *Cat's Eyewitness*

SELF-PROMPTS:

Signs:
Gemini • Deer • Hawthorn
Birthdays:
Scott O'Dell (b. 1903)
Margaret Wise Brown (b. 1910)
Oliver Butterworth (b. 1915)
Susan Cooper (b. 1935)
Jane Kenyon (b. 1947)
Featured Website/Blog:
http://www.suite101.com

MAY 23
SENTENCE PLAY: LONG AND WINDING RHYTHMS

We've spent the past two days focusing on short, punchy sentences and use of punctuation as a visual literary aid. Today, let's take a very deep breath and head in the other direction — towards longer, more mellifluous sentences.

Think of something about which you could dream or contemplate all day long. Write your dreams or thoughts, using long sentences, ellipses, commas and run-on sentences to illustrate the depth, discovery, twists and turns of your process. Think of your sentences as long, winding roads on which you are traveling, checking out all the sites, observing the details, smelling the air and waving to all who pass by. When you are finished, read your piece aloud, and see if you remain as enraptured by the subject as you were while writing.

"Hunch, feel, intuition, a story spinning in different ways — it's a dream pattern. It's also good writing."

— John Barth, author, *The Sot-Weed Factor*

MAY 24
RUNNING WILD

Throw all technique and form to the wind. Toss your long-held ideas and incomplete projects aside. Cut loose the garbs and cloaks that prevent you from fully expressing yourself. Tear down the fences of your yard; become the wild forest for a day. Let your imagination grab hold of your pen and heart and take you in any direction. Don't stop it. Fly with the next thought or whim, and flow with your words. Run wild with your writing today, and see how many new fields you cover. The results may surprise you—and launch an entirely new phase of writing.

"The intuitive mind is a sacred gift and the rational mind is a faithful servant. We have created a society that honors the servant and has forgotten the gift."
— Albert Einstein, scientist-inventor

Signs:
Gemini • Deer • Hawthorn
Birthdays:
Marian Engel (b. 1933)
Joseph Brodsky (b. 1940)
Bob Dylan (b. 1941)
Featured Website/Blog:
http://www.suite101.com

MAY 25
SCALING THE HEIGHTS

In the late 1990s, blind mountaineer Erik Weihenmayer set out to scale the highest points of all seven continents. When he ascended Mt. Everest, he was struck by the desolation and silence atop the world— an entirely different experience than he anticipated. He also noticed how heightened his senses had become.

Think of a time when you sat atop the proverbial world, when you experienced a peak physical, spiritual, intellectual or emotional moment. What did you observe or perceive? How did you feel? *What* did you feel? Were there any parallels in your life between this experience and others? Recall your "scaling of the heights" in an essay. Relive the experience through present tense, stream-of-consciousness writing, to reflect the heightened level of presence during your peak moment. Make your essay an inspiration to seek more peak moments in your life.

"The first secret of good writing: We must look intently, and hear intently, and taste intently."
— James J. Kilpatrick, columnist and commentator

Signs:
Gemini • Deer • Hawthorn
Birthdays:
Ralph Waldo Emerson (b. 1803)
Bennett Cerf (b. 1898)
Robert Ludlum (b. 1927)
Featured Website/Blog:
http://www.wiredforbooks.org

SELF-PROMPTS:

SELF-PROMPTS:

SELF-PROMPTS:

MAY 26
DIRTY GUITARS AND OTHER DE-FRAGGINGS

A flash fiction piece I wrote, "The Dirty Guitar," was based on comments made by popular folk musician Jack Williams at a house concert. Williams talked about the life influences that passed into his guitar, then launched into a 30-minute guitar medley. He called it "de-fragging" himself of 45 years of musical influences that ranged from W.C. Handy to Bob Dylan, Del Shannon to Johnny Mercer, Count Basie to Stephen Foster, The Beatles to Josh White.

Let's de-frag ourselves, Jack Williams style. Begin with a pinnacle moment, one that took some building up. Roll out the memories. Now admit every single memory or fragment of experience or observation that comes to you. Write down a word here, a phrase there, a sentence, verse, stanza. Do this for 15 to 20 minutes, and see how much you cultivate. Don't edit. Let your words meet the memories in your body and go where the exercise takes you.

"Let that voice of the solitary writer or artist speak and you will hear the gratitude of mankind."

— Robert F. Kennedy

Signs:
Gemini • Deer • Hawthorn
Birthdays:
Shelia Greenwald (b. 1934)
Alan Hollinghurst (b. 1954)
Featured Website/Blog:
http://www.wiredforbooks.org

SELF-PROMPTS:

MAY 27
BURSTING BUBBLES

You wake up today, the world at your fingertips. You've been on quite a run of luck and good fortune. Suddenly, you realize that one of five things has happened:
- A long-term romance (or a short, torrid romance) has ended;
- Your string of personal, athletic, creative or business success snaps;
- Your boss is calling—which means vacation is over;
- The baby wakes up when you're curling deeply into an extra hour of sleep;
- It's Monday morning. The weekend is gone.

Your bubble has burst. What does "re-entry" feel like? How does it change your perception of the day? With whom can you talk about this? How will it impact your family, friends, and co-workers? Capture the aftermath of the bubble that has burst—and import the feeling into future or present work.

"People use their own words or their own artistic creations to speak the truth of their lives in a form akin to song."

— John Fox, founder, Institute for Poetic Medicine

Signs:
Gemini • Deer • Hawthorn
Birthdays:
Dashiell Hammett (b. 1897)
Rachel Carson (b. 1907)
John Cheever (b. 1912)
Herman Wouk (b. 1915)
Tony Hillerman (b. 1925)
John Barth (b. 1930)
M.E. Kerr (b. 1932)
Harlan Ellison (b. 1934)
Featured Website/Blog:
http://www.wiredforbooks.org

MAY 28
HE SAID, SHE SAID

"She screamed." "He implied." "She coughed." "He blurted." "She exclaimed."

What about "he said, she said"? We've grown carried away with the use of colorful attributions to identify our speaking characters. These attributions feel crisp and clever when we write them, but they slow down the reader. They also imply a lack of confidence that the dialogue doesn't fully convey the speaker's vocal tone, gestures or meaning.

When your dialogue is incisive and moving, placing "he said" or "she said" intermittently will be enough. Convert your more creative attributions into action verbs. Instead of finishing a quote with, "she screamed," use a series of exclamation points after an obviously heated comment—or *preface* the quote by writing, *She screamed, curdling his blood.*

Write a conversation between two people. Only use "he said" or "she said," or "George said" or "Serena said," to identify the participants. Convert every other potential attribution into a verb to show atmosphere and action. This will spice up all your stories.

"I know that when I step onto this stage, just focusing on technique and what I have played before is not enough. It is being truthful to the moment that counts."

— Michael Jones, author, *Creating an Imaginative Life*

Signs:
Gemini • Deer • Hawthorn
Birthdays:
Ian Fleming (b. 1908)
Patrick White (b. 1912)
Walker Percy (b. 1916)
Featured Website/Blog:
http://www.onpointradio.com

MAY 29
ACTIVATE!

One of the first skills that separates well-published writers from novices pertains to verb use. Well-written fiction and non-fiction utilize action verbs wherever possible. In many cases, they *invent* verbs; *Bird by Bird* author Anne Lamott and *Pilgrim at Tinker Creek* author Annie Dillard create beautiful depictions of sound and observation. The rule of thumb: Use action verbs. Only use "to be" verbs when necessary.

Write a small piece of 150-200 words. When finished, replace all passive verbs with active verbs. Use verbs that properly describe the emotion or action you wish to convey. Invent words if needed— particularly to portray sounds and scents. Compare your revised writing with your earlier work; notice the difference in movement, emotion, and visual presence.

"Life began for me when I ceased to admire and began to remember."
— Willa Cather, author, *My Antonia*

Signs:
Gemini • Deer • Hawthorn
Birthdays:
Mary L. Molesworth (b. 1839)
Willo Davis Roberts (b. 1928)
Featured Website/Blog:
http://www.onpointradio.com

SELF-PROMPTS:

MAY 30
WRITE YOUR HISTORY/HERSTORY

"A people without a history is like wind upon the buffalo grass."

Take this Teton Lakota Sioux proverb to heart—and pen. Write out your personal history/herstory. Start with bullet points of events, and then write 200-word vignettes on each. If the vignettes take you deeper into your history/herstory, explore and write. Use these exercises to plan out memoirs and creative non-fiction pieces, and to work out plots and characters in your forthcoming novels.

"For what we can make of our own experiences, including even our ambivalent feelings about ourselves, is as legitimate a subject as any for fiction."
— Joyce Carol Oates, author, *The Faith of a Writer*

Signs:
Gemini • Deer • Hawthorn
Birthdays:
Millicent Selsam (b. 1912)
Featured Website/Blog:
http://www.onpointradio.com

SELF-PROMPTS:

MAY 31
EMBRACE YOUR WRITING NUCLEUS

Every sentence we write has the potential to touch the nucleus of everything we've lived, breathed, sensed, read, explored or created to this point. This is a profound realization, capable of changing the way we write and how powerful and touching our work can become. Embracing our core nucleus can be frightening, yet once touched, we return for more.

Write a vignette about an experience, place, person, action or thing that completely fills you with life and presence. Write each sentence from the core of your being, from your nucleus. Write until you tire. Continue to practice this form of writing all week—and *always*. This is where great writers go to find their deepest insights.

"This is art, this is writing, this is poetry, it is most profoundly political, this matter of acknowledging the persistence and ineluctable value of the primary, the vernacular, the local, the essential, the simple, the imperfect, the risky, the familial, the potluck dinner, the cleanup, the wild weeds in the vacant lot. I have made this my art, my practice, my homestead."
— Gary Snyder, author, *Turtle Island*

Signs:
Gemini • Deer • Hawthorn
Birthdays:
Walt Whitman (b. 1819)
Elizabeth Coatsworth (b. 1893)
Jay Williams (b. 1914)
Featured Website/Blog:
http://www.salon.com

June

JUNE 1
THE PHILOSOPHER'S MIRROR

Before you write today, take a look in the mirror. Study those wise eyes, the lines and colors of a life filled with experiences, adventures, loves, lessons, pains and joys. Look into those eyes and summon a revelation in your own life, a complete knowing. This revelation is very personal, very deep—it comes from your own experience.

Go into your deepest corners and deepest truths, and see what you find. Describe completely. Chances are, you've hit upon a universal truth, direct from the fount of wisdom, spirit and experience. Write from this depth regularly.

"Whatever the creative urge is, it can only be strengthened by questions and all manners of texts; that it is not fragile; indeed, that it is bottomless."
— Eve Shelnutt, author, *The Musician*

Signs:
Gemini • Deer • Hawthorn
Birthdays:
Dante Alleghiri (b. 1265)
Featured Website/Blog:
http://www.salon.com

JUNE 2
SURRENDER, UNIVERSE

Eighteen centuries ago, the Ancient Chinese poet Lieh Tzu wrote, "To the mind that is still, the whole universe surrenders."

Before writing today, take 15 minutes (or more) to quiet your mind. Say a prayer and ask for clarity. Sit still for 10 minutes. If a thought invades your quiet space, let it pass and move on. Spend the remaining minutes picturing the silence as a window to a universe now open for the business of supporting your writing.

Throw open the doors and windows. Summon everything you've ever learned in your life to become available for *this writing session*. Surrender your thoughts and feelings to your pen or computer; write what comes to you. Write from surrender whenever possible, because it will expand your inner and outer perception—making the universe available to you.

Signs:
Gemini • Deer • Hawthorn
Birthdays:
Thomas Hardy (b. 1840)
Carol Shields (b. 1935)
Featured Website/Blog:
 http://www.salon.com

"Writing is perhaps the greatest of human inventions binding together people who never knew each other, citizens of distant epochs."
— Carl Sagan, astronomer, author, *Cosmos*

JUNE 3
OCCUPYING DIFFERENT HOUSES

A structural challenge for you: Try to write a poem in a different poetic structure. One day, write free verse. The next, try a Japanese form—haiku or tanka. Then, write a sonnet or ballad. See how rhyming couplets work for you. There are many hundreds of poetic structures. Try a few and see if they enhance and crystallize your natural writing rhythm. Transmit the rhythm of moving images to your stories and essays.

Signs:
Gemini • Deer • Hawthorn
Birthdays:
Allen Ginsberg (b. 1926)
Larry McMurtry (b. 1936)
Featured Website/Blog:
http://www.novelspot.com

"The poem is a way of making this wonderful performance of language, of dance. I wanted sounds of the kitchen, of the bedroom, of two people in conversation to come in and become my body. Before I could get to the Muse, I had to go through the violence of language."
— Meena Alexander, poet-novelist, author, *Indian Love Poems*

JUNE 4
ENTHUSIASM BREEDS PASSION

Here's an exercise to breathe fire and desire into your day. Write down the five areas, events, hobbies, people or projects in your life that bring you the most enthusiasm. Take one, two or all five of the topics, and imagine their points of fruition. Write with *passion* as you describe how the topic grew from an item of interest to one that enthralls you. All good writers work from the thresholds of enthusiasm and passion.

"In the writing process, the more a thing cooks, the better."
— Doris Lessing, author, *The Golden Notebook*

SELF-PROMPTS:

Signs:
Gemini • Deer • Hawthorn
Birthdays:
Joyce Meyer (b. 1943)
Featured Website/Blog:
http://www.novelspot.com

JUNE 5
THE WATERS AND THE WILD

"Come away, O human child!
To the waters and the wild
With a fairy, hand in hand…"

Like William Butler Yeats, imagine a fairy taking you by the hand, into an element of nature that both fascinates and scares you. The inside of a tornado? The heart of a hurricane? The depths of a forest? The edge of a thousand-foot cliff? The summit of a great mountain? Write about the excitement and fear that rushes through you, and describe how your perception of your life changes when you "stand" in this place. Remember: The fairy holds your hand. You are safe. Write the magic within the danger.

"You need to ride the linguistic energy of a poem — like riding in a rodeo. You need to let the poem write through you and ride that bucking stallion without being thrown."
— Luis Francia, author, *Eye of the Fish: A Personal Archipelago*

SELF-PROMPTS:

Signs:
Gemini • Deer • Hawthorn
Birthdays:
Richard Scarry (b. 1919)
Bill Moyers (b. 1934)
Ken Follett (b. 1949)
Chuck Klosterman (b. 1972)
Featured Website/Blog:
http://www.novelspot.com

SELF-PROMPTS:

JUNE 6
EXTENDING MY WRITING STRING

Committed athletes use a term to describe consecutive days of working out: *the string*. My high school track coach, now director of a kinesiology center in Montana, once worked out for more than 4,000 consecutive days—11 consecutive *years*. In 2006, a New York playwright wrote a play every single day. While these feats sound certifiably insane to some, they illustrate an important aspect of writing. To write fluidly, openly and prolifically, we must write *daily*.

Start right now, and write a little piece in which you anticipate producing a lengthy string of daily entries, essays, letters, poems or stories. From where will you draw subjects? How will your writing grow? Who will you meet or write about? What new areas of your life do you want to birth? Extend your writing string, now.

"Work every day. No matter what has happened the day or night before, get up and bite on the nail."

— Ernest Hemingway, author, *Old Man and the Sea*

Signs:
Gemini • Deer • Hawthorn
Birthdays:
Thomas Mann (b. 1875)
Will James (b. 1892)
Featured Website/Blog:
http://www.
creativewritingprompts.com

SELF-PROMPTS:

JUNE 7
BURN BABY BURN!

Sometimes, we need a kick-start. A *really hot* idea races through our minds, bodies and souls, blazing its trail to be expressed. We need to *burn*! The results can be amazing: Jack Kerouac wrote *The Subterraneans* in 72 hours. Ray Bradbury crafted *Fahrenheit 451* in nine days. Barbara Cartland wrote romance novels in as few as seven days. Anne Rice wrote her first draft of *The Vampire Lestat* in six weeks. John Keats composed *Ode to a Nightingale* in one hour.

Take an idea that burns through you. Open your journal, and let it rip. Catch yourself on fire, writing quickly, pouring out the words and story. Build your momentum into a bonfire that draws all your air, compels you to give everything inside and outside yourself. Try this for thirty minutes, an hour, or two hours.

Writing like a wildfire is exhilarating. Respond to those special moments. You'll know when they arrive.

"Only those who will risk going too far can possibly find out how far one can go."

— T.S. Eliot, poet-playwright, author, *The Waste Land*

Signs:
Gemini • Deer • Hawthorn
Birthdays:
John Goodall (b. 1908)
Gwendolyn Brooks (b. 1917)
Nicki Giovanni (b. 1943)
Louise Erdrich (b. 1954)
Featured Website/Blog:
http://www.
creativewritingprompts.com

JUNE 8
THE TREE OF (WRITING) LIFE

The writing life bears resemblance to a tree: steady growth of limbs, branches and leaves, flourishing through summer (creative periods); dropping its seeds and leaves in autumn (researching, idea-storing periods); drawing in its sap and lying dormant during winter (contemplative periods).

Think about your own rhythms as a writer, and write an essay about how you work with them. Do you fight them, and try to produce in non-creative times while reading through your most creative rhythms? Or do you move with the flow of your inner nature, spreading yourself across new stories, then drawing in to spend winter nights with a good book or music? Write this essay, and look for ways to adjust your writing life to your own inner rhythms.

"The way to learn to write is to write. Maybe by the time you've written a million words in your life — and that counts letters — you'll begin to discover what you need to know."

— Don James, author, *Vadim*

Signs:
Gemini • Deer • Hawthorn
Featured Website/Blog:
http://www.
creativewritingprompts.com

JUNE 9
THREE POINTS OF YOU

Pick a modern-day event, or recent major occurrence in your life, and describe it from three points of *you* — your present-day self, your teen or young adult self (under 25), and your child self (under 12). Consider how you view(ed) the world, now and then; how you regard yourself, now and then; and political or social views, now and then. Write out the three vignettes, each 200 to 500 words — and reap the revelations!

"Stories move in circles. They don't go in straight lines. So it helps if you listen in circles."

— Naomi Newman, Traveling Jewish Theatre

Signs:
Gemini • Deer • Hawthorn
Birthdays:
Patricia Cornwall (b. 1956)
Featured Website/Blog:
http://www.askaboutwriting.net

SELF-PROMPTS:

JUNE 10
THE EARTH'S WORDS

In *A Song of the Rolling Earth*, Walt Whitman wrote, "The masters know the earth's words and use them more than audible words." What are the words of the earth where you live? Is the nearby hill rolling, rock-strewn, leafy, cracked, steep, pocked or cloaked in green? Look at the earth around you. (If you're in the city, find the nearest park). Feel it, touch it, smell it. Then write about it as though that feature was narrating through you. Personification is the key here. Stay within that frame of writing, never straying to describe your emotions, feelings or others in the area. See if you can write a song of the rolling earth where you live.

Signs:
Gemini • Deer • Hawthorn
Birthdays:
Saul Bellow (b. 1915)
Featured Website/Blog:
http://www.askaboutwriting.net

"The music of the word is never just a matter of sound. It results from the relation of the speech and its meaning. And meaning–content–must always lead."

— Boris Pasternak, author, *Doctor Zhivago*

SELF-PROMPTS:

JUNE 11
TRAN-SITION

A constant writing goal is to create paragraphs that follow each other, smooth as sap running from a just-tapped sugar maple. Sometimes, consecutive paragraphs even cover entirely different material and convey different tones. Why do they seem to merge with each other so well?

It's all about transition, writing that links one paragraph to the next. Very similar to the "bridge" in pop music, the transition relies on the writer's mastery of the subject and ability to identify points in common between paragraphs. Their importance cannot be understated: if you think of pieces of narrative as bones, then transitions are the tendons and ligaments that hold them together.

Practice writing transitions today. Pull in an element or detail from the previous paragraph to light the way to the next—whether it takes a few words, sentence or paragraph to write. Write with subtlety. Work to write transitions so seamless that we view them as the bone of the story, not the ligaments.

Signs:
Gemini • Deer • Oak
Birthdays:
William Styron (b. 1925)
Robert Munsch (b. 1945)
Allan Garganus (b. 1947)
Featured Website/Blog:
http://www.askaboutwriting.net

"The thing is to be venturous, bold, to take every possible fence. One might introduce plays, poems, letters, dialogues: one must get the round, not only the flat. Not the theory only."

— Virginia Woolf, author, *A Writer's Diary*

JUNE 12
WHAT'S IN A WORD?

SELF-PROMPTS:

Mark Twain famously said, "The difference between lightning and lightning bug is just a word." Take a word that produces multiple meanings for you, or a word that can break down into smaller pieces (example: lightning can also break down to "light", and condescending can break down into "con," "descend," or "descending.") Write about how you perceive each part of the word, what it stirs in you, and word strings or sentences you can generate from it. Look up the word's etymological history, where it came from and when. Squeeze all the juice from that word until only the rind remains.

"Words set up atmospheres, electrical fields, charges."
— Toni Cade Bambara, author, *The Black Woman: An Anthology*

Signs:
Gemini • Deer • Oak
Birthdays:
Anne Frank (b. 1929)
Featured Website/Blog:
http://www.refdesk.com

JUNE 13
SEEING THE ACTION

SELF-PROMPTS:

Today, write with a child's trust, allowing the intuition and spontaneity of a trance-like daydream to guide your words, not our controlled thoughts and opinions. Think of something that involves action, movement: a child playing, a sports match, two old lovers embracing on a park bench, sailfish leaping in the sea, a flash flood cascading through a desert wash. Write the action as you see it, allowing the images and movement to form and release themselves in words. Don't offer opinions or thoughts; just see the action and write it. Use action verbs that fit the moment. Observe and write.

"To me, daydreaming is intimately connected with writing. Writing is like daydreaming. It's putting down in dramatic form whatever is on your mind."

— Anne Rice, author, *Christ the Lord: Out of Egypt*

Signs:
Gemini • Deer • Oak
Birthdays:
William Butler Yeats (b. 1865)
Mark Van Doren (b.1894)
Alexandra Sheedy (b. 1962)
Featured Website/Blog:
http://www.refdesk.com

SELF-PROMPTS:

JUNE 14
WRITE A PROFILE

Through their conversational format, profiles open windows into the ways that celebrities and notable personalities think, live, act, dream and feel. The writer chooses questions and topics he or she knows will create an insightful interview. Profiles are one of the best and most available sources of income for freelance writers.

Today, profile someone you know, or with whom you are familiar. Take what you know about the person, or have researched, and form 10 to 15 questions. Make each question open-ended, so it can potentially spread into conversation. If possible, conduct your interview in a place that reflects your subject's environment or interests. Tape the interview, and take notes of the subject's mannerisms and items he or she mentions that you may want to address later. Listen attentively; give the floor to your subject.

When finished, transcribe the tape. Write your profile in one of two ways: As a question-and-answer session, with a 300-word introduction that encapsulates your subject's background and premise for doing the profile; or as a feature, in which you combine narrative and quotes to set the scene, hear the remarks, and capture the spirit of the person and his or her place in life.

Signs:
Gemini • Deer • Oak
Birthdays:
Harriet Beecher Stowe (b. 1811)
Penelope Farmer (b. 1939)
John Edgar Wideman (b. 1941)
Carolyn Chute (b. 1947)
Laurence Yep (b. 1948)
Featured Website/Blog:
http://www.refdesk.com

"The best profile writers are people who can take a small amount of access to the person and amplify it so that it becomes a metaphor for what that person might represent or could represent."

— Chuck Klosterman, author, *Fargo Rock City*

SELF-PROMPTS:

JUNE 15
OPEN MIC NIGHT

Need to test your writing before live audiences a little more? Open Mics provide poets, storywriters, essayists and musicians with a chance to perform their latest works before an audience of kindred souls. It's a wonderful way to work through your stories or poems, hear your voice as it projects the words, and grow comfortable performing before crowds—because you will, again, when your book publishes and you go on a reading and signing tour.

Check out all of the Open Mic nights in your area. Attend one. Sign up, and take a five-minute turn. Build your audience right now.

Signs:
Gemini • Deer • Oak
Featured Website/Blog:
http://www.writersdigest.com

"I think there's a mystical union between music and the sense of a work. I very much believe in reading aloud as the best form of editing, an astringent for a poet's work."

— Mei-Mei Bersenbrugge, author, *Nest*

JUNE 16
NOSTALGIA: TURNING 10 AGAIN

10 years ago. A decade complete. For most of us, turning 10 was a monumental occasion. I blew out candles on a hot, sunny Southern California beach day while getting ready to attend a San Diego Padres baseball game. My heroes, the Apollo 11 astronauts, had recently walked on the moon. Still, my spirit yearned to be 3,000 miles away, sitting on Max Yasgur's farm in upstate New York and attending day two of the Woodstock Music Festival.

Remember turning 10? Take yourself back to that day, and clothe yourself with the sights, sounds, neighborhood, friends, and your favorite things. Give yourself a party in writing. Throw an extra candle on the cake for the things you wish had happened on that day. Write your way into the voice of the 10-year-old, have a party with the child—and see if you can apply this precious moment to an essay, memoir, article or scene in a novel.

"The fantasies of childhood, whether self-invented or acquired by way of popular culture, parallel, in essence, the fantasies of the race."
— Joyce Carol Oates, author, *The Faith of a Writer*

Signs:
Gemini • Deer • Oak
Birthdays:
Joyce Carol Oates (b. 1938)
Featured Website/Blog:
http://www.writersdigest.com

JUNE 17
NOSTALGIA: HIGH SCHOOL DAYS

SELF-PROMPTS:

The surf was up. Constantly. What a senior year of high school for waves! Every morning before school, my friend Enno and I would depart on "dawn patrols." I would show up for my first-period writing class with wet shoulder-length hair, a drippy nose, and tons of ideas.

High school memories instantly attract readers, even if they're your memories. High school is such an emotionally charged time—our passage from childhood to adulthood—that many of the likes and dislikes we form then remain with us for life. Write about your greatest, happiest, saddest or most memorable high school experiences. Who shared your moments with you? What class(es) were you in? What clothes did you wear? What hair styles? Who were your favorite bands? Most and least favorite teachers?

Return to the present moment. Why do these experiences continue to stick with you? Why, when you recount them, do you become somewhat dreamy and warm inside — or chilled? Write about it, and plant the feeling of the experience into a future character or subject.

"History is what scholars and conquerors say happened; story is what it was like to live on the ground."
— Christina Baldwin, author, *Storycatcher*

Signs:
Gemini • Deer • Oak
Birthdays:
John Hersey (b. 1914)
Featured Website/Blog:
http://www.writersdigest.com

SELF-PROMPTS:

Signs:
Gemini • Deer • Oak
Birthdays:
Jerzy Kosinski (b. 1933)
Gail Godwin (b. 1937)
Pat Hutchins (b. 1942)
Featured Website/Blog:
http://www.writersunboxed.com

JUNE 18
NOSTALGIA: FIRST LOVE

Most of us are smitten with memories of our first love. A few of us are even fortunate enough to still be with our first love. To truly fall in love for the first time, whether at age 16, 26 or 36, sits high among the seven wonders of our emotional worlds.

Go back to the moment when you first fell in love. How did you know that you were *in love?* Who was the lucky person? What were some of your experiences together? What dreams, possibilities and feelings raced across your heart?

Write this piece with all the warmth and excitement that your first love engendered. Bring that feeling into this day, and see how it might color or further brighten your life. More importantly, see if you can summon the first-love feeling every time you write a love scene. Bring the sheer, innocent romance of first love into your work — and nestle in the feeling.

"Memoir isn't for remembrance; it's for exploration."
— Patricia Hampl, author, *The Florist's Daughter*

SELF-PROMPTS:

Signs:
Gemini • Deer • Oak
Birthdays:
Tobias Wolff (b. 1945)
Salman Rushdie (b. 1947)
Featured Website/Blog:
http://www.writersunboxed.com

JUNE 19
NOSTALGIA: MY FAVORITE DECADE

We've written about specific nostalgic moments. Let's tackle a bigger fish — an entire decade. Whether we're 15 or 65, we have already lived through a number of decades. So much happens in a 10-year period to shape, define and inform us — and provide us with enormous amounts of material for our writing pursuits, whether fiction or non-fiction.

What was (is) your favorite decade? Start by identifying the decade. List 20 items that make it so defining and memorable for you. Include historic events, social changes, favorite performers who came onto the scene, birthday parties, monumental events (getting a driver's license, voting, getting married, having a child, turning 40) friends who entered your life, spiritual experiences, adventures, things bought and sold. Tie yourself directly to each item on the list. Write an essay or memoir-style vignette about your favorite decade, and conclude it with a paragraph that describes the differences in yourself from the start of the 10-year period to the finish.

"Don't get it right, get it written."
— Ray Bradbury, author, *The Illustrated Man*

JUNE 20
NOSTALGIA: BACK FROM THE FUTURE

Let's return to the year you were born. What were the technological marvels of the day? What cars, electronic and entertainment devices, kitchen appliances or office machines made people exclaim, "Wow…I never thought I'd see this!" List them out. In my birth year, those marvels included Ford Thunderbirds, satellites in space, color television sets and electric typewriters. Items such as CDs, iPods, microwaves, cell phones, personal computers and Bluetooth techology were complete science fiction.

We've come a long way. Now leap ahead 25 years, and imagine how the technology of today will change. Let your imagination race into the future, and list out your predictions. Write a piece that answers these questions: "What would people 25 years from now think of today's most cutting edge technology? And what would people in my birth year think of the items with which I populate my life?"

The answers may surprise you. They will likely be revealing. Most of all, they will enable you to present yourself with a gift: for today, you just wrote today's science fiction, some of which will become tomorrow's science fact.

"Artists and writers are the antennae of the race."
> — Henry Miller, author, *Tropic of Cancer*

SELF-PROMPTS:

Signs:
Gemini • Deer • Oak
Featured Website/Blog:
http://www.writersunboxed.com

JUNE 21
WRITE THE SUMMER SOLSTICE

Summer solstice is the most light-filled day of the year. Trees and plants explode in fullest green, lakes and oceans warm up, and the air heats us — sometimes too much. It kicks off the season of relaxing, vacationing, outdoor recreation, holding get-togethers on porches, under trees, in parks. Summer solstice is one of the most energetically powerful days of the year, which makes it a perfect day to write.

What do you feel like when peaking emotionally and energetically? What experiences, stories, ceremonies, dreams and areas of growth emerge? Write the summer solstice, inside and out. Start with your observations of your outdoor surroundings. Tie those observations into the feelings and aspirations arising from you. Give yourself the next hour or so to celebrate your own summer solstice — and bring forth a writing project or story you plan to complete.

"Observe — Experience — Absorb — Understand — Expand."
> — William Blake, poet, author, *The Marriage of Heaven and Hell*

SELF-PROMPTS:

Signs:
Gemini • Woodpecker • Oak
Birthdays:
Jean-Paul Sartre (b. 1905)
Mary McCarthy (b. 1912)
Patricia Wrightson (b. 1921)
Ian McEwan (b. 1948)
Jane Urquhart (b. 1949)
Featured Website/Blog:
http://forums.writersbeat.com

JUNE 22
DRAW A BEAD ON IT

Let's start with what I believe to be a misnomer: overwriting is bad for your writing health. I somewhat disagree. If you're developing mastery over a subject, experimenting to find the right feelings for characters, or going off on tangents in first draft, overwriting is a good thing. Most of us learn to get to the point by finding nuggets within pages of mellifluous, drawn-out prose. Our maturation as writers comes as we learn to convey more critical information in fewer words.

However, if publishing is your goal, overwriting is a pest that can become a monster. The more we publish, the more precise our writing must become.

Write a vignette, story or essay — or take one you have drafted. Read the sentences aloud, and then start paring words, phrases or entire sentences until you get to the point. Draw a bead on every passage. Replace three- or four-word phrases with single words. Make your points in a clear, convincing way. Cut out the fat.

Signs:
Cancer • Woodpecker • Oak

Birthdays:
Margaret Sidney (b. 1844)
Tess Fragoulis (b. 1964)

Featured Website/Blog:
http:// forums.writersbeat.com

"Overwriting comes of indecision when you are not sure of your target. You haven't drawn a bead on it, so you plaster the whole wall to make sure. That is overwriting."

— Lawrence Durrell, author, *Alexandria Quartet*

JUNE 23
A FLICK? OR A MOVING PICTURE?

You're writing about the Roaring Twenties palace theatre movie scene, or about silent film mega-stars Charlie Chaplin and 'It' girl Clara Bow. Question: What were movies called then?

When writing historical or cultural pieces, our details must match the time period. We must confine ourselves to the products, styles, conveniences (or hardships), modes of transportation and social conventions of that era, and be mindful of the way people talked, interacted, and used nicknames and slang. Writing about unmarried teens kissing publicly is fine in the 21st century, but not if your piece is set in 1902.

Write a one-page essay or vignette about an historical period. Use good details relevant to the time. Go through your piece, and make sure *every detail* illustrates and holds the story's place in time.

Answer to the above question? Movies were called *moving pictures* or *flickers* — both obsolete terms today.

Signs:
Cancer • Woodpecker • Oak

Featured Website/Blog:
http:// forums.writersbeat.com

"When I start describing some character in 18th century Haiti and I want to say what she's wearing or what she's eating for breakfast…I have to somehow find these things out."

— Madison Smartt Bell, author, *All Souls Rising*

JUNE 24
THE 212th DEGREE

At 211 degrees, water retains liquid form, though it is scalding hot. At 212 degrees, it turns to steam—which can power a world. What a difference one degree makes. The same goes for writing. Sometimes, we write a piece and can't quite find the right word, or turn of phrase that we seek. Rather than circling back and making that extra effort, we stop. That single degree often separates good writing from average writing, acceptance from rejection. Today, write a story, essay, poem or vignette. Carefully review it to make sure you're stating the subject exactly as you intended. Look for specific words, phrases, and ways to make the piece clearer. Take that extra step, the 212th degree.

"I want to make the stories interesting on every level, and that involves creating believable characters and situations, along with working the language until it is perfectly clear."

— Raymond Carver, author, *Where I'm Calling From*

Signs:
Cancer • Woodpecker • Oak
Featured Website/Blog:
http://www.gutenberg.com

JUNE 25
SWITCH YOUR POINT OF VIEW

SELF-PROMPTS:

Stuck on a story, scene or essay? Switch your point of view! Imagine the same moment through the eyes of one of your other characters, or an outsider, or even yourself at a different period in your life. Write from that perspective. Then write from the perspective of another character and see how they enhance or enliven the moment. Who knows? Your entire piece may thrive with this different voice!

"I set out to evoke a small world out of a small chaos."

— A.E. Housman, author, *A Shropshire Lad*

Signs:
Cancer • Woodpecker • Oak
Birthdays:
George Orwell (b. 1903)
P.H. Newby (b. 1918)
Yann Martel (b. 1963)
Featured Website/Blog:
http://www.gutenberg.com

SELF-PROMPTS:

JUNE 26
SWIMMING UP A WATERFALL

Sometimes as writers, we come across a subject, belief system, individual or idea that flies in the face of everything we embrace and believe. Imagine the assault on Truman Capote's sensibilities when he first interviewed the two Kansas killers for *In Cold Blood.* When this happens in our writing, do we shy away? Or jump into the other moccasins and listen to that perspective? While the answer appears obvious if we want to grow, it is not easy to swim up the waterfall.

Today, write about something that makes you *bristle,* that thoroughly assaults your values, belief systems and ideas about life. It can be a news story, something you witnessed, a person that turned you off, or a prejudice or belief that disgusted you. Write down the issue, and your point-of-view. Then imagine the other side, and write that out. See if you can bring the two close enough together to explore the differences. You may find resolution, or a peaceful truce. You may not. Regardless, see your stories from all points of view—even if you don't write from them.

Signs:
Gemini • Deer • Hawthorn
Birthdays:
Pearl S. Buck (b. 1892)
Walter Farley (b. 1915)
Featured Website/Blog:
http://www.gutenberg.com

"Often the writing process is filled with a sense of jeopardy because, in essence, with every book I turn myself inside out. You have to give everything away every single time. So there's always the sense of consuming yourself."
— Sue Grafton, author, *T is for Trespass*

SELF-PROMPTS:

JUNE 27
SNAPSHOT BACK STORIES

Whether we're writing novels or articles, we gather far more research about our subjects than we can ever use. Many writers will pore through as many as 500 books and journals—or even more—before they compose a sentence. They might use five percent of their research material to create back story—the subject's life prior to the start of Chapter One. We weave back story into a book carefully: a paragraph here, a page there, just enough to illuminate the subject or character's world.

Think of the many past events that helped create who you are today. Snapshot it—one event, one sentence. In that sentence, state the event and how it affected you or your subject. Then move on to the next event, and the next. No need to write in linear time; it works better to recall your snapshot back stories as they appear to you.

Signs:
Cancer • Woodpecker • Oak
Birthdays:
Helen Keller (b. 1880)
Lucille Clifton (b. 1936)
Featured Website/Blog:
http://www.duotrope.com

"Stillness is dynamic. It is unconflicted movement, life in harmony with itself, skill in action."
— Erich Schiffman, yoga master teacher

JUNE 28
SLEUTH THROUGH OLD JOURNALS

Out of writing ideas? Look through old journals or diaries to reacquaint yourself with ideas you once thought important enough to write down. Take an idea, sketch or life circumstance you haven't written about any further, and bring it to life with your pen. Never mind the fact that years have passed; if anything, that will gird you with additional wisdom and perspective. Where did the idea originally come from? How did you feel when creating the idea? How does it feel now? Let your heart and imagination run wild, and take this old idea into your next writing day.

"The Creative Act is both a rational and intuitive performance. What comes up from within this fissure generally relates to the subject, but for me at least it always seems at first to relate to the essence of the subject."
— John Gardner, author, *Grendel*

Signs:
Cancer • Woodpecker • Oak
Birthdays:
Jean-Jacques Rousseau (b. 1712)
Featured Website/Blog:
http://www.duotrope.com

JUNE 29
SIGN, SIGN EVERYWHERE A SIGN

A pop hit from 1970 certainly nailed the truth: sign, sign, everywhere a sign. No matter where we turn, we see signs — billboards, traffic signs, flashing signs, the signs atop or in front of buildings. They're built and positioned to capture our attention, or prompt us to feel a certain way or buy something. What signs will capture or have captured your attention today?

Start with a list, and then break it down into individual signs. Write a paragraph on each and delve into the reasons *why* a particular sign impacted you. When you're finished, return to the list of signs, and write about your perception of the collective signage.

"Things punctuate the key moments in our lives and serve as reminders of what we value."
— Frederick and Mary Ann Brussat, authors, *Spiritual Literacy: Reading the Sacred in Everyday Life*

Signs:
Cancer • Woodpecker • Oak
Birthdays:
Antoine Sainte-Exupery (b. 1900)
Featured Website/Blog:
http://www.duotrope.com

SELF-PROMPTS:

Signs:
Cancer • Woodpecker • Oak
Birthdays:
Eleanor F. Lattimore (b. 1904)
Czeslaw Milosz (b. 1911)
Mollie Hunter (b. 1922)
David McPhail (b. 1940)
Featured Website/Blog:
http://www.kenyonreview.com

JUNE 30
VITA CONTEMPLATIVA

From the echoes of antiquity arrives today's theme: *Vita Contemplativa,* the Latin translation of a core teaching of Aristotle's. Often, we think of contemplation as passive…kicking back…hey, man, whatever floats through the brain…hanging out with the mind.

Not close. Contemplation involves great activity and discipline, as we mull over and consider topics of consequence in our lives. As writers, contemplation is one of our most important tools.

Actively contemplate something you want to write. Let it billow and spread across your mind. Grow this idea, character, story, poem or vignette for 30 minutes, with no distractions. Then sit down and write. Notice the added vitality and strength of what you've birthed. Practice *vita contemplativa* every possible day.

"You say what you have to say. But you have to learn to say it in such a way that the reader can see what you mean."
— Kurt Vonnegut, author, *Breakfast of Champions*

July

JULY 1
DENSITY OF STYLE

Boris Pasternak, Russian poet and author of the great novel *Doctor Zhivago,* once told an interviewer, "It is the density of style which counts. Through Hemingway's style you feel matter, iron, wood." Added Marianne Moore, "a thing must have intensity."Intensity. Density. Matter. Iron. Wood. These words speak Substance.

Take a story or essay you have written. Review to see if your details reflect the visual imprint in your mind. Most likely, you passed over precise details in some places. Work like a ringsmith placing tiny diamonds into their settings. Choose your words carefully. Give your sentences fluidity and texture that reflect the action you're portraying. Write so that your readers can reach out, touch and feel the details and atmosphere that you describe.

"If by style one means the voice, the irreducible and always recognizable and alive thing, then style is everything."

— Mary McCarthy, author, *A Charmed Life*

Signs:
Cancer • Woodpecker • Oak
Birthdays:
James M. Cain (b. 1892)
Jean Stafford (b. 1915)
Leisel Skorpen (b. 1935)
Featured Website/Blog:
http://www.kenyonreview.com

SELF-PROMPTS:

JULY 2
REDEEM THE CHAOS

Our objective when transforming ideas to finished writing is to "redeem the chaos," to organize our thoughts, notes, perceptions, comments and experiences around and through our subject. We strive to coalesce and distill chaos into clear writing.

Go back through your journals or writings to a passage that came out disheveled, with messy hair and rumpled clothes. Find the central magnet of that piece, the force that pulls you in. Reorganize the passage, writing and revising until it shimmers with clarity. Now compare your writing with the initial creative outburst. When done well, the piece will retain the energy of the original chaos, but the words will be easy to follow and understand.

Signs:
Cancer • Woodpecker • Oak
Birthdays:
Hermann Hesse (b. 1877)
Featured Website/Blog:
http://www.kenyonreview.com

"That is the challenge, the moment of hope: to dance as near the edge of destruction as is possible, to be willing to fall and still not fall."
— Sara Maitland, author, *A Big-Enough God*

SELF-PROMPTS:

JULY 3
FOLLOW YOUR OWN THUMBPRINT

Late novelist Katherine Anne Porter once told the *Paris Review*, "Your thumbprint is not like any other, and the thumbprint is what you must go by." What makes you unique? What mannerisms, habits, points of view, insights, experiences, aspects of your physical appearance and commitments in life create your uniqueness?

Answer these questions. Use a couple of your answers for a 500- to 1,000-word essay or short story that conveys the *tone* and *feeling* of your point-of-view. When you're finished, read the piece aloud and see if it conveys your unique thumbprint. Repeat this exercise whenever you feel the need to strengthen your voice and perspective.

Signs:
Cancer • Woodpecker • Oak
Birthdays:
Franz Kafka (b. 1883)
Dave Barry (b. 1947)
Rohinton Mistry (b. 1952)
Featured Website/Blog:
http://www.wordpress.com

"I am looking not for objective truth but for emotional truth."
— Bonnie Friedman, author, *Writing Past Dark*

JULY 4
WHAT I BELIEVE IN

What do you believe in? What issues, feelings, people and spiritual beliefs form your world and how you live in it? For what would you be willing to risk life and limb?

Our personal beliefs bedrock our writing voice. When we write, we must be very clear about the core beliefs of ourselves and/or our characters—depending upon whether we are writing essays or memoir, creative non-fiction, fiction with autobiographical elements or mainstream fiction.

Answer the above questions with full conviction. Revise and edit your answers until your statements are as clear as your beliefs. Write a story or essay that emanates from the center of your beliefs, and doesn't waver. Read aloud and hear your deepest voice.

"I stare down into the bottomless lake of my mirror."
— Euripides, Ancient Greek dramatist

SELF-PROMPTS:

Signs:
Cancer • Woodpecker • Oak
Birthdays:
Nathaniel Hawthorne (b. 1804)
Neil Simon (b. 1927)
Featured Website/Blog:
http://www.wordpress.com

JULY 5
ORDER THE FACTS

One of my favorite descriptions of being a writer came from Aldous Huxley, author of *Brave New World:* "One has the urge, first of all, to order the facts one observes and to give meaning to life."

Grab a novel or creative non-fiction book from one of your favorite authors. Find a rich narrative passage loaded with facts—at least two pages. Identify and write down the key facts in the passage. Now, shuffle the facts into a different order, but one from which you can trace a story or vignette line. Write a piece that uses the facts in this new order.

Reshuffle the key facts into a third sequence. Compare the piece you wrote and the original passage. See how the re-shuffling of facts created an entirely different story? Return to this exercise when you are having trouble sharpening your point-of-view.

"Language is rich when it is fed by difference."
—Jeanette Winterson, author, *Gut Symmetry*

SELF-PROMPTS:

Signs:
Cancer • Woodpecker • Oak
Featured Website/Blog:
http://www.wordpress.com

SELF-PROMPTS:

JULY 6
PIVOT POINTS

The word "pivot" connotes a sudden change in direction or fortune, taken from a central (pivotal) place. In basketball, players plant their pivot foot and scan the floor in search of a teammate or a shot. In writing, we deal with several pivot points in a story—dramatic climaxes, narrative climaxes, and plot twists. Top authors and journalists are brilliant pivot-point writers. They take us to the moment of truth—or change—and make us part of the change.

Think of a crucial moment in yours or a friend's life, or the crucial moment in a piece on which you're working. Write your way to that moment. Ask yourself: What's on the line? What feelings and thoughts does it trigger? Does my intuition or gut seek one way over the other? What are the options? How will others be affected by each possible decision? When I take that step, do I look back? Can I look back? What does it look like back there?

When you're finished, revise your piece by compressing it to the fewest possible words. See how your perspective or the direction of your story has changed.

"Be submissive to everything, opening, listening."
— Jack Kerouac, author, *On the Road*

Signs:
Cancer • Woodpecker • Oak
Birthdays:
Dhan Gopal Mukerji (b. 1890)
Gloria Skurzynski (b. 1930)
Featured Website/Blog:
http://www.edutopia.org

SELF-PROMPTS:

JULY 7
REAL PLUMS, IMAGINARY CAKE

Many times, fiction serves as a direct reflection of the author's life. The author creates characters that are alter-egos of himself/herself, family members or friends, and sets the story in a familiar, real setting. In many ways, the story is non-fiction, an exaggerated memoir.

Let's try to create something entirely fictional—but with real qualities. Create a character that does not resemble you in any way. Give the character a setting you have experienced, but fictionalize its identifying features. Now place the character into a situation or conflict you have personally experienced.

Write out a scene from your personal knowledge. Give the character feeling and movement; make every bit of your story feel real. Bring the setting to life, so that we can't imagine it any other way.

"(When you're writing a novel,) you can only see as far as the headlights, but you can make the whole trip that way."
— E.L. Doctorow, author, *Loon Lake*

Signs:
Cancer • Woodpecker • Oak
Birthdays:
Robert A. Heinlein (b. 1907)
Featured Website/Blog:
http://www.edutopia.org

JULY 8
CLOSING LINES THAT BLOW READERS AWAY

Write closing lines that blow your readers away. Seal your essay or story with a bang. Make your endings so potent and unforgettable that the story, or the imagined continuation of it, will shimmer in readers' minds for days or weeks afterward.

Take an essay or story on which you're working, or recently worked. Rewrite the final paragraph, either creating a narrative summation or piece of dialogue that resolves the story and leaves a dramatic or intellectual imprint on the reader. Work on these final 20 to 200 words as though they were the most precious you've ever written.

When finished, read the paragraph to a trusted friend who is willing to offer honest feedback. Ask if it made him or her think or ponder the issue, theme or message of the story. If so, then you've closed well.

"Focus is so important that you have to be able to work for 48 hours straight if that's necessary. Have nothing standing in your way."
— Marsha Norman, playwright

Signs:
Cancer • Woodpecker • Oak
Birthdays:
Shirley Ann Grau (b. 1929)
Marianne Williamson (b. 1952)
Featured Website/Blog:
http://www.edutopia.org

JULY 9
BEING NATURE

Go to a lake, forest, desert oasis or mountain. Sit quietly for 15 to 30 minutes and tune into the prevailing sounds—birds and insects chirping, wind whistling through trees, maybe a deer scurrying through underbrush. Now, *become* the object of your study. Become a tree. Become a bird. Become the wind. How does your environment feel now? What is it like to glide on cloud-currents? To carry food twice your bodily weight? To be a piece of bark that guards an entire tree?

Write from an omniscient point of view. Try to leave all human emotion out. Dissolve the perceived separation between you and your environment.

"If I had my druthers, every prose book I wrote would be like inhaling jungle."
—Diane Ackerman, author,
An Alchemy of Mind: The Marvel and Mystery of the Brain

Signs:
Cancer • Woodpecker • Oak
Birthdays:
Barbara Cartland (b. 1901)
Dean R. Koontz (b. 1945)
Featured Website/Blog:
http://www.asle.org

JULY 10
A DAY OFF! (SORT OF)

Take today off from writing. "But," you ask, "isn't this a book of writing exercises for *every* day of the year?"

Now for the exercise: Read a page or two from many different books. Read from genres you like—and genres with which you're unfamiliar. Read authors you have always followed. Read someone unfamiliar. Read a translated author. Read both women and men—and a teen-aged author. Read from books that have been unopened for years, or decades. Read a short and long poem. Read books of different genres but similar subjects.

Make your day the ultimate readers' smoothie. Taste and savor the styles, voices and images of these authors. Close your eyes and absorb the words. *Experience* the words. Then return for another taste. Try to repeat this day of deep nourishment and rejuvenation many times every year. The results can be incredible.

"When you start reading in a certain way, that's already the beginning of your writing."

— Tess Gallagher, poet, author, *Dear Ghosts*

Signs:
Cancer • Woodpecker • Holly
Birthdays:
Marcel Proust (b. 1871)
Alice Munro (b. 1931)
Featured Website/Blog:
http://www.asle.org

SELF-PROMPTS:

JULY 11
GREATEST CHILDHOOD SUMMER

Recall your greatest childhood summer. Did you go to camp? Visit your grandparents on the other side of the country? Vacation in exotic places? Stay home and discover the natural wonders and adventures nearby? Go surfing or lie on the beach every day? Play until you dropped from exhaustion every night? Or sit under shade trees and read, write and draw, oblivious to everything but the warm breeze and the world of your imagination?

Find your most splendid childhood summer and write about it *from your heart*. Dive into the feelings, hopes and insights you experienced. Sometimes, writing our best childhood memories leads to great memoirs, children's books, chapters in young adult novels, or essays on reclaiming elements of our pasts. Most of all, sweep back into that moment and enjoy the innocence and wonder of your most magical summer.

"Writing is not writing skills, but knowing how to see. Tune in and notice all the details."

— Carolyn Chute, author, *Merry Men*

Signs:
Cancer • Woodpecker • Holly
Birthdays:
E. B. White (b. 1899)
Featured Website/Blog:
http://www.asle.org

JULY 12
CUBIC CENTIMETER OF CHANCE

Through mythic Yaqui shaman Don Juan, anthropologist/author Carlos Castaneda (*Tales of Power*) introduced the "cubic centimeter of chance." The premise: when universal realization hits or an amazing opportunity drops on our laps, it can changes our lives. What do we do with it? We have a tiny window of opportunity, our cubic centimeter of chance.

The more we write, the more our creative minds open to these universal realizations and insights. When they arrive, they feel like divine gifts. Treat them as such. Run with them in both words and actions.

Recall your most recent insight, realization or moment of particular clarity. For the next 30 to 60 minutes, write everything that comes to mind and heart. Follow your words wherever they go; don't stop to edit or revise. When finished, take the next step indicated by your words.

"The great enemy of clear language is insincerity."
— George Orwell, author, *1984*

SELF-PROMPTS:

Signs:
Cancer • Woodpecker • Holly
Birthdays:
Henry David Thoreau (b. 1817)
Pablo Neruda (b. 1904)
Featured Website/Blog:
http://www.fmwriters.com

JULY 13
INDULGE YOUR (WRITER'S) CRAVINGS

Recently, I read an interview with Boris Pasternak. His precise description of snow-covered trees, fireplace warmth and frozen sunlight at his Russian home made me long for winter. I arrived home, turned off my cell phone, stoked the fire and read *Doctor Zhivago* in near-complete silence.

It is vital that we indulge our writer's cravings, whether by reading or writing what grabs our mind. This spontaneity gives our brain greater flexibility and pliability, makes us more open to receive new information, observe unusual details and create deeper insights. We become better writers when we throw down our guards and indulge. We grow into what late poet Alan Ginsberg called "spontaneous mind."

Write about the first person, thought, moment, memory, observation or activity that grabs you today and won't let go. Afterward, go outside, take an observant walk, and note the first author who comes to mind. Read something by that author—either from your bookshelf, or an excerpt online.

"It was a garage sale ... vignettes, odds and ends of scholarship, bits of memoir, short bursts of sociology, apostrophes, epithets, moans, cackles, anything that came into my mind."
— Tom Wolfe, author, *The Right Stuff*

SELF-PROMPTS:

Signs:
Cancer • Woodpecker • Holly
Birthdays:
Wole Soyinka (b. 1934)
Cameron Crowe (b. 1957)
Featured Website/Blog:
http://www.fmwriters.com

SELF-PROMPTS:

JULY 14
CREATING MY WRITING SANCTUARY

If you could build a writing sanctuary, what would it look like? Where would it be located within your house—or property? What furnishings and plants would it contain? What books, paintings and pieces of music would surround you? What quoted words would you post on the wall or bulletin board?

Create your sanctuary. Sketch, draw and write everything you envision in your sanctuary. "Build" the structure of your literary dreams. Let your imagination run wild. Once you're finished with physical description, write the *atmosphere* — the sanctuary's energy, the feeling you need to write and commune with your thoughts.

Add one item from your dream sanctuary to your current writing environment. Tomorrow, add another. Start to build the dream today.

Signs:
Cancer • Woodpecker • Holly
Birthdays:
Irving Stone (b. 1903)
Featured Website/Blog:
http://www.fmwriters.com

"We live at the edge of the miraculous."
— Henry Miller, author, *Stand Still Like a Hummingbird*

SELF-PROMPTS:

JULY 15
ONGOING CONTEMPLATION

What issue, person or thought have you contemplated recently? Call it to mind, sit quietly, and contemplate it more deeply. Return to this subject several times today.

Pick up your journal and write what you have contemplated. Use words that reflect the depth of what you are thinking and feeling. Remain in this emotional and intellectual immersion while you write.

Read what you wrote, and see if you can expand it into an essay, short story or vignette—or implant it into a book-in-progress.

Signs:
Cancer • Woodpecker • Holly
Birthdays:
Iris Murdoch (b. 1919)
Clive Cussler (b. 1931)
Featured Website/Blog:
http://www.essaypunch.com

"Unexpectedly you find it, welling upwards in the empty tree."
— Rainer Maria Rilke, author, *Letter to a Young Poet*

JULY 16
DISPATCHING INNER LONGINGS

The Chinese philosophy of Taoism instructs, "Dispatch inner longings with a hunter's accuracy." When we long for something, and the longing consumes our thoughts and feelings, we must bring it forth. It serves not only as our deepest emotional impulse, but also informs our characters. Many stories live on inner longing.

What is your greatest inner longing? Let's dispatch it with a hunter's accuracy. Identify the longing. Think about *why* you need it and *how* it will enhance your life. Write the action steps you will take, the changes you will embrace, and your envisioned result of taking this leap. Or, write out the inner longing of a character. Move through your draft, and revise so that its clear, precise words radiate intent—the hunter's accuracy.

"I finally discovered the source of all movement, the unity from which all diversities of movement are born."

— Isadora Duncan, dancer-choreographer

SELF-PROMPTS:

Signs:
Cancer • Woodpecker • Holly
Birthdays:
Anita Brookner (b. 1928)
Arnold Adoff (b. 1935)
Featured Website/Blog:
http://www.essaypunch.com

JULY 17
THE EYES HAVE IT: EYESCAPES

You've probably heard the expression, "Eyes are the windows of the soul." Our windows to our literary subjects—real or imagined—are their eyes. We can reveal a character with the eyes. If I write, "The sea-farer's eyes shone like penlights on a roadmap," you would likely guess the sea-farer is a salty old skipper with leathered skin (roadmap), yet his eyes and mind are constantly attentive and alert (penlights). You might write another 500 words about the skipper—all from one sentence that described his eyes.

Describe someone's eyes. Are they deep? Big? What color? Set back in their sockets? Wrinkles? How deep—and where? Framed by arching eyebrows? Animated when the person is expressing himself/herself? Use physical features as comparisons (caves, stones, clouds, etc.). *Landscape* your subject's eyes with your words. Keep writing until the description feels complete.

"Such was the beginning of that course from which I have been unable throughout my life to deviate: I mean the conversion of whatever delighted, distressed or otherwise preoccupied me in to an image, a poem, thus finishing with it; so as both to rectify my notions of exterior things, and to tranquilize myself within."

— Johann Wolfgang Goethe, author, *Autobiography of Goethe*

SELF-PROMPTS:

Signs:
Cancer • Woodpecker • Holly
Birthdays:
Erle Stanley Gardner (b. 1889)
Featured Website/Blog:
http://www.essaypunch.com

SELF-PROMPTS:

JULY 18
THE EYES HAVE IT: ILLUMINATION

As within, so without. When we *really* want to know what someone is thinking or feeling, we turn to their eyes. Writing about the inner eye gives us — and our readers — direct access to the heart and soul that form the character's or subject's thoughts, motivations and actions. Sometimes, a sentence or two suffices. "I saw Grandpa picking at that heart on his plate with a certain look," Louise Erdrich wrote in her novel, *Love Medicine.* "He didn't look appetized at all, is what I'm saying."

Write about the quality of light in someone's eyes when that person is happy, joyous. How bright is the light? Do the person's eyes seem to enlarge? Does it attract everyone around the person? What does the light in the person's eyes resemble? Now switch gears, and write about the eyes of a morose subject. Do you sense darkness, foreboding inside his or her pupils? Do you feel blocked from access to the soul? Try an angry person. Are his or her eyes simmering, molten? Strive to write the inner and outer eye masterfully.

"I suppose the best occupation for a writer is meeting a great many different people and seeing what interests them."

— Aldous Huxley, author, *Brave New World*

Signs:
Cancer • Woodpecker • Holly
Birthdays:
Margaret Laurence (b. 1926)
Hunter S. Thompson (b. 1937)
Elizabeth Gilbert (b. 1969)
Featured Website/Blog:
http://www.authorsinyourpocket.com

SELF-PROMPTS:

JULY 19
DUMPED IN A FIELD

How would you feel if someone swooped down, blindfolded and whisked you to a location you'd never seen before — and dumped you off? What would you say? How would you spend your first hour in the new location?

Transfer this scenario to a fictional character — or write it from your perspective. Be sure to include the initial sense of horror and the feeling of being lost. Also reach into your emotions and thoughts to provide the interior monologue of what it feels like to be abandoned, uprooted from everything that is comfortable. Finally, the last question: How would you spend that first hour? Fretting — or acting? Write a compelling story or personal account.

"By the end of a poem, the reader should be in a different place from where he started. I would like him to be slightly disoriented at the end, like I drove him outside of town at night and dropped him in a cornfield."

—Billy Collins, author, *The Art of Drowning*

Signs:
Cancer • Woodpecker • Holly
Birthdays:
John Newbery (b. 1713)
Eve Merriam (b. 1916)
Featured Website/Blog:
http://www.authorsinyourpocket.com

JULY 20
PICKING UP DROPPED STITCHES

The eminent 1960s educator-artist-poet Mary Caroline Richards taught the "philosophy of the dropped stitches." In order to continue expanding our strengths, we must revisit and embrace qualities and weaknesses we left behind. For instance, a veteran distance runner finds that, after age 40, running alone can no longer improve performance. He or she looks back, sees a lifelong aversion to stretching, the gym and good diet, and realizes those three areas must be integrated in order to continue racing well.

Likewise with writing. Start a piece that emphasizes your strengths — whether lyrical language, writing about nature, or delving into feelings. Introduce an area you've shunned, avoided or toward which you've felt bias; for instance, if you like writing about feelings but have trouble with nature, place yourself or your character in the woods and work it out while observing forest life. Or, if you like describing food but avoid descriptions of herbs, tell us about how thyme and rosemary remind you of a childhood garden.

Pick up a dropped stitch. Then another. Reclaim as many as you can.

"Life shrinks or expands in proportion to one's own courage."
— Anais Nin, author, *Little Birds*

Signs:
Cancer • Woodpecker • Holly
Birthdays:
Francesco Petrarch (b. 1304)
Cormac McCarthy (b. 1933)
Featured Website/Blog:
http://www.authorsinyourpocket.com

JULY 21
SELF-CULTIVATION: PLANT DIVERSITY

Sometimes, we use up so much creative energy that our wellsprings of inspiration and ideas dry up. It happens to everyone, no matter how many books or articles they write. When this happens, we must self-cultivate.

The best way to keep the writing flame stoked, even when writing constantly, is to plant diversity. Write about every subject that comes to you. Experiment with different genres. Read new material constantly. Hook up your brain of ideas to your journal, and jot them down. Observe something new. Talk with someone with whom you wouldn't otherwise associate.

Write one sentence from each book, magazine article, poem or letter you read today. Throw in a few sentences from today's favorite observations or conversations. Put the sentences together, then write an original story or essay that presents the diverse images in another way.

"Let us be silent that we may hear the whispers of the gods."
— Ralph Waldo Emerson, author, *The Works of Ralph Waldo Emerson*

Signs:
Cancer • Woodpecker • Holly
Birthdays:
Ernest Hemingway (b. 1899)
Marshall McLuhan (b. 1911)
Catherine Storr (b. 1913)
John Gardner (b. 1933)
Tess Gallagher (b. 1943)
Featured Website/Blog:
http://www.nanowrimo.org

SELF-PROMPTS:

JULY 22
SELF-CULTIVATION: WATER VOCABULARY SEEDS

Remember those nagging vocabulary exams in school? We'd receive the words on Monday, practice using them in sentences, then take our quizzes on Friday. No one will admit to liking vocabulary quizzes, but everyone remembers them.

For the committed writer, vocabulary building never ends. It is one of the most important ways to self-cultivate—but a lot more fun than the weekly school variety.

As you read a book, write down *all* the words you don't know. Look up their meanings. Return to the book, and study how the author utilizes each word. *Feel* the word rising through the prose and into your vocabulary. Grab your journal and write a vignette that includes the newly learned word—or a collection of words. Make this a regular practice.

Signs:
Cancer • Woodpecker • Holly
Birthdays:
Tom Robbins (b. 1936)
Paul Lewis Quarrington (b. 1953)
Featured Website/Blog:
http://www.nanowrimo.org

"A word is the quintessential symbol. Its power comes from the fact that every member of a linguistic community uses it interchangeably in writing, speaking and understanding."

— Stephen Pinker, author, *The Language Instinct*

SELF-PROMPTS:

JULY 23
SELF-CULTIVATION: HOMEGROWN WORDS

Grow your own words. Go outside, and write about the movements of nature—or the streets—for 20 to 30 minutes. Capture the action, atmosphere and landscape. If a particular sound, mood, color, shape or movement surges through you, and you don't have a description to suit it, make up the word. Don't worry if it sounds outrageous, weird or different—it *is* different. It's brand new! Use the new word in a sentence. Plant it into a story that needs a jolt. Keep a list of your homegrown words; use them to add uniqueness to your voice and spice up your stories.

Signs:
Leo • Salmon • Holly
Birthdays:
Raymond Chandler (b. 1888)
Patricia Coombs (b. 1926)
Robert Quakenbush (b. 1929)
Featured Website/Blog
http://www.nanowrimo.org

"Originally all words were poems, since our language is based, like poems, in metaphor."

— Willard Funk, *Word Origins and Their Romantic Stories*

JULY 24
SELF-CULTIVATION: TASTE-TEST WRITING

Taste-test writing offers a wonderful way to deepen our voices, become more versatile, spin off stories from the inspiration of our favorite authors, and broaden our reading horizon.

Start by picking six to ten books from your shelf—preferably by authors you really like. Turn to the middle of each book, and read two to three pages. When you're finished reading, write an original piece that launches from your favorite passage or passages. Try to write three or four mini-pieces from the same number of excerpts. Work entirely in your voice. Keep your story and slant original.

"There are as many kinds of essays as there are human attitudes or poses, as many essay flavors as there are Howard Johnson ice creams."
— E.B. White, author, *Charlotte's Web*

SELF-PROMPTS:

Signs:
Leo • Salmon • Holly
Birthdays:
Alexandre Dumas (b. 1802)
John D. MacDonald (b. 1916)
Featured Website/Blog:
http://www.languageisavirus.com

JULY 25
SELF-CULTIVATION: HARVEST YOUR IDEAS

We opened the self-cultivation exercises by putting our ideas on paper. Now, let's harvest them.

Choose five ideas you wrote down. For each, write a one-sentence takeoff point from which the idea can blossom into a story, essay, article, poem or song. Which sentence jumps at you? Start writing. Don't stop until your creativity and the idea begin to wind down.

Harvest your ideas—even when working on a book or major project. Picking ideas is like harvesting crops: the more we pay attention to them, the greater our food supply. In any writer's world, ideas *are* food. Nourish them constantly.

"Twenty years from now you will be more disappointed by the things that you didn't do than by the ones you did do. So throw off the bowlines. Sail away from the safe harbor. Catch the trade winds in your sails. Explore. Dream. Discover."
— Mark Twain, author, *The Adventures of Tom Sawyer*

SELF-PROMPTS:

Signs:
Leo • Salmon • Holly
Birthdays:
Elias Canetti (b. 1905)
Featured Website/Blog:
http://www.languageisavirus.com

Signs:
Leo • Salmon • Holly
Birthdays:
George Bernard Shaw (b. 1856)
Aldous Huxley (b. 1894)
Bernice Rubens (b. 1928)
Steven Cosgrove (b. 1945)
Rick Bragg (b. 1959)
Featured Website/Blog:
http://www.languageisavirus.com

JULY 26
MY THREE VOCABULARIES

Prolific novelist James Michener (*Tales of the South Pacific*) once offered a *Washington Post Book World* interviewer his five suggestions for gaining a foothold as a writer. His second suggestion was "acquiring an individualized vocabulary on at least three levels, including modern street lingo."

Three vocabularies? Isn't it tough enough to build one? Yes, but Michener was urging writers to learn languages or variations of language to develop better narrative and character voices.

What are your three vocabularies? Do you have lingo or slang you use? Work-speak? How do your written and spoken vocabularies differ? Write down 10 to 20 words from each vernacular. Write a piece in which you use several words from each of your three vocabularies.

"Language is the road map of culture."

— Rita Mae Brown, author, *Sour Puss*

SELF-PROMPTS:

Signs:
Leo • Salmon • Holly
Birthdays:
Kathleen Norris (b. 1947)
Featured Website/Blog:
http://www.fanstory.com

JULY 27
BOOMERANG STORIES

The boomerang story starts and ends at the same place. Among today's finest writers of high-impact, high-economy boomerang stories are Sandra Cisneros (*Women Hollering Creek and Other Stories, The House on Mango Street*) and T.C. Boyle.

Choose a subject and situation that can only be resolved by returning to the starting point. Write out the entire scene, including interior monologue, a moment of distraction, detail and the action of your protagonist. Make sure you capture everything. Then, "sweep" your story toward its conclusion by creating a scenario whereby we return to the opening lines.

"The poet sees the end and beginning of days."

— Anne Waldman, poet, author, *Fast Speaking Woman*

JULY 28
CROSSING THE INTERSECTION

SELF-PROMPTS:

Intersections are to books what stereos are to cars—an essential accessories. Intersections strongly suggest choices will be made with major consequences; their appearance in print is always dramatic. An intersection is the one place where the author says, "Let's look at all points of view thus far." It creates perspective.

Choose a piece of writing on which you've been working. Imagine its focal point is an intersection—of streets, buildings, vehicles, social policies, inner emotions or spiritual beliefs. Rewrite its focal point to illustrate the intersection and show the choices symbolized by its four directions. Practice writing in a point of view that differs from your own. *Show* why the intersection is where the critical next choice takes place.

"Good writing takes place at intersections, at what you might call knots, at places where the society is snarled or knotted up."

— Margaret Atwood, author, *The Handmaid's Tale*

Signs:
Leo • Salmon • Holly
Birthdays:
Beatrix Potter (b. 1866)
Natalie Babbitt (b. 1932)
Featured Website/Blog:
http://www.fanstory.com

JULY 29
CAPTURE THE FLASH POINT!

SELF-PROMPTS:

The next time a conversation or encounter piques your emotions, observe your emotional flash point—whether you feel rage, euphoria, horror, joy, depression, ecstasy, disappointment or devastation. Write from this place. Mince no words. Use the punctuation of the emotion— exclamation points! Ellipses...Colons: Em dashes—to set dramatic pauses—. *Feel* the energy and emotion in your words. Unload them onto paper.

"You learn a lot when you put down what people said and how they acted in great crises in their lives."

— Marjorie Kinnan Rawlings, author, *The Yearling*

Signs:
Leo • Salmon • Holly
Birthdays:
Eyvind Johnson (b. 1900)
Featured Website/Blog:
http://www.fanstory.com

SELF-PROMPTS:

JULY 30
CANDID CAMERA

Writers over 45: Remember *Candid Camera,* that wacky television show from the late 1960s that anticipated *America's Funniest Videos* and the paparazzi by a few decades? Within its premise lies a tremendous writing exercise.

Go to a place filled with commotion—a busy park, sports event or concert, crowded mall or congested city street. Sit down with your journal amidst the bustle (without getting hurt or run over!), and jot down candid snapshots of what you see—Faces! Cars! Balls! Swings! Crazed shoppers! Spend no more than two sentences on each image, then jot down the next image. When you've written 10 to 20 such sketches, put them together into a piece—but keep the candidness intact with short sentences and quick cutaways to the next moment.

Signs:
Leo • Salmon • Holly
Birthdays:
Emily Bronte (b. 1818)
William Gass (b. 1924)
Featured Website/Blog:
http://www.mostlyfiction.com

"Writing for an audience it is necessary to decide whether or not explanations are necessary. They are not necessary. Explanations murder like a knife the perception. Explanations are the lie making it possible to accept the truth. Explanations are invented as the apology for the action."
— Kay Boyle, author, *Monday Night*

SELF-PROMPTS:

JULY 31
CONTAINERS AND VESSELS

The joy of ceramics comes from shaping pieces of clay into containers and vessels of shapes that reflect the potter's vision and skill. We can experience this process by writing a piece and molding it to the shape, texture and voice that we imagined when we began to write. This works especially well with poetry, lyrics, essays and slice-of-life vignettes.

Write down a moment that occurred recently. Capture the mood, atmosphere, emotion, pace and action. Review the piece and cut out all unnecessary words. Start with adverbs and conjunctions. Next, delete words or phrases that slow down the story's movement.

Read the piece out loud, to yourself or others. "Brush off" any phrasing that seems awkward or off-key. Step away for a while, then observe the container or vessel you've created.

Signs:
Leo • Salmon • Holly
Birthdays:
J. K. Rowling (b. 1965)
Featured Website/Blog:
http://www.mostlyfiction.com

"Journaling is discovery, excitement, the unchartable high of monkeying around with time and traveling through it."
— Al Young, poet, author, *The Sound of Dreams Remembered*

August

AUGUST 1
FIRST THOUGHT, BEST THOUGHT

The thought hits like a comet streaking through the night. Borne of intuition, divine gift, heart or mind, it glows with richness and power. Maybe it's a song melody, the opening line of a novel or poem, or the subject of a book or story.

Many let these thoughts fade, then regret the loss of their ideas. Others grab the nearest object and scribble. One of rock music's dearest souls, Jefferson Airplane and Jefferson Starship singer Marty Balin, scribbled the lyrics to the great song *Miracles* in 45 minutes after *darshan,* or spiritual honoring, with revered Indian "miracle maker" Sathya Sai Baba. The love Marty felt both for his then-partner and Sai Baba converged; he wrote as fast as the words flowed.

Let's try something. Walk in nature, look at a colorful piece of art, or listen to an engaging song. Write down the first thought or inspiration that comes to you. Carry that thought either to its conclusion, or to a place where you can tend to it later. Be sure to convey the *central message* and the *energy* of that thought. Feel the energy, close your eyes, and imagine the perception lodging in your cells, heart and mind. House it in your body.

Never let an earth-shattering thought slip past you again. Often, that is the material you've been seeking.

"When you are a songwriter connected to Spirit, or your Muse, or whatever you want to call it, you tap into a dimension of our world. You try several things, and then something whacks you in your guts. What is it? Don't ask — just follow."
— Marty Balin, singer-songwriter, Jefferson Airplane/Jefferson Starship

Signs:
Leo • Salmon • Holly
Birthdays:
Herman Melville (b. 1819)
Madison Smartt Bell (b. 1957)
Featured Website/Blog:
http://www.mostlyfiction.com

115

Signs:
Leo • Salmon • Holly
Birthdays:
P.D. James (b. 1920)
James Baldwin (b. 1924)
Isabel Allende (b. 1942)
James Howe (b. 1946)
Featured Website/Blog:
http://www.advancedfictionwriting.com

SELF-PROMPTS:

AUGUST 2
SYNESTHESIA: Cross-Sensory Perception

Five centuries ago, visionary Italian inventor Leonardo DaVinci coined a new term, *synesthesia,* to describe cross-sensory perception. Suffice it to say that DaVinci constantly viewed his Renaissance-era world in this manner.

Let's embark on a two-day adventure with synesthesia. Use the questions below as prompts, and write answers that can later be expanded into vignettes, poems or little stories:

- What does loneliness taste like?
- What do you feel when listening to a concert?
- What does the sound of breaking glass look like?
- How does a dissipated ocean wave smell when it swirls around your feet?
- In silence, what does your heart hear and see?

"When you walk into a room and you get a certain feeling or emotion, remember back until you see exactly what it was that gave you the emotion. Remember the noises and smells, and what was said. Then write it down, clearly."

— Ernest Hemingway, author, *For Whom the Bell Tolls*

Signs:
Leo • Salmon • Holly
Birthdays:
Ernie Pyle (b. 1900)
Leon Uris (b. 1924)
Mary Calhoun (b. 1926)
Featured Website/Blog:
http://www.advancedfictionwriting.com

SELF-PROMPTS:

AUGUST 3
SYNESTHESIA: Writing the Connections

The best similes, metaphors and instances of synesthesia occur when we're open and receptive. The greater we attune to our surroundings, the more our writing minds will indulge cross-sensory perceptions and cross-connections.

Take one of the five questions you answered yesterday, or one of the examples of synesthesia you jotted down, and write a small story or essay. Guide the story or essay entirely with the opening line, the experience of synesthesia. Think of yourself as an artist mixing colors (senses) on the palette to arrive at a new color, a new image, a new experience. Write the experience. Open your mind to receive new cross-sensory perceptions.

"Writing is the willingness to see."

— Natalie Goldberg, author, *Banana Rose*

AUGUST 4
SIMILE DRILL

Let's spend today working on similes, comparing objects in the same sentence. Take the 10 sentences below and turn them into similes, using the words "like," "as" or "than" to connect the two objects. When you're finished, turn one of your similes into a story, essay or poem.

Example: A man's radiant smile: "His smile warmed her like a hundred suns."

1. A boss who gets under your skin
2. A favorite teacher that challenged (or challenges) you
3. Comparison between a lake and a mood
4. Comparison between a book scene and a movie scene
5. A powerful woman making a point
6. A sports star returning home
7. Comparison between a flower garden and a single potted flower
8. Comparison between a surfer and a hiker
9. It's colder than…
10. You're funnier than…

Write similes of your own in your journal. Practice using them.

"The thrill is working a miracle, making life where there was none."
— Tobias Wolff, author, *This Boy's Life*

SELF-PROMPTS:

Signs:
Leo • Salmon • Holly
Birthdays:
Percy Bysshe Shelley (b. 1792)
Featured Website/Blog:
http://www.advancedfictionwriting.com

AUGUST 5
THE SPREADING VINE

Since ancient times, grapevines have fascinated everyone from winemakers to botanists, artists, and writers. Their many directions, twists, textures and fruits suggest wild expression, yet they all come from tap roots that reproduce for many decades—if not centuries. We can use the metaphor of the grapevine to find unique writing perspectives and angles on subjects that fascinate us.

Start by drawing a grapevine. Make sure to include a tap root and plenty of vines. Think of the taproot as your subject and each vine as an aspect or slant about the subject. Try to make these angles as unique and new as the grapes of a new season's vine. Write pieces from the two angles that resonate most within you.

This is a great exercise for freelance writers who hit upon a subject, but must develop a hook and angle that will draw editors—and readers—from several different publications.

"Words cluster like chromosomes, determining the procedure. Spontaneous initial originality seems difficult to reproduce consciously later."
— Marianne Moore, author, *Fables of La Fontaine*

SELF-PROMPTS:

Signs:
Leo • Salmon • Hazel
Birthdays:
Ruth Sawyer (b. 1880)
Conrad Aiken (b. 1889)
Robert Bright (b. 1902)
Featured Website/Blog:
http://www.bookbrowse.com

SELF-PROMPTS:

AUGUST 6
INTERCUTTING

In the middle of a movie scene, the action suddenly shifts. A long shot of a rock band zooms down to a close-up of fans cheering. An overhead view of a flooded town switches to tears streaming down a single victim's face. A shot of two women talking about their daughters fades to their daughters doing — or not doing — what they imagine.

A cinematography editing technique, intercutting involves sudden picture changes in order to switch or intensify point-of-view. It forces the viewer (reader) to approach the experience differently, to perceive in another way. A variation of this technique is also used in literary fiction, memoir and, more rarely, in journalistic non-fiction.

Write a paragraph about the most exciting, dramatic, poignant or important thing you did yesterday. Now, skip a space, and write the next paragraph from a different perspective: What if I hadn't done this? Your tone should be more intense and the writing more intimate than the previous paragraph. When finished, skip a space and return to your initial point-of-view. You've just successfully intercut your vignette.

"When I try to explain, I write the story. The story must write me. The story must create me."

— h.d., author, *Bid Me To Live*

Signs:
Leo • Salmon • Hazel
Birthdays:
Alfred, Lord Tennyson (b. 1809)
Matt Christopher (b. 1917)
Barbara Cooney (b. 1917)
Piers Anthony (b. 1934)
Featured Website/Blog:
http://www.bookbrowse.com

SELF-PROMPTS:

AUGUST 7
RESEARCH LIKE A SPIDER

Let's form a research pattern to match our creative minds. Think of a spider that catches insects in all parts of its circular silk before it chooses food from the entire web. When you research a topic, simultaneously draw from books, interviews, articles, DVDs or audio clips, and Internet sources. Source journals, diaries, special collections, newsletters and museums. Follow link chains in search of deep research. If you're working on a musical subject, listen to tunes while researching. If your subject concerns travel or adventure, then participate. Focus your research: *How does the information pertain to my subject, my character and my work?*

Today, choose a topic to research. Collect all available resources, spread them on your desk, attune to the way your mind is assembling the information, and take notes. Go where the research and your mind lead you. Write notes in all directions, and then bring them together. Research like a spider.

"No story is the same to us after the lapse of time; or rather we who read it are no longer the same interpreters."

— George Eliot (Mary Ann Evans), author, *Silas Marner*

Signs:
Leo • Salmon • Hazel
Birthdays:
Maia Wojciechowska (b. 1927)
Betsy Byars (b. 1928)
Featured Website/Blog:
http://www.bookbrowse.com

AUGUST 8
STORYCRAFTING: Foreshadowing

Let's start with a distinction: foreshadowing and forecasting are polar opposites. Forecasting is telling the readers what is to happen shortly before you reveal it. Why continue to read if you already know what's going to happen?

Conversely, foreshadowing is a great literary device. By using a piece of dialogue, sentence or paragraph, the writer provides a clue as to what will happen to a character, setting or event later in the story. Foreshadowing is used most often in novels and non-fiction works that build toward major concluding events. It can happen 200 pages before the actual event, or 10 pages before. Either way, the reader looks back: "I remember the author clueing me in…"

Write a story or essay, or use one you've already written. Somewhere in the first third of the piece, drop a clue that tells us what a character might do, experience or conclude later. Drop another hint in the next third of the piece—a sentence or quick comment. Then show what happens.

"I make some assumptions about my readers, that they would understand certain things. You can't write explaining everything to the outsider."
— Sapphire, author, *Push*

Signs:
Leo • Salmon • Hazel
Birthdays:
Marjorie Kinnan Rawlings (b. 1896)
Featured Website/Blog:
http://www.writing-world.com

AUGUST 9
IMAGINE YOUR ANCESTRAL PAST

Mark Twain once remarked that without an active imagination, our judgment comes into question. Let's practice imaginative writing by turning to…our own ancestral pasts. We carry the DNA seeds of all our direct ancestors in our bodies, which means that we have cellular links to the dawn of humankind.

So let's imagine past times in which our ancestors lived, faraway lands and eras for which we secretly yearn. Write about yourself in that setting, and what captivates you in that place—whether it is the sanctum of a castle, a heather-covered English hillside, or a sumptuous Greek banquet with court poets, musicians and dramatists providing entertainment. Go to a place and time where an ancestor once lived, and make that world your own.

"What kind of poems are our cells writing?"
— Li-Young Lee, author, *Behind My Eyes*

Signs:
Leo • Salmon • Hazel
Birthdays:
John Dryden (b. 1631)
P. L. Travers (b. 1899)
Tove Jannson (b. 1914)
Patricia McKissack (b. 1944)
Featured Website/Blog:
http://www.writing-world.com

SELF-PROMPTS:

AUGUST 10
IN MY CHILD'S FOOTSTEPS

Parents: Ever watched your child play, express a feeling or mannerism, then say to yourself, "That's what I wanted to do when I was that age," or "Why is he/she so good at this thing that fascinated me when I was a kid?" We all have those moments. It could happen while your child is playing music, excelling in a sport, or giving a teen boy or girl looks that you once gave.

Recall an "in my child's footsteps" moment. Grab your journal, and describe the activity, gesture or expression. Then, describe your experience with it while a child. Compare and contrast. Finally, ask yourself: "What inspires me about my child's experience with this?"

Turn a vicarious experience into direct written contact with the *spirit* of that experience—and play like you did as a child.

Signs:
Leo • Salmon • Hazel

Featured Website/Blog:
http://www.writing-world.com

"Keep your focus, keep plugging, follow your heart, and don't get caught up in everyone's plan for you."
— Ann Bancroft, polar explorer, author, *No Horizon Is So Far: Two Women and Their Historic Journey Across Antarctica*

SELF-PROMPTS:

AUGUST 11
CREATE YOUR OWN MYTH

Time to bring up our secret treasures: the most dangerous, heroic or adventurous things we've ever done. Time to write our own myths.

Recall such an event in your life. Remember details, the pace of the action, others present … how it started, how you acted, how your action changed the situation or another person's life in a good way. Jot these notes down.

Write a short story of up to 2,000 words that chronicles your feat. Keep the central action, motive and details intact, but dramatize the story. Ramp up the intensity and excitement beyond what it actually was. Turn every moment into a breath-holder—especially toward the climax. End the piece by stating how the recipient of your action was changed.

This technique provides a great way to write subject or character back story. Furthermore, it illustrates how far and thin the truth is stretched in order to accommodate the danger, heroism and lesson giving found in myths.

Signs:
Leo • Salmon • Hazel

Birthdays:
Alex Haley (b. 1921)

Featured Website/Blog:
http://www.stories.com

"There's a parallel in some ways between superstition and the way fiction works, the way fiction can produce these rather magical moments, which aren't entirely impossible, aren't entirely beyond belief."
— Graham Swift, author, *Waterland*

AUGUST 12
THE SIZZLING ANECDOTE

Great non-fiction writing thrives on anecdotes, true stories about the subject that build the story or article. The anecdotes can be either tasty *hors d'oeuvres* or the main ingredients—depending upon the subject and the way you write it. Anecdotes can range in length from 50 words to many pages. They relate directly to the theme or subject, providing slice-of-life details. Well-written anecdotes carry the pace, tone, rhythm and narrative arc of all good prose.

Write a sizzling anecdote today. Think of an incident or experience in which your passion was tested or fully expressed. Write the experience as a story. Include all necessary details; put us inside your skin. We want to feel like you did. Make sure every word is true and every fact accurate.

Become a dynamic anecdote writer. You will use them for the rest of your writing days.

"People hunger for stories, good language and books about serious things that aren't huge scholarly tomes that are hard to read."

— Kathleen Norris, author, *Amazing Grace*

Signs:
Leo • Salmon • Hazel
Birthdays:
Robert Southey (b. 1774)
Edith Hamilton (b. 1867)
Ruth Stiles Gannet (b. 1923)
Deborah Howe (b. 1946)
Sue Monk Kidd (b. 1948)
Featured Website/Blog:
http://www.stories.com

AUGUST 13
WHAT HAPPENS NEXT?

Write down an incident or situation, then ask yourself: *What happens next?* Write another incident or situation, and then repeat the question. Try to answer *what happens next?* at least 10 times, creating ten scenarios that arose from the previous description.

Use *What Happens Next?* when your narrative feels too plodding, or you don't have enough climactic points or dramatic moments to drive the plot forward. This is also a proven outlining technique for memoir, narrative non-fiction and biography.

"I need something driving down the center of a book like a magnet to draw everything to it--that's what I look for during the first months of writing something new. I often have to write a hundred pages or more before there's a paragraph that's alive."

— Philip Roth, author, *The Human Stain*

Signs:
Leo • Salmon • Hazel
Birthdays:
Charlotte Younge (b. 1823)
Walter Crane (b. 1845)
Featured Website/Blog:
http://www.stories.com

Signs:
Leo • Salmon • Hazel
Birthdays:
John Galsworthy (b. 1867)
Danielle Steel (b. 1947)
Featured Website/Blog:
http://www.writingfix.com

SELF-PROMPTS:

AUGUST 14
CROSS-DRAFTING

A movement has sprung up within the San Francisco literary scene — cross-drafting. A writer steps completely outside her/his chosen genre to write in an entirely different form. For example, a poet might write science fiction, a mystery writer might choose romance, or a novelist might opt for magazine photo captions. The results are not only entertaining, but also extremely beneficial to the writer who has just expanded his/her range.

Pick a genre that is not your own. Find a recent journal entry, essay or short story that can be redirected; better yet, utilize a new idea. Take the plunge, and write for an hour in a genre you've wanted to try, but never have before. See if the experience energizes and expands your writing.

"At a certain point in the life of the writer, the works, the art and the life become identical. The person merges with his artwork."

— Allen Ginsberg, author, *Mind Breaths*

Signs:
Leo • Salmon • Hazel
Birthdays:
Sir Walter Scott (b. 1771)
Featured Website/Blog:
http://www.writingfix.com

SELF-PROMPTS:

AUGUST 15
STORYCRAFTING: IMAGES WITH WINGS

Virtually all poets, lyrical and literary writers live for the moment when the perfectly formed concrete image appears on their page. Powerful images set the tone for the rest of the page … or entire piece.

Create strong imagery that will take wing and fly with your writing. Make a list of 40 nouns that invoke a feeling in you — good or bad. Then jot down ten flexible adjectives — colors, height/weight comparisons (tall, light), your favorite descriptive, *active* words. Mix up the words. Bring nouns and adjectives together in groups of three or four, some with your conscious effort to make the right combination, some at random. When you arrive at a particularly powerful image, set it aside. See how many you can craft.

Finally, write a few paragraphs in which your images set the color, tone and mood for what is to follow. Make image-writing a major part of your writing practice.

"I have my head, thank God, full of visions. One has never too many — one has never enough."

— Henry James, author, *The Turn of the Screw*

AUGUST 16
POWER ANGLES, POWER SLANTS

In the journalism world, they're called "angles." In creative non-fiction, memoir and fiction, they're known as "slants" or "hooks." Regardless, every new piece of writing must enter the stage from a direction—usually the author's or a character's perspective on the matter.

Write a story, article or journal entry that begins with a specific slant. It can be an opinion, an observation or something another person said that changed your view of a situation. If you have trouble finding a topic, go with the tried and true: love, religion or politics. Make sure you feel strongly about the slant you're taking. Write from that perspective. When finished, review your writing and ask, "Does each paragraph describe and illustrate my slant on the subject?"

"A factual piece of work can explore whole new dimensions in writing that would have a double effect fiction does not have—the very fact of it's being true would add a double contribution to strength and impact."

— Truman Capote, author, *In Cold Blood*

Signs:
Leo • Salmon • Hazel
Birthdays:
Charles Bukowski (b. 1920)
Featured Website/Blog:
http://www.writingfix.com

AUGUST 17
WRITE DANGEROUSLY

Throw away all decorum about writing style, propriety and technique. Tear down the walls of your inner censors. Throw open the windows for those thoughts and ideas that would have been deemed outrageous at work, school, home or out with friends. Time to live dangerously on paper!

Spend an hour or two writing outrageous material—dreams, fantasies, romance, crime, horror. Think of delicious plots, schemes and conspiracies. Write paragraphs and pages you've always *wanted* to write, but for whatever reason—choice of language, kids seeing your work, possibility of embarrassment—you never laid down on paper.

Stretch your comfort zone. Write beyond what makes you comfortable. Rub your sentences on razor wire. Take your paragraphs behind closed doors. Scare the heck out of yourself with the most haunting thing you've ever written. Write from the danger zone. Chances are, you'll meet a future character or the subject of several essays and stories.

"I insist on writing whatever has to be written. You write what you can write."

— Louise Erdrich, author, *Love Medicine*

Signs:
Leo • Salmon • Hazel
Birthdays:
Ted Hughes (b. 1930)
V.S. Naipaul (b. 1932)
Ed Sanders (b. 1939)
Jonathan Franzen (b. 1959)
Featured Website/Blog:
http://www.8-2-6valencia.org

SELF-PROMPTS:

AUGUST 18
HONOR THY TITLE

How important is the title of your book or story? Bookstore owners, editors, literary agents and publishers generally agree that the title makes up 50 percent—or more—of a browser's buying decision. Novelist Jeanette Winterson noted, "A book or story deserves the best title that the writer can imagine and it has to be a title that will stick in people's minds."

Think of a title for your next story, poem, essay or book. If something appears that is powerful enough to knock you off your feet, stop there: You probably have it. Otherwise, consider the meanings and layers of your book. Think of phrases that suggest the theme. Look for *double entendres,* titles with more than one meaning. The more a reader feels that your title reflects the narrative, the greater your title. Make every title you write, now and in the future, instantly eye-catching. The first impression runs deep with readers.

Signs:
Leo • Salmon • Hazel
Birthdays:
Paula Danziger (b. 1944)
Featured Website/Blog:
http://www.8-2-6valencia.org

"I think almost every writer in the world would hope that books would always be talked about with respect and civility and depth and seriousness."
— Dave Eggers, author, *A Heartbreaking Work of Staggering Genius*

SELF-PROMPTS:

AUGUST 19
CONTINUATION PLAY

In basketball, the continuation play occurs when a player is fouled while shooting. Even though the whistle blows, he or she can continue; if the ball goes in the basket, the points count.

Writing's version of the continuation play is *suggestion,* in which we infer what will happen next, but we don't *write* it. Suggestion is critical to the pacing of any good fiction or non-fiction story. It's a question of knowing when to take your feet off the narrative gas pedal and let the reader fill in the blanks.

Write a vignette in which you build to a conclusion, and let the reader take it from there. Use crisp details. Resist all urges to write the punch line. Instead, make a strong final suggestion.

Signs:
Leo • Salmon • Hazel
Birthdays:
Ogden Nash (b. 1902)
Featured Website/Blog:
http://www.8-2-6valencia.org

"That's where all my fiction starts, with that fundamental yearning inside each of us."
— Robert Olen Butler, author, *Mr. Spaceman*

AUGUST 20
LAUGHING TO THE GROUND

Besides making people laugh, humor allows authors to give readers a chance to breathe after dramatic scenes. That's why, in everything from sci-fi to mainstream, crime and horror, a particularly intense scene will be followed by a joke, or a humorous exchange between different characters.

Take a newspaper headline, incident in your life, or a joke or comment you heard, and put your best comedic spin on it. Write a funny dialogue or scene. Include jokes or puns. Show characters in slapstick moments, such as chasing a ball across a lake — that just froze yesterday. Laugh as you "wipe off" the soaked pursuer.

Regularly try to add humor to your writing. Practice in your journal. Even if you don't think you're funny, you'll attract laughs simply by observing life, and knowing when to lighten the mood of your piece with a quick joke or humorous aside.

"Advice to aspiring humor writers: listen."
— Christopher Buckley, author, *Supreme Courtship*

Signs:
Leo • Salmon • Hazel
Birthdays:
Edgar Guest (b. 1881)
Salvatore Quasimodo (b. 1901)
Featured Website/Blog:
http://www.encyclopedia.com

AUGUST 21
FEEDING OUR LITTLE DARLINGS

Every novelist or creative non-fiction author faces difficult cutting choices when editing first drafts. Perhaps the most difficult is removing their "little darlings," tangents on which they spent a lot of time, but don't specifically add to the story. They are *the* hardest bits to remove from the manuscript; we sometimes scratch, claw and want to fight to the death to save them.

We all have little darlings — stories we started and didn't finish, pieces of drafts, segments from scenes, moments of complete clarity and insight for which we cannot find a home.

This time, let's feed them. Take an edit you made from a story or book draft, or a past journal entry you liked very much, but didn't pursue further at the time. Give it a twirl on the dance floor, and develop the fragment into a full piece. See what your little darling looks and feels like with added expression.

"In that last editing stage, I am outside myself. I'm looking at it much more clinically, and saying, okay, get out of this scene quicker."
— Michael Ondaatje, author, *The English Patient*

Signs:
Leo • Brown Bear • Hazel
Birthdays:
Robert Stone (b. 1937)
Featured Website/Blog:
http://www.encyclopedia.com

AUGUST 22
STORYCRAFTING: Spin-Off Stories

A book, movie or play contains the overall story, of course, but every character or situation brings along mountains of additional stories — past, present, future. Furthermore, good works always seem to contain one or more storytelling characters that spin yarns through the pages. Once, I broke down a 300-page novel by T.C. Boyle, one of America's finest novelists and short-story writers. It contained more than 50 mini-stories.

Become a story weaver today. Brainstorm for 20 minutes. Write whatever comes to mind. When finished, review your work sentence by sentence. Find three places from which you can begin side stories. Write them.

Signs:
Leo • Brown Bear • Hazel
Birthdays:
Dorothy Parker (b. 1895)
Ray Bradbury (b. 1920)
Annie Proulx (b. 1935)
Featured Website/Blog:
http://www.encyclopedia.com

"I'm sort of a showman, I love to perform, I love to go on stage, and I love an audience. So do many of my characters. We're all storytellers."
— T.C. Boyle, author, *Riven Rock*

AUGUST 23
STORYCRAFTING: Layering Stories

When I read a novel or memoir that builds upon its own well-layered stories, I feel like I've died and gone to a Swiss chocolate factory. These books are *sweet,* no matter the subject. Layering is the *crème de la crème* of story writing, the particular skill of creating relationship between the stories in a book. The stories work together in a literary version of the Native American Medicine Wheel: past, present, future, interpersonal, outside and inside oneself.

Let's layer. Brainstorm for 20 minutes. Read your work and spin off two stories. Next, create two past, present or future stories from each of the side pieces you just wrote. Extend a "branch," a detail, fact or action, from one take to the next. Establish a link, then deepen the relationship. See if these pieces provide layers of context to each other and your original story.

Signs:
Virgo • Brown Bear • Hazel
Featured Website/Blog:
http://www.fundsforwriters.com

"For us, there is not just this world, there's also a layering of others. Everything has presence and meaning within this landscape of timelessness."
— Joy Harjo, poet, author, *She Had Some Horses*

AUGUST 24
UNFINISHED STATUES

We all have stories we didn't finish, ideas we never germinated, slice-of-life essays we never sliced into essays, brilliant story plots we never pursued. At the time, we lacked the desire, time or energy — or courage — to complete. Perhaps these unfinished statues are best left buried…but what about the idea you've always wanted to revisit? The one that would cause you regret if you don't finish it?

Grab that idea and look for the point that draws you in. See if you can pick up its impulse — then dive in with renewed energy. Try to complete one of these fragments — even if it is a five-line poem or letter. Take it to the finish line.

"It takes a long time to bring excellence to maturity."

— Syrus, Ancient Roman writer

SELF-PROMPTS:

Signs:
Virgo • Brown Bear • Hazel
Birthdays:
A.S. Byatt (b. 1936)
Paulo Coelho (b. 1947)
Orson Scott Card (b. 1951)
Oscar Hijuelos (b. 1961)
Featured Website/Blog:
http://www.fundsforwriters.com

AUGUST 25
THE CULTURE (REFERENCE) CLUB

Cultural references are the life's blood of strong topical and time-based narrative nonfiction writing. They give us benchmarks on time, setting, place, current (to the piece) events, and how those references shape the story and the writer's experience in the world. When written in properly, they work very well.

Here's an example I wrote some years ago:

While I discussed construction bids, the Amish man's wife and kids sat in a candlelit corner of their hewn log home, books open, immersed. One kid read Dickens, the other Mark Twain. They beheld the slower moving, less distracting environs of 19th century England and Missouri, when readers enjoyed languorous passages and adventures that developed slowly, rather than racing through literary sound bytes. What attention spans; what depth. It was the best of reading times. Dickens would agree.

Write a piece about something that happened recently to which you can attach historical, social, or cultural context. Drop in one or two cultural references, stamping the moment with a fact, perception or observation relatable to most. Be careful not to "show what I know"; rather, add to the depth of the passage.

"I write about nature and human nature. And most often about that twilight zone where the two meet and have something they can teach each other. I like that best."

— Diane Ackerman, author, *I Praise My Destroyer*

SELF-PROMPTS:

Signs:
Virgo • Brown Bear • Hazel
Birthdays:
Brian Moore (b. 1921)
Featured Website/Blog:
http://www.fundsforwriters.com

SELF-PROMPTS:

Signs:
Virgo • Brown Bear • Hazel
Birthdays:
Christopher Isherwood (b. 1904)
Patricia Beatty (b. 1922)
Featured Website/Blog:
http://www.creativenonfiction.org

AUGUST 26
WHAT'S IN? WHAT'S OUT?

Agony wears many masks. Few are more emotionally or mentally gruesome than deciding what stays in your work—and what comes out.

Grab the first draft of your most recent work. Run it through this quick six-point "trim list":
- Remove superfluous adjectives, adverbs and adverbial phrases.
- Change passive to active verbs whenever possible.
- Trim unnecessary details—and phrases or clauses that contain them.
- Remove back story unrelated to the subject's motive and situation *in your story*.
- Remove extra conjunctions, prepositions and other connective words.
- Remove spin-off or tangential stories that don't feed a plot or sub-plot.

Try to remain as detached as possible when editing your work. That eases the agony.

"I like the mental puzzle involved with dealing with a real situation rather than one you can arbitrarily choose to change."
— Susan Orlean, author, *The Orchid Thief*

SELF-PROMPTS:

Signs:
Virgo • Brown Bear • Hazel
Birthdays:
William Least Heat Moon (b. 1939)
Jeanette Winterson (b. 1959)
Featured Website/Blog:
http://www.creativenonfiction.org

AUGUST 27
AVOID STEREOTYPES

Originality and uniqueness are critical to our success. We must always work to avoid stereotypes by finding unique wrinkles to even the most common person, situation or circumstance…or the way we write a detail or re-state a commonly known fact.

Let's embark on a "road to uniqueness" exercise. Ponder the first two questions. Write a vignette in response to the third:
- Three-word description of your subject or character
- Write three adjectives to support a stereotype of that subject or character. For instance, if the character is a reclusive artist, write "quiet," "creative," "private."
- What characteristics would shatter all assumptions of stereotype? What makes your character unique?

"There are so many selves in everybody, and just to explore and exploit one is wrong, dead wrong, for the creative person."
— James Dickey, author, *Deliverance*

AUGUST 28
DISCOVER AND CREATE UNIQUENESS

Identify one unique element, quality or characteristic of a subject or character in your current or next story or essay:

- How does this characteristic define your character in the eyes of others? How does your character use it?
- Outline a scene in which you reveal deeper layers of character through this trait.
- Write the scene.

"I write about hunger because I am perpetually hungry. I write about greed because I always want more. I write about emptiness because I too often feel empty..."

— Mary Sojourner, author,
Bone Light: Ruin and Grace in the New Southwest

Signs:
Virgo • Brown Bear • Hazel
Birthdays:
Johann Wolfgang von Goethe (b. 1749)
Leo Tolstoy (b. 1828)
Robertson Davies (b. 1913)
Rita Dove (b. 1952)
Featured Website/Blog:
http://www.creativenonfiction.org

AUGUST 29
STORYCRAFTING: Echoes

Echoing is the repeated use of a catch phrase, exclamation or endearment that reminds us of the theme or connections between characters while simultaneously driving the story forward. It differs from foreshadowing, which hints at future events.

Let's try echoing. Write a story or essay of at least 1,000 words. Find a catch phrase that, if you repeat it more than once, will remind the reader of your character or situation. For example, if I were writing a robbery chase scene, I might repeat, "They're getting closer!" See if you can "hear" the echo bounce off the walls of your story and beg you to listen more closely.

"Everything's got to do with listening."
— W.S. Merwin, author, *The Ends of the Earth: Essays*

Signs:
Virgo • Brown Bear • Hazel
Birthdays:
Oliver Wendell Holmes (b. 1809)
Eve Shelnutt (b. 1941)
Featured Website/Blog:
http://papercuts.blog.nytimes.com

SELF-PROMPTS:

AUGUST 30
I, STORYTELLER

My friend Emory DeWitt likes to say to me, "You write stories. I tell them." A masterful oral storyteller in the classic Southern tradition, Emory continues a practice that dates back to our cave dwelling ancestors. "You get up there and stretch some facts, throw in some invented details ... and make it sound *just beyond* what's real," he says.

Take a break from writing today. Tell a story. Create an idea that feels nonsensical, or can be stretched into something fictional, and start reciting. Every time it sounds like you're coming to the end of the road, add something new. Don't worry about the twists and turns; enjoy telling the story, feeling the cadence of your voice and how it can speed up or slow down the action. After about 10 minutes, bring your story to an end. Remember the rhythm of the story in everything you write for the next week.

Signs:
Virgo • Brown Bear • Hazel
Birthdays:
Mary Shelley (b. 1797)
Donald Crews (b. 1938)
Featured Website/Blog:
http://papercuts.blog.nytimes.com

"(Storytellers) created a world for me. Not only did they create a world, but they created a kind of sensibility – something to measure myself against."
— John Edgar Wideman, author, *Damballah*

SELF-PROMPTS:

AUGUST 31
CROSS-TRAINING: WALKING

Dedicated athletes swear by cross-training, the use of another sport or series of exercises to bolster their fitness level and performance in their specialty. Baseball players will play golf, lift weights or run; basketball players will use balance board trainers, mini-trampolines or even dance; runners will swim, bike or add a battery of core muscle exercises. As writers, we serve ourselves by engaging in activities that feed and energize our minds and bodies, open our creative channels and promote greater writing.

Today, take a long walk. Smell the air, listen to the sounds, feel your feet contact the earth, and *unwind*. Engage your mind in your current writing project, a letter you want to write, or a piece you want to organize or journal. When you get home, write it out. Use walks as extensions of your writing life. They are invaluable allies.

Signs:
Virgo • Brown Bear • Hazel
Featured Website/Blog:
http://papercuts.blog.nytimes.com

"If you're roaming the world as an outsider, then you are an explorer and you write as an explorer...in the sense of coming into a strange situation and gaining some insight into it."
— Kurt Vonnegut, author, *Slaughterhouse Five*

September

SEPTEMBER 1
BECOME A TABLOID WRITER (FOR A DAY)

Think of a real or imagined event that would make a sensational newspaper or tabloid headline. Collect the basic facts. Then write to your wild imagination's content, but contrast the preposterous parts of the story with the mundane, the ordinary. Make at least some of the story believable so that readers will "take the leap" and find your most fantastic statements and claims to be plausible.

"Rumor can run all the way around the world while Truth is still putting on his pants."

— Mark Twain, author, *Life on the Mississippi*

SELF-PROMPTS:

Signs:
Virgo • Brown Bear • Vine
Birthdays:
Edgar Rice Burroughs (b. 1875)
Allen Stuart Drury (b. 1918)
Featured Website/Blog:
http://www.42explore.com/journl.htm

SEPTEMBER 2
TRAVELING THROUGH TIME

When we travel, our creative juices and senses are on high alert, we're emotionally high from the newness of the place and its people, and we tend to be uninhibited in what we think or feel. Once, while traveling through Italy, I sat for hours at the Lago di Garda blufftop ruins of Roman poet Catullus. I imagined myself to be Catullus, looking out every morning at the majestic lake from his villa, which was larger than a football field. I wrote romantic, elegiac poetry in his style to strengthen the connection, and then wrote an essay.

On your next journey, find a place or a moment and write about it. Imagine its tactile history — who walked, recited a poem, made pottery, canoed or played flute where you sit? What did they think and feel? Go *deep.* Your cellular memory will be your guide.

"Authors understand and convey feeling and emotion, the inner dynamics of cultures."

— Dr. Norman Sims, author, *The Literary Journalists*

SELF-PROMPTS:

Signs:
Virgo • Brown Bear • Vine
Birthdays:
Lucretia Hale (b. 1820)
Eugene Field (b. 1850)
Allen Stuart Drury (b. 1918)
Featured Website/Blog:
http://www.42explore.com/journl.htm

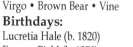

SEPTEMBER 3
SUSPEND TIME & SPACE

One of the most magical elements of writing lies in its ability to suspend time and space. Write a narrative of at least eight paragraphs that takes your from Point A to Point B. Be sure to include time references. Now, take a pair of scissors and cut up your paragraphs, then throw them on your desk or into a box. Pick them up randomly. From this new order, write a story or an essay. When you sense a circular motion in the narrative, you've taken a leap forward *and* produced a truly original piece of writing.

"Why do we write? You are desperate to communicate, to edify or entertain, to preserve moments of grace or joy or transcendence, to make real or imagined events come alive. But you cannot will this to happen. It is a matter of persistence and faith and hard work. So you might as well just go ahead and get started."

— Anne Lamott, author, *The Blue Shoe*

SELF-PROMPTS:

Signs:
Virgo • Brown Bear • Vine
Birthdays:
Sarah Orne Jewett (b. 1849)
Alison Lurie (b. 1926)
Featured Website/Blog:
http://www.42explore.com/journl.htm

SEPTEMBER 4
METAPHORICALLY SPEAKING

SELF-PROMPTS:

Metaphors are powerful expressions of imagery in which one object is given the properties of another. One of the greatest metaphors in American literature came from Stephen Crane, who opened *The Red Badge of Courage* with the immortal, "The sun was a red wafer in the sky." He described a Civil War battlefield by summoning images of blood, smoky sunrise, the Catholic sacrament of communion, the presence of Christ (sun-red wafer-sky) and death — all in the same sentence.

Write a metaphor and story it out. Give an object the properties of another (e.g. "My garden was a swamp"). Write out possible directions you can take the metaphor. Use the metaphor as your topic sentence, and describe/extend the metaphor through an active scene. Write one to three paragraphs, until the metaphor runs out of gas. As part of your writing practice, try to compose new metaphors at least once per week.

"Get the readers to care, to listen to your story, and you can make up a whole new dialect of your own if you like."

— Nickole Brown, poet, author, *Sister: Poems*

Signs:
Virgo • Brown Bear • Vine
Birthdays:
Richard Wright (b. 1908)
Syd Hoff (b. 1912)
Joan Aiken (b. 1924)
Featured Website/Blog:
http://www.associatedcontent.com

SEPTEMBER 5
POV WORKSHOP: 'Where Am I Coming From?'

SELF-PROMPTS:

Emily Bronte worked out the issues of her soul through her characters in *Wuthering Heights*. Jack Kerouac chronicled his growing devotion to Buddhism in *The Dharma Bums*. Jane Smiley laid out the idiosyncracies of the academic life—both likes and dislikes—through *Moo*. Robert Olen Butler told his experience of Vietnam through a dozen different lenses in *A Good Scent from a Strange Mountain*.

As you consider whose or what point of view to use, ask this question: *Where am I coming from?* How does the image that burns in your mind wish to be presented? What message, or theme, are you going for? *Who* will embody this? Will it be one person, or several?

Consider which of your characters will tell the story. Maybe it will be one character. Maybe several. Perhaps *you* will tell the tale. Or be the narrator for everything, the omniscient storyteller. Try to arrive at your starting point.

"You can't make all your characters come from the same neighborhood and have them only know what you know. You just can't."

— Gail Godwin, author, *A Mother and Two Daughters*

Signs:
Virgo • Brown Bear • Vine
Birthdays:
Paul Fleischman (b. 1952)
Featured Website/Blog:
http://www.associatedcontent.com

SELF-PROMPTS:

SEPTEMBER 6
STORYCRAFTING: Parallel Construction

5:15 p.m.: A young artist walks into the store. She grabs a shopping cart, starts piling groceries into the cart, stops to admire the color combination of a label, and *pow*—she collides with the man of her dreams.

5:15 p.m.: A workaholic rushes out of his car. He runs into the store to grab a six-pack of Red Bull. His mind fixates on aisle and location; everything else is a blur. He rounds the corner. *Smack!* The most beautiful woman he's ever seen rubs her head.

Parallel construction uses simultaneous but separate scenarios to create a point of convergence: a meeting, occurrence, realization or conclusion. It provides a powerful, immediate view of the story that delights readers to no end.

Write about two best friends about to make major decisions at the same time. Parallel their thoughts, then convene them for a final goodbye or dinner. Keep everything very present, in each character's point of view. Don't reveal their closeness until the end, when you bring them together.

Signs:
Virgo • Brown Bear • Vine

Featured Website/Blog:
http://www.associatedcontent.com

"You have to take pains in a memoir not to hang on the reader's arm, like a drunk, and say, 'And then I did this and it was so interesting.'"
— William Zinsser, author, *Inventing the Truth: The Art & Craft of Memoir*

SELF-PROMPTS:

SEPTEMBER 7
CROSS-TRAINING: Reading

While reading seems like an obvious sidekick to writing, a lot of writers reduce or even discontinue reading while working on major projects. Never stop reading; it germinates new thoughts, ideas and ways of putting words together. Plus, it's fun and entertaining.

A cross-training secret: If you're writing fiction, read non-fiction, biographies and poetry. If you're writing articles and essays, read memoir and fiction. If you're writing dry, work-related material, try reading science fiction and adventure, or romantic adventure. Read outside the genre you're writing. And read materials you wouldn't ordinarily touch.

Pick up something out of your reading zone. Read it for an hour, and look for style or a passage that suits you.

Signs:
Virgo • Brown Bear • Vine

Birthdays:
Arthur Knight (b. 1887)
Taylor Caldwell (b. 1900)

Featured Website/Blog:
http://www.theshortstory.org/uk

"I have learned not to laugh at the books written by others…The point was to read these books — strange, and indifferent, and interspersed with moments of astonishing beauty — so as to put myself in their authors' shoes."
— Orhan Pamuk, author, *Snow*

SEPTEMBER 8
POV WORKSHOP: Voicing the Protagonist

Many authors (including me) spend six months to a year—or more—playing their protagonist's imagined words in their minds. They will work out language, culture and dialect, and create a point of view other than their own. After that, they will write the story.

Let's work on your main character's point of view. Think of every situation in which your protagonist will appear, or in which you can imagine him or her appearing. Be sure to include moments of drama, conflict, joy, sorrow, growth, danger or difficulty, and resolution. Sketch out five to ten of these situations, writing entirely in the protagonist's voice. *Keep your voice out of the conversation.* Keep writing sketches until you polish the character's voice.

"If you can hear the voice, you can speak in that voice, and you can imagine the speaker."

— Russell Banks, author, *Rule of the Bone*

Signs:
Virgo • Brown Bear • Vine
Birthdays:
Frederick Mistral (b. 1830)
Featured Website/Blog:
http://www.theshortstory.org/uk

SEPTEMBER 9
MY STORY CARAVAN

I've always wanted to caravan with a circus or band of gypsies, camping beneath the open sky, sharing stories in front of a fire, enjoying the diversity of each other's lives. One of the pivotal songs in my novel *The Voice,* "Gypsy's Prayer," conveys this dream. While I won't be joining any circuses or gypsy bands, I will be attracted forever to the idea of the caravanserai, tribal pow-wows, Arabian Nights, Scherezade and roaming, and hearing new and ancient stories that have been told once…or 10,000 times.

Imagine yourself around a campfire after a day of travel, and you're holding the storyteller's stone. What stories would you tell? What types of stories could others tell that would engage you?

Write about an event you have told and retold. When you're finished, look for sentences that could spin off into smaller stories, vignettes or poems. Write a few of those pieces. Imagine that you're writing for a few elders, some children, a couple of musicians, several cooks, and a leader. Create your own caravan of stories.

"Why does anybody tell a story? It does indeed have something to do with faith, faith that the universe has meaning, that our little human lives are not irrelevant, that what we choose or say or do matters, matters cosmically."

— Madeleine L'Engle, author, *A Swiftly Tilting Planet*

Signs:
Virgo • Brown Bear • Vine
Birthdays:
Phyllis Whitney (b. 1903)
Aileen Fisher (b. 1906)
Featured Website/Blog:
http://www.theshortstory.org/uk

SELF-PROMPTS:

Signs:
Virgo • Brown Bear • Vine
Birthdays:
H.D. (Hilda Doolittle) (b. 1886)
Robert McClung (b. 1916)
Mary Oliver (b. 1935)
Featured Website/Blog:
http://www.verlakay.com

SEPTEMBER 10
A NIGHT AT THE FOLLIES

During our great-grandparents' time (and before), American audiences laughed and sang at vaudeville shows, joining in the performers' keen ability to take bad turns of luck or choices in life and find the folly in them. The early 20th century version of comedy clubs, vaudeville produced the man who made self-deprecating slapstick humor universal—Charlie Chaplin.

Let's look at our own follies today. Think of a decision you made that avalanched into four or five bad decisions. Which of those decisions led to another half-dozen questionable choices? Write them down. Now, seek to find the humor in your follies. It's there. We can't help but laugh at some of our past mistakes. Write a vignette that offers a slapstick view of your errant choices—but also reveals what you learned from them. Use this technique to lighten up fiction or narrative non-fiction after an intense scene.

"You will do foolish things, but do them with enthusiasm."

— Collette, author, *Gigi*

SELF-PROMPTS:

Signs:
Virgo • Brown Bear • Vine
Birthdays:
O. Henry (b. 1862)
D.H. Lawrence (b. 1885)
Alfred Slote (b. 1926)
Anthony Browne (b. 1946)
Featured Website/Blog:
http://www.verlakay.com

SEPTEMBER 11
POV WORKSHOP: Minor Characters, Major Voices

Minor characters are often the trickiest points-of-view to write. Each minor character has a specific role to play in the plot, and in the lives of the protagonist(s). They own distinct voices, but their voices can never overtake the main characters—only enhance their significance.

A scenario: You are in a bind or dilemma. A sticky situation. Four people come to you—one relative, one friend and two complete strangers. Two women and two men. Include a teenager as one of your four characters. Each has a different voice and world view. They will give you advice or direction. Write a quick paragraph about the bind you're in. Next, in two sentences apiece, introduce each minor character. Speak of their perspective, and their feeling about your situation, so we can establish their uniqueness. Finally, write an ensemble sketch in which they take turns speaking with you. Have them enter and leave the scene at different times. Make their points of view easy to identify, and vital to the story.

"The knowledge of characters who are utterly not yourself is vital; other people, people who aren't you."

— John Irving, author, *Until I Find You*

SEPTEMBER 12
SELF-PORTRAIT: THE NAVAJO WAY

Years ago, naturalist Joseph Cornell (*Sharing Nature with Children*) visited students on the Navajo Indian reservation. The assignment he gave: draw a self-portrait. Joseph expected to see various renderings of faces and bodies. What he received was far different—most of the drawings depicted a child surrounded by large mesas, corn, rain, clouds, sun, kachina dolls, eagles and other symbols. The students drew their self-portraits; they did separate themselves from their home environment.

Write or draw a character sketch, non-fiction subject study or self-portrait the Navajo way. Describe your place amidst your immediate surroundings, and how you and the environment interact in a way that defines you. Keep the writing centered. Be incisive; seek deeper insight and wisdom. Use the material for a current or future work.

"I have to think of a way where someone in the book, if not the person herself, could tell where she came from and why and so on."
— Elmore Leonard, author, *Get Shorty*

Signs:
Virgo • Brown Bear • Vine
Birthdays:
Alfred A. Knopf (b. 1892)
Michael Ondaatje (b. 1943)
Featured Website/Blog:
http://www.verlakay.com

SEPTEMBER 13
STORYCRAFTING: Unforgettable Endings

I will never forget the last chapter of Anne Rice's magnum opus, The Witching Hour. While vampires are not my things, I voraciously devour Anne's magical imagery, irresistible characters and constant sense of presence. She spent nearly 1,000 pages prepping for this climax, taking the story to a conclusive confrontation between Rowan and Lasher. I read in abject horror, yet could not put the book down because the imagery and action were riveting. It is the only book I have read as an adult that kept me awake for two nights. So haunting, so distressing—yet here I am, a decade later, writing about it. That is an unforgettable ending.

Take a story or essay you've written—or, write a new story. Look at your final page, and seek to accomplish the four (of many) skills Anne Rice has mastered: 1) Create your ending from the dynamics of the story, characters and plot; 2) Make sure your story moves toward this point; 3) Make it unique to the story, a new moment; and 4) It must be realistic, or at least plausible.

"Style must always have an organic relation with the story. If you're telling a simple tale, then the style should be simple, but if you're dealing with very complex people, I don't think you can capture the quality of their minds without a style that is complex."
— Norman Mailer, author, *Harlot's Ghost*

Signs:
Virgo • Brown Bear • Vine
Birthdays:
Sherwood Anderson (b. 1876)
Roald Dahl (b. 1916)
Featured Website/Blog:
http://www.sfwa.org

SELF-PROMPTS:

SEPTEMBER 14
CROSS-TRAINING: Gardening

Another great "cross-training" discipline grows from the earth—your garden. Whether you plant a vegetable garden that produces year-round, rim your office window with indoor plants, create a water garden in your pond or bury a few rows of flower bulbs, try to develop a green thumb. Not only does it clear the mind and allow contemplation time, but it also forms a relationship between you, the earth and the elements—all of which belong in good writing.

Write about the act of planting, memories it invokes and how the earth and seed feel in your hands. Then write about the relationship between the beginning of stories, essays or poems, and the beginning of a garden. Do something in your garden every day. Nurture your writing.

Signs:
Virgo • Brown Bear • Vine
Birthdays:
Hamlin Garland (b. 1860)
Edith Thacher Hurd (b. 1910)
Featured Website/Blog:
http://www.sfwa.org

"Those who persist that they live in a garden will find their carrots veering off to join or intersect the lettuce, while weeds and animals from the forest insinuate themselves through the slackening fence wire."

— Joseph Meeker, ecologist

SELF-PROMPTS:

SEPTEMBER 15
POV WORKSHOP: To Be Omniscient...

The omniscient point of view serves as both a catch-all and a reliable safety net. The author—you—speaks through all the characters and narrative, creating a story in which every viewpoint is explored in the third person. The omniscient point of view populates most epic and historical novels, classic literary works, and topical non-fiction.

Today, write an original story, either fiction or about a recent incident in which you were involved. Include two or three characters, a situation, point of conflict and resolution. Write in third person, capturing all the characters' views and actions from the point of view of the *story itself*. You are omniscient, able to sit inside the skin of the characters, the situation and the setting. Give us a panoramic view.

Signs:
Virgo • Brown Bear • Vine
Birthdays:
James Fenimore Cooper (b. 1789)
Agatha Christie (b. 1890)
Robert McCloskey (b. 1914)
Featured Website/Blog:
http://www.sfwa.org

"Maybe every writer, read with care, reveals his shortcomings."
— Jorge Luis Borges, author, *Death and the Compass*

SEPTEMBER 16
LIGHTING THE ROOM

The quality or type of light in a room often changes our perception of its contents, or alters our moods, thoughts or feelings when we're inside. Accomplished writers set the tone of many scenes by describing the light. For instance, a bedroom suffused with candlelight presents a different tone than an office illuminated by fluorescent lights.

Go to a room in your home and describe its contours, features, contents, moods, angles, shadows and surprises. Consider in your descriptions:

    a. Sunlight
    b. Moonlight
    c. Fluorescent light
    d. Everyday lights or lamps
    e. Lamps of unusual design or style

"Great writing to me is, you open the book and you are surprised each time out. That's what I want to do. That's literature."

— T.C. Boyle, author, *East Is East*

Signs:
Virgo • Brown Bear • Vine
Featured Website/Blog:
http://www.identitytheory.com

SEPTEMBER 17
FLASH!

Write a complete story or memoir vignette, with one or more characters, a conflict, resolution, plot and setting, in 200 words or less. Choose your words carefully; write with precision. If you have more than one character, guide your story with dialogue. See how many flash fictions you can write in the next month—and have a lot of fun doing it!

"The universe is made of stories — not atoms."

— Muriel Rukeyser, poet, author, *Breaking Open*

Signs:
Virgo • Brown Bear • Vine
Birthdays:
William Carlos Williams (b. 1883)
Elizabeth Enright (b. 1909)
Ken Kesey (b. 1935)
Featured Website/Blog:
http://www.identitytheory.com

SELF-PROMPTS:

Signs:
Virgo • Brown Bear • Vine
Featured Website/Blog:
http://www.identitytheory.com

SEPTEMBER 18
WRITE THE RIVER

A few years ago, my Ananda College students and I drove ten miles from our campus in the Sierra Nevada Foothills to the Yuba River. We grabbed our towels and journals, and edged down a deer path that would shake the knees of mountain goats. After that steep descent, we sat atop flat slabs of granite, refugees of the last Ice Age.

I invited my students to "write the river." "There are five different currents in motion right now," I told them. "You can only see three from above. Dive underwater and open your eyes to see and feel the other two. How do all five work together? How does each express itself?"

You can do the same. Sit for thirty minutes in a place of natural beauty. Immerse yourself in the setting, and then describe how the moving elements interact. Write as if everything is in relationship. How does each moving part shape the principal natural object (river, mountain, lake, ocean, wildflower patch)? How do you feel within this movement?

When you're finished, sit for a moment and take in your surroundings. Do they feel more alive? In concert with you? How has your relationship to them changed in the last 30 minutes?

"Facts are eloquent."

— Norrie Epstein, author, *The Friendly Shakespeare*

SELF-PROMPTS:

Signs:
Virgo • Brown Bear • Vine
Birthdays:
Rachel Field (b. 1894)
Sir William Golding (b. 1911)
Featured Website/Blog:
http://www.autocrit.com

SEPTEMBER 19
POV WORKSHOP: Multiple Viewpoints

Pick up the story that involved you and the four minor characters. Walk the four minor characters "off-stage," and bring in two major characters, people very close to the narrator. Write another scenario in which you explore the perspectives and prejudices of the characters. Reflect their positions in their dialogue, how they react to opposing viewpoints. Fuse their comments to their personalities so we do not doubt the viewpoint. Switch to the other character, then the narrator. Play with this for a while, and develop multiple viewpoints.

"The rocks in the water do not know how the rocks in the sun feel."
— Haitian proverb

SEPTEMBER 20
FILLING THE HOLES

SELF-PROMPTS:

Let's switch to a particular form of editing—filling the holes. Take a piece of writing on which you've been working. Read it through, and then examine each sentence and paragraph to see if any detail or expression is hidden or omitted. If you find one, does it invite further exploration or discussion? Does it welcome the exposure of added details? Does it grab the reader and say, "I've got something *else* to tell you"?

Turn your writing into a two-part invitation: for the reader, deeper engagement; for you, deeper revealing of your truth. Fill the holes.

"Whatever has been told to you will be full of holes and omissions and things that are hidden. A narrative line will make all these things pop out in the open."

— Luisa Valenzuela, author, *He Who Searches*

Signs:
Virgo • Brown Bear • Vine
Birthdays:
Upton Sinclair (b. 1878)
Featured Website/Blog:
http://www.autocrit.com

SEPTEMBER 21
CROSS-TRAINING: Adventure

SELF-PROMPTS:

What seems like an outrageous adventure—but possible? Is it skydiving? Surfing? White-water rafting? Summiting a mountain? Spending a week distributing relief supplies in an impoverished country—or a less fortunate part of this country? Walking 20 miles in a fund-raiser? Attending a rock or hip-hop concert?

Take the leap! Put your fullest attention, spirit and energy into the event, and *participate*. Write about the adventure, the people, the risk (if any), the thrill of trying something new—and *how* it might expand what you consider possible. If you write fiction, assign this adventure to a character.

Adventures are great ways to stretch our limits, extend our comfort zones, and provide tremendous amounts of new material to which we can circle back for years.

"A journey is time suspended. All decisions await arrival, and one travels on, day after day, accepting each as it comes."

— Louis L'Amour, author, *Jubal Sackett*

Signs:
Virgo • Brown Bear • Vine
Birthdays:
H.G. Wells (b. 1866)
Fannie Flagg (b. 1944)
Stephen King (b. 1947)
Marsha Norman (b. 1947)
Featured Website/Blog:
http://www.autocrit.com

SEPTEMBER 22
BOCCACCIO'S EXERCISE

In his masterwork, *the Decameron,* pre-Renaissance Italian novelist Giovanni Boccaccio combined narrative, dialogue, lyrics, poetry, slang and colloquialisms to tell 100 traveling stories through the eyes of many characters. Some say *The Decameron* loosened the mores and spirits of enough readers to be a contributing factor in The Italian Renaissance. It's a tremendous example of throwing everything on the table and writing.

For the next hour or two, fill Boccaccio's shoes. Write a story in which you explore something—a new country, forest, cave, yours or another's heart, or an old building. Combine narrative, dialogue, poetry and slang as you travelogue. If you feel like saying something, say it. If you observe something amazing, write a poem or song. Bring in other characters (or real people) if you'd like. Run all of these forms together.

"You have to make (your story) up every day as you go along. Then you have to play the cards you already have on the table — you have to deal with what you've already said. Quite often, you've gotten yourself into things that seem to lead nowhere, but if you force yourself to deal with them…"
— Joan Didion, author, *The Last Thing He Wanted*

SELF-PROMPTS:

Signs:
Virgo • Crow • Vine
Birthdays:
Esphyr Slobodkina (b.1908)
Featured Website/Blog:
http://www.blogspot.com

SEPTEMBER 23
BLOGGING: Write What You Know

Do you live in the blogosphere yet? If not, consider joining the many who write or contribute to blogs online. It's a great way to publish your writing and promote your books or book aspirations!

Blogs can range from journal-like free association to well-structured, well-illustrated articles—and everything in between. A posting can run 50 to 2,000 words, or more. It can also include photos, video and other imported items. Your perspective, commentary and opinion matters—after all, it is your blog.

Pick a subject about which you can write many times, and continually find new material. Spend 10 or 15 minutes jotting down article ideas.

Now write your first entry. When you write, include plenty of keywords—specific references that will attract search engine visitors looking for material on your subject.

"As long as the plots keep arriving from outer space, I'll go on with my virgins."
— Barbara Cartland, author of 853 romance novels

SELF-PROMPTS:

Signs:
Libra • Crow • Vine
Birthdays:
Euripides (b. 480 B.C.)
Featured Website/Blog:
http://www.blogspot.com

SEPTEMBER 24
BLOGGING: Find Your Host, Then Post!

At first glance, it's like shopping for specific grains of sand while standing on the beach: Where to place your blog entries?

Spend today researching blogs that pertain to your subject. Many blogs offer bulletin boards, some form of chat, or the opportunity to post guest blogs. You can also add a blogging feature to your website (if you have one). Social networking sites such as MySpace (www.myspace.com) and FaceBook (www.facebook.com) contain the busiest blogs on the Internet. Maybe your blog belongs here, too.

Locate a blog host. Registration is simple, but be sure to put unique passwords on each blog. Consider Wordpress (www.wordpress.com), TypePad (www.typepad.com), BlogSpot (www.blogspot.com), Thoughts (www.thoughts.com), Blogstreet (www.blogstreet.com) or Google Blogs (www.googleblog.blogspot.com). All contain built-in features that enable you to blog, post, and import photos, video, audio or other files with ease and convenience.

"I just go where my unconscious leads me and wait for whatever it throws up on the shore of my imagination. It always surprises me."
— Robert Olen Butler, author, *Tabloid Dreams*

Signs:
Libra • Crow • Vine
Birthdays:
Frances Harper (b. 1825)
F. Scott Fitzgerald (b. 1896)
Wilson Rawls (b. 1913)
Featured Website/Blog:
http://www.blogspot.com

SEPTEMBER 25
BLOGGING: Viral Blogging

Your blog is up, you've already received emails from friends and readers, and you're feeling good about what you've started. Now comes the tough part: producing fresh material.

Let's work with two specific techniques to keep your blog strong. First, take the original list of subjects, and brainstorm for more ideas. Write down anything related to your blog's focus currently happening with you, your community, or the world. Develop stories and write.

The other technique, and today's exercise, is to write a "blog cluster" — several articles in short succession. Start with a 150- to 200-word entry. Review the entry, and look for a key sentence or phrase from which you can write another entry. Compose that entry. Now think of other topics, angles, or advice you can give that is related to the two articles. Write a couple more articles. While clustering, be sure to keep your list handy — other ideas will pop out to be addressed later.

"I do not understand the capricious lewdness of the sleeping mind."
— John Cheever, author, *Falconer*

Signs:
Libra • Crow • Vine
Birthdays:
William Faulkner (b. 1897)
Featured Website/Blog:
http://www.blogtopsites.com

SELF-PROMPTS:

SEPTEMBER 26
BLOGGING: Read Great Blogs

Some of the most creative writing and graphic design takes place on blogs. It behooves us to study the best.

Search for five top blogs in areas that interest you. Read and study them. Post a comment. As you study, openly brainstorm and mind map ideas for your blog, ways you can add new features into your presentation. Study the feature, experiment with it, shape or remodel it to your blog material, and create a new feature that is of *your* making. We're after originality, not copying and plagiarism.

A few search sites: http://www.topbloglists.com, http://www.worldtopblogs.com, http://usa.blogranking.us, http://blog505.com, and http://www.blogelites.com.

"The library is a sacred place, a clinic for the soul."
— Ramses II, Egyptian pharaoh

Signs:
Libra • Crow • Vine
Birthdays:
T.S. Eliot (b. 1888)
Jane Smiley (b. 1949)
Featured Website/Blog:
http://www.blogtopsites.com

SELF-PROMPTS:

SEPTEMBER 27
BLOGGING: Tell the World!

Your blog rocks. You know it, your friends and family know it, and you truly have something to say that reflects the uniqueness of your mind, voice and writing skill.

How to get the world to respond? It's time to put together announcement emails and texts, as well as notifying chatrooms, discussion groups and social networking sites on which you might have a page.

Write a linked announcement about your blog today, no more than 50 words (25 is even better) stating your blog's topics and your mission. Read it aloud. Work until it sounds smooth as a radio commercial. Anchor the announcement with a link to your blog. Example: *Explore the inner world of the writing life at* http://366writing.wordpress.com. E-mail and post on chat rooms.

Finally, go online and learn some tricks of the blog publicity trade — which will also help you promote your articles, essays, stories and books.

"We have it in our power to begin the world again."
— Thomas Paine, author, *Common Sense*

Signs:
Libra • Crow • Vine
Birthdays:
Paul Goble (b. 1933)
Featured Website/Blog:
http://www.blogtopsites.com

SEPTEMBER 28
CROSS-TRAINING: Retreat

Sometimes, we need to push away the pace and stimuli of daily life and take time for ourselves. However, we're not talking about idling away the days or staring dead-eyed at a flat screen. Retreats are exceptional cross-training activities for anyone seeking greater contact with their feelings, lives and spiritual persuasions.

Think of a retreat you would like to take. It might be a writing residency workshop or camp. Maybe it's a church or yoga retreat. Perhaps you want to take an adventure or trek, or attend a fitness retreat. Decide what you'd like, and write about some of the things to which you'd look forward at a retreat. Later, when you're there, take along ideas or pieces you've begun, and develop them while you're away from daily responsibilities.

"Writing requires, for me, not only the actual time when I am writing, but a span of time for dreaming, taking notes, reading, meditating in the bathtub, walking alone. The peripheral time is just as crucial."
— Frances Mayes, author, *Under the Tuscan Sun*

Signs:
Libra • Crow • Vine
Birthdays:
Kate Douglas Wiggin (b. 1856)
Featured Website/Blog:
http://www.about.com

SEPTEMBER 29
POV WORKSHOP: I, Memoir

Over the past 40 years, the proliferation of creative non-fiction, memoir and first-person essays and fiction has suggested that first-person is both easy and profitable to write. Fact is, well-done first-person is an art form. The simplicity: You either write about your own experiences or assume the persona of your protagonist. The challenge: If you write any non-fiction in first person, you must scrutinize facts to make sure they match your truth—or state a compelling reason why they don't. You must also be mindful of others who may appear in your *true* story in a less than glowing way.

Find a subject that deeply interests, attracts, repulses, angers or delights you. Write about your viewpoint on that subject, how long you've held it, why you formed it, and how both your viewpoint and the subject have intermingled with your life. Peel away the surface layers of rote opinion. Dive in and *write your heart and soul as it pertains to that subject.* Keep writing until you can write no more. Write like a memoirist.

"It's like building a house. You get to a certain part and you realize you need a different gauge of lumber or something, and you have to go get it."
— Ian Frazier, author, *Family*

Signs:
Libra • Crow • Vine
Birthdays:
Miguel de Cervantes (b. 1547)
Featured Website/Blog:
http://www.about.com

SELF-PROMPTS:

Signs:
Libra • Crow • Vine

Birthdays:
Rumi (b. 1207)
Elie Wiesel (b. 1928)

Featured Website/Blog:
http://www.about.com

SEPTEMBER 30
FINISH YOUR WRITING DAY *HOT!*

When your writing session nears its end, don't sprint to a hasty finish. Rather, write until you arrive at a particularly juicy, poignant, steamy or dramatic moment, then *stop.* Carry the heat and gravity of that moment into the next day, when you sit down and resume. Finishing "hot" is one of the greatest antidotes for writer's block and tired writing.

"Creations are places where caring and daring come together."
— Adriana Diaz, author, *Freeing the Creative Spirit*

October

OCTOBER 1
WRITE SOMEONE ELSE'S DIARY

OK, amateur snoops, curiosity addicts, viewers of *Inside Edition* and gossip lovers: today is your lucky day. We're going deep into the character's most secret drawer and pulling out his or her diary—a diary that *you* have written.

Occupy the heart, mind and skin of your character or another person. Write their diary. Be realistic. Make some entries lengthy and others short, some emotionally evocative and others contemplative, some observant and others gossipy.

Diary pages make awesome novel excerpts. They also help you get to know your characters intimately, to write well in another's persona, or to gain deeper insight into those you know—even if your "entries" differ from the truth.

"The human family has all the same secrets, which are both very telling and important to tell."

— Frederick Buechner, author, *Telling Secrets*

Signs:
Libra • Crow • Ivy
Birthdays:
Tim O'Brien (b. 1946)
Featured Website/Blog:
http://www.aar-online.org

SELF-PROMPTS:

OCTOBER 2
GATHERING COLLECTIONS

Many of us will not write non-fiction books or novels. Instead, we will produce numerous short stories, essays or poems. What to do when we have enough pieces to create a book-sized collection?

Look at your grouping of stories, essays or poems. Is there a theme or a string, a direction that the works seem to take? Is there a dominant piece that serves as the nucleus around which the other pieces rotate? Does *every* piece have a catchy title and a first paragraph (or stanza) that grabs the reader by the heart or mind? Is it self-contained—yet part of the larger overall theme or direction?

Some collections are arranged chronologically. Most are not. For today, if you don't already have a solid order of contents, spread the first pages of each piece on your floor. Move them around, as though arranging a photo album, until your combinations feel and look right. Use this mosaic approach to build the collection.

Signs:
Libra • Crow • Ivy
Birthdays:
Jan Morris (b. 1926)
Featured Website/Blog:
http://www.aar-online.org

"Strive for that state of knowing that eventually becomes luminous."
—Stanley Kunitz, poet, author,
The Wild Braid: A Poet Reflects on a Century in the Garden

SELF-PROMPTS:

OCTOBER 3
FORM A WRITER'S GROUP!

We all need community, especially with our oft-lonely life of writing for weeks, days and hours on end.

So form a writer's group! Contact five or six people you know to be writers (the local library is a good place to check), and ask them to inform some friends. Host an introductory meeting, find out how far everyone has progressed in their writing (and *what* they're working on), and organize a more regular get-together. You can host it salon-style, where everyone reads and comments on the work, plus literary topics in general. You can create it as a community organization, a clearinghouse for readings, fairs, sales, signings and open houses at different writers' houses. Or, you can have a working writer's group, in which one writer reads from his or her manuscript and receives *constructive* feedback from others in the room.

Write about the features you would like to see in a writer's group, what you would like the group to accomplish, what *you* would like to gain, and how you envision the group forming. Then, get to work!

Signs:
Libra • Crow • Ivy
Birthdays:
Gore Vidal (b. 1925)
Featured Website/Blog:
http://www.aar-online.org

"Forming a circle is a symbolic way of asserting that the true teacher is always invisible in our midst."
— Alice O. Howell, author, *The Web in the Sea: Jung, Sophia, and the Geometry of the Soul*

OCTOBER 4
JUST SAY IT!

Take a productive working writer's vow: *I will never again allow my inner censor to stop me. I will write what I need to say, simply and clearly.*

Think of a challenging exchange or scene in a recent essay, story or article you wrote, one in which you couldn't say exactly what you needed to say. Either you avoided the statement, or you danced circles around it with circuitous writing. Read the selection again. What jumps out at you that needs to be said?

In one sentence, write the point or statement you need to make for the story to work best. Now write a paragraph leading from that sentence … and a paragraph leading back to it. Write sharp, concise sentences, full of substance. Do not mince words. When finished, return to your story, and rewrite the difficult segment so that it reads exactly as you intended.

"The way to say it is to say it."

— Gertrude Stein, author, *Tender Buttons*

SELF-PROMPTS:

Signs:
Libra • Crow • Ivy
Birthdays:
Donald Sobol (b. 1924)
Jackie Collins (b. 1937)
Anne Rice (b. 1941)
Featured Website/Blog:
http://www.bonnieneubauer.com/ssonline.shtml

OCTOBER 5
CROSS-TRAINING: Daydreaming

When we grew into adulthood, we left many aspects of childhood behind. Sometimes, as our lives hurry along in their regimented miasma of schedules, events, job duties and kid duties, we inadvertently shed parts of ourselves we'd like to reclaim — especially when we get into something creative or engaging, like writing.

Today, let's welcome back a great friend of childhood: the daydream. Remember lying beneath trees, staring up at leaves or clouds? Or looking at the Moon and wondering what it would be like to see it up close? Spend the next 15 or 20 minutes daydreaming. Don't stop the flow of the dream; let it form and grow. Write out the daydream, putting yourself in the middle.

Daydream often. We are never too old to wish upon stars. Or touch them.

"I've always used dreams the way you'd use mirrors to look at something you couldn't see head-on — the way that you use your mirror to look at your hair in the back."

— Stephen King, author, *The Shining*

SELF-PROMPTS:

Signs:
Libra • Crow • Ivy
Featured Website/Blog:
http://www.bonnieneubauer.com/ssonline.shtml

OCTOBER 6
VOICE OF THE ESSAY

The essay serves a number of purposes, ranging from deep and personal to incisive and informative. Sometimes, it is all of the above. The most important decision we make in preparing a strong essay occurs in the first sentence: How are we going to voice the essay? Will we make it an intimate account of a first-person experience that branches out to include a larger view of the subject? Or will we write in third person, and focus on delivering our key points through studious observation and objectivity?

Write a 1,000-word essay about a subject of great importance to you. Gather your facts and research, connect it to your personal experience with the subject, and give the material time to percolate. Set your voice in the first sentence. Seek to establish yourself as an authority on the subject, but rather than delivering an authoritarian essay, invite your readers to participate. Even though essays are non-fiction, the way your voice "sounds" in delivering the piece matters tremendously to readers.

"The essay narrator is also a construction. The person who speaks from the page is made of words."

— Scott Russell Sanders, author, *Cloud Crossing*

Signs:
Libra • Crow • Ivy
Birthdays:
Thor Heyerdahl (b. 1914)
Lee Kingman (b. 1919)
Featured Website/Blog:
http://www.bonnieneubauer.com/ssonline.shtml

OCTOBER 7
OBSERVATION POST: Tuning In

Observation is to a writer what breath is to a drowning man. Always seek something to observe: sunrise, dogs or kids playing, cars speeding down the highway, hawks circling in the sky.

Write an observation. Emphasize the relationship between what you see, what you feel, and the thoughts or ideas it stirs within you. Try to observe the same subject for the next 10 days, writing what you see, feel and think. Your writings will differ slightly as you notice nuances and fine details about your subject.

10 days from now, compare the first and last pieces. Glean the best material from all 10 vignettes and write a mosaic that reads like time-lapse photography.

"We influence things greatly, but when you're standing out in the prairie and there's just this open sky and open land around you, you realize how small you are. How vulnerable."

— Kathleen Norris, author, *Dakota*

Signs:
Libra • Crow • Ivy
Birthdays:
James Whitcomb Riley (b. 1849)
Alice Dalgliesh (b. 1893)
Robert Westall (b. 1929)
Susan Jeffers (b. 1942)
Diane Ackerman (b. 1948)
Featured Website/Blog:
http://www.chacha.com

OCTOBER 8
OBSERVATION POST: Every Shade and Nick

Poet-fictionist Harvey Stanbrough once told his students to write the shades of a birch tree's bark. If someone came back with a monochromatic piece, only writing about one color, he sent the person back to the woods to observe again.

Write about someone's face. Get beyond simple descriptions of the eyes, mouth, cheeks, jaw and forehead. Where are any wrinkles? What do they look like—and suggest? How are the eyes set on the face? What is the skin's texture? Do the cheeks rise and fall when the person laughs? How does the mouth set when the person concentrates? Cries? Cracks a joke? How heavy is the beard (if a man)? Any recent cuts from shaving (Because of hurry? Inattentiveness? Singing to himself?)? How full or thin are the lips? How do *they* move?

Write down every shade and nick of your subject's face. Match each detail with a sentence about what it suggests to you. Make your observation more precise as you write.

"I care more about what is being said in a poem than how it is being said."
— Nikki Giovanni, poet, author, *Blues: For All the Changes*

Signs:
Libra • Crow • Ivy
Birthdays:
Barthe DeClements (b. 1920)
Frank Herbert (b. 1920)
R.L. Stine (b. 1943)
Featured Website/Blog:
http://www.chacha.com

OCTOBER 9
OBSERVATION POST: Inside the Circle

Here's an observation exercise that led to one of the most popular poems at my readings, "The Riverstone Runes." It germinated beside a cottonwood-shaded stream in southeastern New Mexico where, in the 1870s, Billy the Kid hid out from Pat Garrett and his posse.

Grab your journal, and walk outside to a place where nature abounds. If you're in the city, go to a sizable park, lush riverside, or forest. Measure out a circle about 10 steps in radius (30 feet). Sit in the center. For the next thirty minutes, write what you see, interactions or relationships that develop between you and anything within that circle, and how the circle might flow, co-exist. Write down *everything*. Let the material percolate overnight.

"As you begin to write and develop voice, musicality happens over time, but eventually, it becomes part of the essential motion of how you use the language. It's a continual sense of adventure and discovery."
— Mei-Mei Bersenbrugge, poet, author, *Four Year Old Girl*

Signs:
Libra • Crow • Ivy
Birthdays:
Johanna Hurwitz (b. 1937)
John Lennon (b. 1940)
Featured Website/Blog:
http://www.chacha.com

SELF-PROMPTS:

OCTOBER 10
OBSERVATION POST: Writing the Circle

Take the rich material you wrote in the circle yesterday. Review and rearrange it into a poem, story or series of sketches. Or, use the setting as a backdrop to write reminiscences or dreams, always coming back to your observations when they remind you of a point to make, or a connection with nature or another person.

Use your time in the circle to produce deeply observant writing that implants your observations of that spot of earth in your heart and mind forever. Then create another circle, and capture every physical detail—and the emotional details welling from within you at the same time.

"With maturity, our horizons should broaden from the narrow circle of those known to us to include all those in need of suffering, whole nations as well as individuals."

— Margaret Guenther, author, *Toward Holy Ground*

Signs:
Libra • Crow • Ivy

Birthdays:
Ivan Bunin (b. 1870)
Claude Simon (b. 1913)
James Marshall (b. 1942)
Nora Roberts (b. 1950)

Featured Website/Blog:
http://www.freelancewriting.com

SELF-PROMPTS:

OCTOBER 11
THE OBSERVATION POST: Refresh!

Observe the same subject(s) as you did in the first Observation Post exercise. Write out what you see, feel and think, and how you and the subject interact during your period of writing. Strive for nuances and fine details. Look for subtleties in color, texture, tone, movement and the way the subject fills space or time. Compare the first and last pieces in this series, and note the difference.

If you want to take this exercise even further, glean the best material from every Observation Post exercise. Write a sequence of vignettes, in mosaic (non-chronological) style, that reads like a time-lapse presentation of your evolution as a keen observer and author of fine detail.

"Writing is really rewriting—making the story better, clearer, true."

— Robert Lipsyte, author, *The Contender*

Signs:
Libra • Crow • Ivy

Birthdays:
Russell Freedman (b. 1929)
Richard Paul Evans (b. 1962)

Featured Website/Blog:
http://www.freelancewriting.com

OCTOBER 12
CROSS-TRAINING: Museums and Galleries

Writing involves yearning. We yearn for that perfect phrase, choice of words, perfect description of a sound, building, animal, person's face or situation. The visual arts give us the opportunity to study creativity in myriad forms, but more importantly, to attune with the skill and vision it took to produce the work.

Take a trip to an art gallery, museum, pottery shop or sculpture garden—a place where artists or artisans show their work. Use your senses to feel what the artist expressed, tracing the lines with your eyes as though they were fingertips. When you get home, write about the "field trip" in your journal—and see if you can produce a piece of written art. Visit museums, galleries and artisan shops often. They are renewable, ever-changing resources of creative inspiration.

"I keep thinking we'll wake up someday and everyone will remember that every memorable piece of art we've ever had surprises us in its form."
—Dave Eggers, author, *How We Are Hungry*

Signs:
Libra • Crow • Ivy
Featured Website/Blog:
http://www.freelancewriting.com

OCTOBER 13
OLD LETTERS

Old letters offer rich, exquisite material. Letters create windows of deep, private moments and intimacy for readers, as they have for many centuries. They also provide new writing subjects and a way to review our place in others' lives—and vice versa. They are tried and true literary devices, whether in their entirety or excerpted.

Grab a stack of letters—the older, the better. Read the letters, and write down 5 to 10 possible story ideas. Write a story.

Think of characters or subjects who might write or receive one of the letters. Write a scenario showing the character or subject utilizing the letter. Or, determine how to weave the letter into your present work, and integrate it.

Finally, note the letters' intimacy and languaging. Write a story in which the letter defines and provides seed material for the plot (or, if a short-story story, the central action).

"You can't wait for inspiration. You have to go after it with a club."
— Jack London, author, *Call of the Wild*

Signs:
Libra • Crow • Ivy
Birthdays:
Eugene Michael Richter (b. 1890)
Featured Website/Blog:
http://www.agentresearch.com

SELF-PROMPTS:

OCTOBER 14
ROMANCE THE UNKNOWN

Part of our perceptual duty is to reach into the unknown, explore it, journey through it and bring back the elements that feed our work. We expand the sphere of our writing, we grow wiser, and we write more authentically. Witness visionary poet William Blake's comment about the ultimate unknown: "The man who never in his mind and thoughts traveled to heaven is no artist."

Today, tackle something about which you know next to nothing. Research the subject, read three or four articles or blogs, and ponder the material for a few minutes. Return to your journal, and write a couple of paragraphs about the subject. See if you can relate the subject matter to a personal experience or piece of knowledge. Make the comparison, either in a few sentences or as a simile. End with two or three questions that will inspire or motivate you to dig further into the subject. Have fun digging.

Signs:
Libra • Crow • Ivy
Birthdays:
Arna Bontemps (b. 1902)
Featured Website/Blog:
http://www.agentresearch.com

"Not only write about what you know, but about what you don't know. It extends the imagination."

— Toni Morrison, author, *Song of Solomon*

SELF-PROMPTS:

OCTOBER 15
FOLLOW THE CHARACTERS

Find a subject or character about which you're writing, or one you are thinking about developing. A real person works, too—anyone but you. Your subject has just learned he/she must change his/her lifestyle to survive. Sink into your character's point of view, and start writing. Follow your character's every thought, feeling, hesitation, decision and action. Leave out your own editorial wishes. Immerse in his/her world. Work for about an hour, but don't let the clock stop you.

Signs:
Libra • Crow • Ivy
Birthdays:
Italo Calvino (b. 1923)
Featured Website/Blog:
http://www.agentresearch.com

"I don't think there was ever a moment where, before writing, I said, well, this is what the character is going to do. You just see possibilities."

— Graham Swift, author, *Last Orders*

OCTOBER 16
THE WELL-PACED STORY

The best-paced stories mix the fast and slow, the heated and calm, the serious or funny. Authors intentionally vary the pace to take the readers into the depths, screech through dramatic moments or create emotional space through humorous exchanges.

Write an essay or story that features fast action, a dramatic emotional exchange, and a moment of contemplation. Use short sentences for fast action and drama. Use. Fragments. When. Making. An. Emotional. Point. (can you envision a finger pointing from this page?) Write long, exploratory sentences when pondering, contemplating, or explaining issues that require thinking. Slow the pace so the reader can grasp the material—then kick it back into high gear with dialogue or a statement. See if you can create three changes of pace. Make well-paced work an objective of everything you write.

"Pace to me is a great deal more than just turning the pages fast. Sometimes the pace needs to be slowed down. Sometimes you want that change in texture. I'm conscious of pace. It's a thing that I think about when I write."

— Jean Auel, author, *Clan of the Cave Bear*

Signs:
Libra • Crow • Ivy
Birthdays:
Oscar Wilde (b. 1854)
Eugene O'Neill (b. 1888)
Gunter Grass (b. 1927)
Featured Website/Blog:
http://www.poynter.org

OCTOBER 17
VISUALIZE...THEN WRITE

After the morning brainstorm, look out your window and visualize your writing for the day. Fill in the setting, characters (real or fictional), colors, emotions and scents of the moment, and attach it to the goal of the scene or story. Jot down this mental sketch, grab your "paint brush" (computer or pen) and "paints" (words), and bring your visualization to written life.

"Get that story down before you lose sight of it. It may not look so good tomorrow."

— Raymond Carver, author, *Fire: Essays, Poems, Stories*

Signs:
Libra • Crow • Ivy
Birthday:
Jimmy Breslin (b. 1929)
Wally Lamb (b. 1950)
Featured Website/Blog:
http://www.poynter.org

OCTOBER 18
TAPPING INTO THE DREAM WORLD

Jot down your dreams as soon as you wake up. If you don't remember specifics, write down images, moments, high and low points. Tap into the *spirit* of what was happening, *your* spirit, as well as the symbolism. How do you feel? Who made you laugh or cry? Was someone taking you on a journey? What thoughts did it provoke? Write a poem, essay, article, scene or short-short story from your dreams.

"I have been waked up in the night sometimes by a plot advancement or solution of a problem that I had not even been dreaming about."

— Patricia Highsmith, author, *Strangers on a Train*

SELF-PROMPTS:

Signs:
Libra • Crow • Ivy

Birthdays:
Henri-Louis Bergson (b. 1859)
Nancy Winslow Parker (b. 1930)
Terry McMillan (b. 1951)

Featured Website/Blog:
http://www.poynter.org

OCTOBER 19
O LANGUAGE MY LANGUAGE!

There are thousands of spoken languages and dialects. From the working writer's standpoint, this number shrivels to insignificance: Everyone on the planet has his or her own spoken and written voice, a unique language. That's almost 7 billion languages.

Write down your first language. Add a second, third or fourth language you know. Then add: phrases you learned from your parents or grandparents; slang or colloquialisms you use; military or job-based jargon; abbreviated languages (for older folks, shorthand; for younger people, probably texting); any sports or hobby-based terminology.

Quite a list, isn't it? These are the seeds of your unique language.

Write a page or two that combines words from your terminologies so that they make perfect sense. Enrich your writing by integrating your full language.

"The language that we have available to us as American writers is a chorus of voices; it's not officially classified as upper or middle or lower, it moves in and out, it invades itself."

— Russell Banks, author, *The Sweet Hereafter*

SELF-PROMPTS:

Signs:
Libra • Crow • Ivy

Birthdays:
Ed Emberly (b. 1931)

Featured Website/Blog:
http://www.writersbreak.com

OCTOBER 20
MISUNDERSTANDING

Misunderstandings fill our lives and those of our circles of family, friends and acquaintances. In writing, misunderstandings lead to conflict; conflict leads to dramatic events; eventually, resolution occurs.

Create a misunderstanding on paper, or recall a misunderstanding you experienced with someone. What was the situation? The misunderstood remarks? The prevalent emotions? The actions taken—or not? *How* and *why* were the remarks misunderstood—what was the missing piece that would have resolved the matter? Why wasn't it present at the moment?

Write the misunderstanding with an eye toward resolution—or disaster. See if you can apply this touch to a work in progress.

"It pains me very much that people are not trying to redeem, transform, heighten and intensify language."

— Jeanette Winterson, author, *The Passion*

SELF-PROMPTS:

Signs:
Libra • Crow • Ivy
Birthdays:
Crockett Johnson (b. 1906)
Wylly Folk St. John (b. 1908)
Art Buchwald (b. 1925)
Michael McClure (b. 1932)
Elfriede Jelinek (b. 1946)
Featured Website/Blog:
http://www.writersbreak.com

OCTOBER 21
WRITING IN SLANG

Let's veer off to another type of language expansion—slang. These are the cut-up, hackneyed words and phrases (some crude or obscene) unique to specific regions or peoples. While slang doesn't add intelligence and eloquence, it does season the story or article with distinct local flavor. For novelists, short story writers, creative non-fiction authors, journalists and memoirists, slang is crucial to know—but use sparingly.

Write down 20 to 25 slang terms that you can speak and understand effortlessly. Now create a story, travelogue or journal entry in which you use each of the words. If you have a hard time fitting them into narrative, switch to the greatest delivery vehicle for all slang, all language—dialogue.

For the next few days, listen to passersby as they talk. Be especially mindful when you hear slang that is unfamiliar to you. Grow your slang vocabulary. It will serve you well.

"Slang is a language that rolls up its sleeves, spits on its hands and goes to work."

— Carl Sandburg, poet, author, *Rootabaga Stories*

SELF-PROMPTS:

Signs:
Libra • Crow • Ivy
Birthdays:
Samuel Taylor Coleridge (b. 1772)
Ursula K. LeGuin (b. 1929)
Featured Website/Blog:
http://www.writersbreak.com

SELF-PROMPTS:

Signs:
Libra • Crow • Ivy
Birthdays:
Deepak Chopra (b. 1946)
Featured Website/Blog:
http://www.writingforums.org

OCTOBER 22
REWRITING HISTORY FROM THE OUTSIDE

Why do readers of historical fiction and memoir keep coming back for more, even though the basic facts behind the stories have been known for decades or centuries?

There will always be a market for nostalgia; we love to reminisce and know our roots. Furthermore, no historian knows *all* of a subject's possible acquaintances, friends or enemies. This opens the door to creating stories that have yet to be told. Authors work between the cracks—the unrecorded periods of their characters' lives—to dig up new material.

Find an historical period with which you're familiar. Visualize a scene involving a person who was there. What was he or she doing? Trying to figure out? What secret conversations did he/she have with others that we don't know about? When you write the scene, be sure to include a few facts to establish time, place and atmosphere.

"The story is the armature of the novel. You can't have a good novel without a good story. You must have that frame to build the novel around."
— Erica Jong, author, *Fear of Flying*

SELF-PROMPTS:

Signs:
Scorpio • Snake • Ivy
Birthdays:
Marjorie Flack (b. 1897)
Michael Crichton (b. 1942)
Featured Website/Blog:
http://www.writingforums.org

OCTOBER 23
REWRITING HISTORY FROM THE INSIDE

Historical fiction writers work from within the imaginary psyches of people who actually lived. The ground is always fertile, since no historian knows *all* of the interior monologue, struggles, thoughts, silent joys or sufferings historical figures experienced.

That's where we come in, like sleuths in the night. Think of a historical figure that intrigues you, and enter that person's mind *before* he or she makes the decision or takes the action we know as historic fact. What was he/she worrying about? Happy about? Where was his/her heart? Was the person's *inner life* serene, or tumultuous? What motives or conflicts run through this person? What does he/she hope to achieve? Has it happened yet?

Write the person's interior monologue, while observing the natural setting. Put your reader in the middle of this walk—and write in an active voice, to convey a feeling of presence.

"Even if you research everything available, you are still way short of a full understanding of an individual, because thousands of hours of interior monologue are unrecorded — the worry and anxiety and frustration and taking time to solve a problem…this is where the imaginative leap is important."
— Irving Stone, author, *Passions of the Mind*

OCTOBER 24
MAKING HISTORY PRESENT

Harken back to a moment of history in which you wanted to live, or in which you want to set a story. Write from that place as though it were the present day. What does the landscape feel like? What do the people smell like? How does food taste? What concerns people? Who do you love? Who loves you? How do the times change your views? What remains the same? Indulge in your desired moment of history, and see how much presence you can bring to it through your words.

"That's what we're here for: to make the world new."
— Nancy Mairs, author, *Ordinary Time*

SELF-PROMPTS:

Signs:
Scorpio • Snake • Ivy
Birthdays:
Brenda Ueland (b. 1860)
Bruno Munari (b. 1907)
Barbara Robinson (b. 1927)
Featured Website/Blog:
http://www.writingforums.org

OCTOBER 25
VISITING AND REVISITING CHILDHOOD

Our childhood memories hold the seeds we brought into adulthood. To return to childhood is not only a wonderful nostalgic journey for those harboring good memories, but also a repository for writing material. So are childhoods that were difficult; they might conceal even more substantial and valuable content. By visiting our earliest touchstones, we keep the ever-inquisitive "inner child" alive and bring our entire lives to the page, no matter what we're writing.

What is your fondest childhood memory? For the next hour, revisit it. Jump into the setting, laughs, screams, adventure and discovery within the experience. Make your writing all-inclusive, so rich and full that readers connect to the sense of being a child. Remember: when we played, *nothing* distracted us. Reflect that complete focus.

"I'll always return to the landscape of childhood. No matter how long I live somewhere else, those images are imbedded in ways I can't escape."
— Melanie Rae Thon, author, *Girls in the Grass*

SELF-PROMPTS:

Signs:
Scorpio • Snake • Ivy
Birthdays:
Gilbert Patten (b. 1866)
Anne Tyler (b. 1941)
Featured Website/Blog:
http://www.typepad.com

The Write Time

SELF-PROMPTS:

OCTOBER 26
SETTING THE WRITING TABLE

To write consistently, it is essential that we become creatures of routine. This starts with setting the writing table—the room, desk, tools and surroundings of your daily plunge into the relationship between words, mind, heart and creation.

Write an essay on what you consider to be your ideal writing space. Music? Plants? Knick-knacks? Open windows? Storyboards and character sketches pasted on the walls? Inspirational sayings from your favorite authors? Your cat curled up in the corner? Once you've written the essay, incorporate as many elements as possible into your current space. Set your writing table—and keep refining and changing it to suit your taste, feed your routine.

Signs:
Scorpio • Snake • Ivy
Birthdays:
Ellen Showell (b. 1934)
Steven Kellogg (b. 1941)
Featured Website/Blog:
http://www.typepad.com

"Volume depends precisely on the writer's having been able to sit in a room every day, year after year, alone."

— Susan Sontag, author, *Under the Sign of Saturn*

SELF-PROMPTS:

OCTOBER 27
KNICK-KNACK STORYTELLERS

Due to their sentimental, historical or collecting value, and their unique designs, knick-knacks provide stories of their own. They also serve as wonderful props for scenes. We just need to dig them out.

Check out a knick-knack shelf in your house, or a friend's house. Study the objects, their design and origins—perhaps their history—and the way they are arranged. Now rearrange the objects. What are the stories behind the objects? What do they tell you in this new arrangement? Who held them before you? How did they live? What mythical creatures live inside them?

Let the knick-knacks take you away for countless hours of story writing fun. Occasionally rearrange the knick-knacks, and continue to import these little treasures into your future works.

Signs:
Scorpio • Snake • Ivy
Birthdays:
Enid Bagnold (b. 1889)
Constance C. Greene (b. 1924)
Fran Leibowitz (b. 1950)
Featured Website/Blog:
http://www.typepad.com

"Literature isn't a closed circuit. It's a universe full of intersecting dialogues."

— Tess Gallagher, author, *The Lover of Horses*

OCTOBER 28
THE POWER OF A (UNI)VERSE

Astronomy has fascinated me since childhood: new star and galaxy discoveries, shadow or parallel universes, the light reaching earth from stars that exploded 5 billion years ago. Every time I read about a discovery, I'm reminded that writers explore and create new universes with every story or book they write.

Dive deeply and freely into your subject. Make your subject the center of your universe. Or, create a new world or universe! *Immerse.* Lose track of space and time; emerge from the writing session thinking, "Where am I? *That* much time passed?"

"For the sake of a single verse…one must be able to think back to roads in unknown regions, to unexplained meetings and partings one had long seen coming; to days of childhood still unexplained; to days in rooms withdrawn and quiet and to mornings by the sea, to the sea itself, to seas, to nights of travel that rushed along on high and flew with all the stars."
— Rainer Maria Rilke, author, *The Duino Elegies*

Signs:
Scorpio • Snake • Ivy
Featured Website/Blog:
http://www.education-portal.com

OCTOBER 29
DIMENSIONS OF A PERSON

Every person carries dimensions entirely their own, through the interaction of their cultural, environmental, spiritual, educational, emotional, social, family and community influences. A great literary example comes from *Dimensions of a Life,* an anthology of more than 70 pieces that show different angles and dimensions of Pulitzer Prize-winning poet Gary Snyder.

Think of two people you know best—a spouse or partner, relative, best friend. Write down every fact you know. Go back to when they were born, or stories they told you about their earlier years. Next, choose five to 10 facts, and write a paragraph from each. Search for the *dimension* of that person, their deeper character, that generated the action or trait about which you wrote. How does the dimension enhance that person's character?

Take note of the variety of dimensions, the aspects revealed. Use this exercise to develop characters that grow deeper during the course of your book or story.

"You have to know people. You have to know the dimensions in which they have lived, do live, and yet may live."
— Morris L. West, author, *Daughter of Silence*

Signs:
Scorpio • Snake • Ivy
Birthdays:
Dominick Dunne (b. 1925)
Featured Website/Blog:
http://www.education-portal.com

SELF-PROMPTS:

OCTOBER 30
DELICIOUS OBSESSION

Sixteenth century German religious leader Martin Luther admitted that he couldn't halt one obsession: "It is a fever that does not break, this writing."

The fever has gripped many noteworthy authors. Barbara Cartland wrote 853 romance novels. Isaac Asimov completed 500 science fiction novels. Joyce Carol Oates has written 80 books and several thousand short stories. Louis L'Amour wrote 100 western novels. Ray Bradbury has written 100 sci-fi and essay books…and counting.

When the writing bug bites, nothing can scratch it. We write about *everything.* Our journals become laboratories for ideas and expressions. We experiment with different genres, forms and styles. We become voracious readers, consuming subjects that we may integrate into our writing. We study people and events, deeply.

Most of all, we write and write and write. So let's do it. For the next hour or two, obsess. Write about anything and everything. Go wherever the Muse takes you. Crank it out.

Signs:
Scorpio • Snake • Ivy
Birthdays:
Fjodor Dostoyevsky (b. 1821)
Ezra Pound (b. 1885)
Timothy Findley (b. 1930)
Featured Website/Blog:
http://www.education-portal.com

"It is possible to get a kind of obsession, so that one can work on a book forever in order to perfect it and get in everything he wants to get in, but I believe it is more important to get done and go on to other work."
— Thomas Wolfe, author, *Look Homeward, Angel*

SELF-PROMPTS:

OCTOBER 31
Halloween
'I DIDN'T SEE THAT COMING'

Unexpected feelings happen. We think that something will strike us one way, but it doesn't. We expect to celebrate over a big sports victory, but our team loses. We nurture a romantic feeling, only to be shunned. Or, we begin another lonesome night—only to meet someone who changes our life. Jolts to the heart serve up strong stories.

Develop a scenario in which the lead subject or character (or you) passes through the scene fielding one set of emotional expectations—only to be dealt another. Good or bad; doesn't matter. Write about the change in feeling, and how it comes out in their ensuing comments, gestures or actions. *Show* the changed, unexpected feeling through action and/or dialogue.

Now change a scene or two in a work-in-progress to invite the unexpected. Surprise and intrigue your reader at the same time.

Signs:
Scorpio • Snake • Ivy
Birthdays:
John Keats (b. 1795)
Susan Orlean (b. 1955)
Featured Website/Blog:
http://www.book-in-a-week.com

"Readers don't want to hear about predictable feelings, but unexpected feelings. Why would they read your story if they could anticipate the feelings?"
— Rachel Howard, author, *The Lost Night*

November

NOVEMBER 1
PLOT LINES: The Situation

SELF-PROMPTS:

Nearly 90 percent of all books contain variations of themes or situations first explored 2,500 years ago in the Ancient Greek theatre of Aeschylus, Pindar, Euripides, Sophocles and others. *Ninety percent!* The implication: All stories originate from a finite number of universal themes.

When a story starts to shimmer in your mind, ask this question: *What's the situation?* It needs to be strong enough to move your real-life or fictional characters forward — and begin your story. It also must establish the theme, and feed the plot through present developments, back story and potential future outcomes.

Write a situation, a premise for your story or essay. Show what happens to set off the story. The opening situation must be in place for the story to begin.

"I went around looking for a situation where those questions of devotion and service and things being out of control and things being in someone else's hands would be more central than they were in mine."
— Francine Prose, author, *Household Saints*

Signs:
Scorpio • Snake • Reed
Birthdays:
Stephen Crane (b. 1871)
Charlaine Harris (b. 1951)
Featured Website/Blog:
http://www.book-in-a-week.com

163

SELF-PROMPTS:

NOVEMBER 2
MUSICAL ACCOMPANIMENT

The oldest artistic marriage in civilization is the union between music and writing. Western civilization's first creative writing, in Sumeria and Egypt, was poetry. Centuries later, poetry and music merged in Ancient Greece. Homer wrote the first epics, or story-poems, at this time. The popular term Muse, originally a pantheon of nine inspirational beings, led to the word *music.* The word for song-verse, *lyric,* comes from a stringed instrument, the lyre.

Write a piece in your journal, or on your computer, that feels musical to you. Try to feel the rhythm. Use imagery and write from the heart. Make your piece *move;* dance in its sentences and phrases. See if you can *hear* your words thrumming. Write in constant motion. Don't edit; don't censor, but write at the same beat, the same pace, as the words come to you. Write like you're dancing and singing in front of 20,000 screaming fans, or conducting the London Philharmonic.

See how your musical voice may differ from your normal writing voice. Integrate some of that musical voice. It is your deepest natural rhythm.

Signs:
Scorpio • Snake • Reed
Birthdays:
Odysseas Elytis (b. 1911)
Featured Website/Blog:
http://www.book-in-a-week.com

"A musician must make his music, an artist must paint, a poet must write if he is to ultimately be at peace with himself."
— Abraham Maslow, author, *New Knowledge in Human Values*

NOVEMBER 3
WRITING THE 'OTHER' SENSES: Thought

SELF-PROMPTS:

Austrian scientist and anthroposophist Rudolf Steiner, founder of the Waldorf School educational system, believed that we perceive our inner and outer environment not with five senses, but with 12. Steiner stressed that each sense had an inner and outer expression, which becomes more obvious when looking at the "other seven." When incorporating them into writing, the added senses create rich layers and texture to characters — as well as studies of living people. They are incredible tools.

We'll cover all seven of the "other" senses. Let's start with the sense of thought. This covers not what a person thinks about, but the *effects* of thought on his sense of well-being and his walk in the world. Write a sketch about a character, non-fiction subject or person you know, and ask: Does he think his way through everything — to the exclusion of his heart feelings? Does she populate her mind with thoughts that expand and grow — or sharp conclusions, opinions? Is he judgmental or non-judgmental? How do her lofty thoughts inspire those around her? How do his thoughts of earth-as-living-organism inform his manner of living and comporting himself? How does a person's base, crude thoughts reflect in what he watches, listens to? How he talks to others?

"The novel is the greatest example of subtle interrelatedness that man has discovered."

— D.H. Lawrence, author, *Lady Chatterley's Lover*

Signs:
Scorpio • Snake • Reed
Featured Website/Blog:
http://www.ezinearticles.com

SELF-PROMPTS:

NOVEMBER 4
PLOT LINES: What's Happening? The Hook

Once the situation is stated and the story opens, something happens that "gets the ball rolling" (or bleeding or romancing, as the case may be). It could be reminiscence, a tragedy, an old love interest rolling back into town or the commission of a mysterious crime.

What about the situation, and your main character's (or narrator's) involvement with it, prompts your character to make a final decision or to change something? What is the specific thing said, or done, to push the character forward?

Answer these questions, and you will arrive at your hook. Write a few paragraphs in your journal about the hook, how it works, and how you imagine it weaving in and out of the plot and your key characters' (or real people's) lives through the story.

Make your book grab us so we start turning pages.

Signs:
Scorpio • Snake • Reed
Featured Website/Blog:
http://www.ezinearticles.com

"There was a story and a romance that was colorful and ebullient, and there was also an avoidance that was disturbing. A matter of unfinished business."
— Suzanne Lessard, author,
The Architect of Desire: Beauty and Danger in the Stanford White family

SELF-PROMPTS:

NOVEMBER 5
EVOLVING LIFE LESSONS

We bring into adulthood the life lessons of our childhood and adolescence — direction and guidance (or not) from our parents, advice from our grandparents, the influences of relatives and friends. Each of us uses some of these life lessons that have served as our launching pads, lessons we transformed into our own ways through trial, error and wisdom.

Think of a habit you picked up from one of your parents — then changed or transformed. Write about the habit as they practiced it, how and why you assumed it, then the series of events that led to you evolving or transforming the habit. How have you expressed this trait in life situations? Draw back to your parent's habit, to show how far the lesson has come.

Apply this scenario to a story or essay character or subject.

Signs:
Scorpio • Snake • Reed
Birthdays:
John Berger (b. 1926)
Featured Website/Blog:
http://www.ezinearticles.com

"The sage within a writer is one who cultivates his or her own nobility, using the teaching that has been handed down as guidance, but evolving and maturing from the private compound of affinities that was seeded at conception."
— Robert Aitken, author,
Zen Master Raven: Savings and Doings of a Wise Bird

NOVEMBER 6
OUTSIDE THE MARGINS

To find the material that makes us grow as people and writers, we need to veer outside the margins — often. Our craft requires us to talk with people with disparate views, explore ideas and books with which we don't always agree, look at objects or events from a variety of angles — literally — and seek out newness while honoring our lives and interests. Our craft requires us to write these new ideas and concepts, sharpening and widening our perception as we do.

Grab some paper without any lines. Copying or typing paper will do. Think of something you read or heard about that seemed outrageous, well out-of-bounds to you. Write about the event as though *you* participated in it. Imagine the thrill of danger, of heading outside your comfort zone. Imagine knowing the others who participated, and embrace their eccentric ways. Write beyond what you thought to be your margins, where fertile places and unimagined growth await. Afterward, see if you feel or think more expansively.

"Vision looks inward and becomes duty. Vision looks outward and becomes aspiration. Vision looks upward and becomes faith."
— Stephen S. Wise, religious scholar

Signs:
Scorpio • Snake • Reed
Birthdays:
James Jones (b. 1921)
Michael Cunningham (b. 1952)
Featured Website/Blog:
http://www.artellaland.com

NOVEMBER 7
PLOT LINES: Issues, Motive, Conflict

We all have issues — some very serious, others little quirks. We can push all these issues, and others, on our characters.

Plot thrives on conflict. In everyday life, most of us seek to avoid or work through conflict. In story, essay, memoir, topical non-fiction and novel writing, conflict drives the plot. While they may not want it in their personal lives, working writers embrace conflict with open arms and bear hugs.

What conflict or conflicts beset your character(s)? What conflicting issues have arisen from the situation that launched your story? What conflicts can you see coming? Write scenarios. Build your plot with an initial conflict that centers your story.

"I have a little piece of paper that says, 'Have I written something that will humiliate me?' This is exactly the kind of abandon you must write with."
— Marsha Norman, playwright, author, *'Night, Mother*

Signs:
Scorpio • Snake • Reed
Birthdays:
Albert Camus (b. 1913)
Featured Website/Blog:
http://www.artellaland.com

SELF-PROMPTS:

Signs:
Scorpio • Snake • Reed
Birthdays:
Bram Stoker (b. 1847)
Margaret Mitchell (b. 1900)
Ben Bova (b. 1932)
Kazuo Ishigro (b. 1954)
Featured Website/Blog:
http://www.artellaland.com

NOVEMBER 8
TRIBE OF POTENTIAL CHARACTERS

While sitting at a sidewalk café one afternoon in New York City's bustling Union Square, a friend noticed my discomfort at the swarm of pedestrians. "Look at them as 2,000 potential characters walking by every 15 minutes," she said.

Who makes up your tribe of potential characters? Think of 10 people you know who would make good major or minor characters. Write five known traits about each. Add one strength and one weakness for each (to your knowledge). *Invent* five traits for each person. Describe a face as well—one that doesn't look like your acquaintance. Take one of the 10 characters and write a two-page story, blending known and imagined traits. Create a narrative scene, with a beginning, middle and end. Keep the other lists for future stories—and look for more people to "sketch"!

"The novel is a genre that would have us believe that its characters might have a life beyond the pages."
  — John Mullan, author, *Eighteenth Century Popular Culture*

SELF-PROMPTS:

Signs:
Scorpio • Snake • Reed
Birthdays:
Anne Sexton (b. 1928)
Carl Sagan (b. 1934)
Featured Website/Blog:
http://www.romancejunkies.com

NOVEMBER 9
LOVE SCENES THAT TRANSFORM

Love scenes can strike many poses, from early teenage attraction to deep, involved interchanges between adults. They range from purely emotional to purely physical, from subtle to direct, from short to lasting, from love of another to love of God. They cross the gamut of age-appropriate suitability. We'll focus on scenes that can transform readers—and you.

Think of an act of heartfelt love with a spiritual depth and quality to it. Bring in your subjects, and write the scene. Use long and short sentences to simulate breathing and speaking patterns. Try to be suggestive at times, rather than direct. Use dialogue and narrative to deepen the exchange. Show the layers of love between the subjects by the way they kiss, their utterances to each other. Write with strong nouns and verbs so that the reader *feels* the love. Your goal: for the reader to walk away from your scene with a heightened heart.

"To write a good love letter, you ought to begin without knowing what you mean to say, and to finish without knowing what you have written."
  — Jean-Jacques Rousseau, author, *Reveries of a Solitary Walker*

NOVEMBER 10
PLOT LINES: Character-Driven Issues

A major part of good plotting is to match specific issues with characters most likely to harbor them. Make sure your characters' personalities and tendencies are consistent with the issues they undertake. Or, if you have unpredictable characters, assure that the issues are plausible, within the realm of reason.

Look at two or three characters in your story. Examine the issues in your plot. Which characters bring forth these issues? How do they handle them? What issues do your characters bring to the story?

Seamlessly integrate characters and their issues. These are the behavioral tendencies that drive the plot.

"If you focus on who the people in your story are, if you sit and write about two people you know and are getting to know better by day, something is bound to happen."

— Anne Lamott, author, *Tender Mercies*

Signs:
Scorpio • Snake • Reed
Featured Website/Blog:
http://www.romancejunkies.com

NOVEMBER 11
WRITING THE 'OTHER' SENSES: Balance

Freewrite in your journal or on your computer about a person or character's relationship with balance. Do they tilt to one side when they walk? Lean their head one way or the other when listening? What is their state of emotional and spiritual balance? Are their lives balanced? How do they adjust to difficult situations? How is their outer balance affected by heights? Depths? Do they lose "center," or balance, when they become excited or angry?

"Caress the detail, the divine detail."

— Vladimir Nabokov, author, *Lolita*

Signs:
Scorpio • Snake • Reed
Featured Website/Blog:
http://www.romancejunkies.com

SELF-PROMPTS:

NOVEMBER 12
THE INVERTED PYRAMID

One of the first lessons aspiring reporters learn in journalism school and newspaper offices is to write in inverted pyramid style. While this style is the polar opposite of narrative writing, it prompts the writer to insert the most important facts and details first: "Most important facts up top, B matter down below; we cut from the bottom-up." Thus, the origin of its name.

The inverted pyramid style is an effective exercise device to curb overwriting, and to organize details and scenes so that they keep moving.

For a day, let's occupy a newspaper desk. Think of something that happened today (or yesterday). Write down the 10 facts that best describe and illustrate the event or occurrence. Prioritize them in order of importance. Write a 250- to 400-word story, with a strong *lead* — the most defining fact. Then write your story, inserting all nine of the other important facts. Don't elaborate; just connect the facts with crisp description and good transitions. Close with a strong *tag* – a parting comment or fact.

"Probably never before in human history have so many been so keenly aware of what our troubles are and what causes them and what can be done about them…great things for a writer to explore and do something with."
— Edward Abbey, author, *The Monkey Wrench Gang*

Signs:
Scorpio • Snake • Reed
Birthdays:
Anne Parrish (b. 1888)
Marjorie W. Sharmat (b. 1928)
Tracy Kidder (b. 1945)
Featured Website/Blog:
http://www.midwestbookreview.com

NOVEMBER 13
PLOT LINES: Complication Ladder

SELF-PROMPTS:

What intrigues you more—someone who has led a problem-free life, or someone who has walked tough, adventurous, colorful roads and come through to tell the story?

Oral and written storytelling thrive on complications. Readers *crave* the next complication, the next issue in which they can immerse with you and see if your (or a character's) solution matches their way of handling it.

Add a complication to the life of one of your characters today. Pull it out of the blue. Make it sudden—a car crash, visit from an old love interest, out-of-town promotion that involves moving the family, sudden death of a close friend. Introduce it by writing a long paragraph that describes the complication and where it originated. End with a dramatic, declarative sentence, such as: "Bruce stared into the mirror. His open mouth swallowed back."

"I like to think of what happens to characters in good novels and stories as knots—things keep knotting up. And by the end of the story—readers see an 'unknotting' of sorts, a reproduction of believable emotional experiences."
— Terry McMillan, author, *Waiting to Exhale*

Signs:
Scorpio • Snake • Reed
Birthdays:
Robert Louis Stevenson (b. 1850)
Nathaniel Benchley (b. 1915)
Featured Website/Blog:
http://www.midwestbookreview.com

SELF-PROMPTS:

NOVEMBER 14
MY JOURNAL, MY GOLDMINE

I have two chests stuffed with 32 years of journals—about 100 notebooks. They are full of ideas, word experiments, deepest secrets and feelings, facts, dialogue, interior monologue, contemplative writing, manic writing, poems, songs, and the beginnings of countless stories, essays and novels. By now, I might have 15,000 ideas in my journals—some good, many useless, with a select few gold nuggets waiting for me to rediscover them.

As a working writer, your journal may be your most important possession. Make it your private goldmine, your laboratory. Write material you never imagined committing to print — deepest secrets and fantasies, crazy observations, newly invented words, doodles, new ideas … explorations and adventures you've undertaken. Write the good, bad and ugly. If you don't test the new material, how will you write about it with authority and authenticity later?

Use your journal for every writing adventure you want to take. Fill it with ideas, visions, perceptions. Make it your most indispensable resource.

Signs:
Scorpio • Snake • Reed
Birthdays:
P.M. Mart (b. 1899)
P.J. O'Rourke (b. 1947)
Featured Website/Blog:
http://www.midwestbookreview.com

"When I write in my journal I'm not just writing back at me, I'm justifying the day, and I'm asking questions, and I'm going on intellectual sorties without having to worry about sounding silly."

— Gail Godwin, author, *Queen of the Underworld: A Novel*

SELF-PROMPTS:

NOVEMBER 15
AN HOUR TO…

What if someone told you that you had one more hour to write? Or to live? Or to dance, sing, play basketball, run, garden, play with the kids, visit your best friend or love, or shop?

We've heard this rhetorical question countless times. Let's answer it while armed with a pen and our clearest, deepest thoughts. Write about how you would spend that hour, with a twist: Think of the one activity that defines you, the activity at which you dream of perfection. Use this "final hour" to rise to the highest height of who you are, the moment you are swept off the summit while in your personal glory. Go the final step. *Know* what 100 percent looks and feels like.

Refer to this essay every time you are unsure of what you're seeking. Also see if you can incorporate an "hour to live" scenario into an existing piece, or write something new that addresses it.

Signs:
Scorpio • Snake • Reed
Birthdays:
Marianne Moore (b. 1887)
Featured Website/Blog:
http://www.writerthemag.com

"O creator of being, grant us one more hour to perform our art and perfect our lives."

— Jim Morrison, musician, poet, author, *The Lords and the New Creatures*

NOVEMBER 16
PLOT LINES: Discovery!

SELF-PROMPTS:

I recently moved decades of accumulated books, art works, files, photographs, heirlooms and old articles and stories I wrote into my new home office. To see some of these things again about which I'd forgotten…what a thrill! The love of discovery resides within me just as strongly as when I was a nine-year-old hiking through forests.

Discovery is crucial to plot. Your characters will make discoveries in themselves, or in whatever they might be investigating or seeking. By seeding these discoveries throughout your story, you create many places to advance the plot and add further intrigue to your piece.

Take your character, or characters, through a discovery. Add a scene in which they find something—whether an object, or a characteristic or hidden secret about another person. Or themselves. *Show* the discovery. Write how it feels, first impressions, first thoughts. Where will the discovery lead? Write it out.

"Examine nature accurately, but write from recollection, and trust more to your imagination than to your memory."
— Samuel Taylor Coleridge, author, *Rime of the Ancient Mariner*

Signs:
Scorpio • Snake • Reed
Birthdays:
Jose Saramago (b. 1922)
Featured Website/Blog:
http://www.writerthemag.com

NOVEMBER 17
LISTEN, LISTEN, LISTEN

SELF-PROMPTS:

Try something very simple…yet very challenging. Find a sound or group of sounds you have never really listened to, or that you haven't heard in many years. Sit down, close your eyes, and *listen*. Listen for rhythm, tone, subtleties, and amplitude. Listen to how the sound moves, how its volume changes, how it informs you when the wind and distance start to sweep it away. Become so immersed that you embody the advice of Beat novelist Jack Kerouac (*On The Road)*: "Be submissive to everything, opening, listening."

Grab your journal or computer, and write what you experienced. When finished, go into a work-in-progress, or a story or essay you'd like to write, and find or develop a scene that involves listening. Either write the scene anew, instilling the depth you just experienced from your period of listening, or enhance an existing narrative with this deeper observation.

"For now, I'll just be here, alone, watching and listening."
— Susan G. Wooldridge, author, *Poemcrazy*

Signs:
Scorpio • Snake • Reed
Featured Website/Blog:
http://www.writerthemag.com

Signs:
Scorpio • Snake • Reed
Birthdays:
Jessamyn West (b. 1902)
Margaret Atwood (b. 1939)
Alan Dean Foster (b. 1946)
Featured Website/Blog:
http://www.mywriterscircle.com

SELF-PROMPTS:

NOVEMBER 18
WRITING THE 'OTHER' SENSES: Movement

Movement is a fascinating *sense,* one that can be explored forever in writing. Movement reflects a person's comfort level with their outside environment.

Write about someone you know, and integrate answers to these questions: Does the person flow, move with grace? Or nervously? Is he or she in a hurry? Plodding along? Or keeping an even pace? How long or short is the person's walking stride? How does he or she run when pressed for time? How slow or fast (and *how*) does the person move his or her hands when speaking? How does the pace of movement change when the person is happy? Sad? Excited? Depressed? In love? Recently out of love?

"You must write on the human breath. You should write the way you breathe."

— James Joyce, author, *Ulysses*

SELF-PROMPTS:

NOVEMBER 19
PLOT LINES: Doin' The Twist

The twist funnels surprise into your story. It emerges at a key plot point to send the story in another direction—or change the reader's opinion of a character.

Twists are both fun and enticing. Have your star football player admit he'd rather practice yoga all day (true story: ask Miami Dolphins star Rickey Williams). Have an old boyfriend or girlfriend walk in and say that they still love you. Trot out the commander of the alien planet bent on your destruction … and see that he's human. Walk down a mountain path … into an enclave of people who weren't supposed to be alive. Or a spiritual retreat imbued with deepest love and compassion.

Build your twist by creating a scene at which the key people will be present. Next, have a character say or do something—or witness an event—that unsettles the story, twists it around, and creates a different perception. Write until you've just sprung the most delicious secret or surprise.

Signs:
Scorpio • Snake • Reed
Featured Website/Blog:
http://www.mywriterscircle.com

"What do you do when you've done everything that comes 'naturally'? It's really more exciting after that point."

— Eve Shelnutt, author, *The Writing Room*

NOVEMBER 20
A LYRICAL HISTORY

Many people find history fascinating, while others find it boring and stilted to a narrow point-of-view. Often, the writing makes the difference. A fun way to bring our own history to life—and to use in our work—is by creating lyrical poetry from it. Songwriter and 1960s activist/musician Ed Sanders of The Fugs turned lyrical epics into an art form and a dozen books.

Recall an event that sends a charge through you. Write out the images the experience conjures. Write what you did, how you acted/reacted—only the movements. Describe features of the place—only the physical description. When you're finished, pull all of these sentences and phrases together into a lyrical poem.

"Fame to me is not writing a bestseller, but knowing that someone, somewhere is reading one of my books."

— May Sarton, author, *At Eighty-Two: A Journal*

Signs:
Scorpio • Snake • Reed
Birthdays:
Nadine Gordimer (b. 1923)
Donald Hall (b. 1928)
Don DeLillo (b. 1936)
Featured Website/Blog:
http://www.mywriterscircle.com

NOVEMBER 21
WRITING LOSS

It happens: someone we know and love dies. How do we cope and move on? As writers, we can process loss through our pens and computers—and create deep emotional content from that experience. Since most literature either deals with love or death, or both, our ability to write loss is a valuable asset.

Think of the most recent person you've lost. Why does the world feel emptier? What characteristics made the person so special? What do you miss most about your relationship? How did the person handle the final months? Or was death sudden? What was *your* last visit with the person like? What legacy did the person leave? What thoughts and feelings have come to you since the person passed—and where have they led? Follow every thought and every feeling to the end of its string, and write it down. Cry. Sniffle. Shake your head. Be raw, red, sad and angry. This is not only grief processing, but also rich material gathering.

Well-written pieces will spread tears, grief and sadness across a page—but also seeds of hope that the departed one's legacy will live on. Write loss in your chosen genre or form.

"I've come to realize that almost everyone over a certain age has lost someone — through death or distance or some kind of emotional struggle — whom they long to have back in their lives."

— Margo Livesey, author, *House on Fortune Street*

Signs:
Scorpio • Snake • Reed
Birthdays:
Isaac Singer (b. 1902)
Featured Website/Blog:
http://www.sparknotes.com/writing/style

Signs:
Sagittarius • Snake • Reed
Birthdays:
George Eliot (Mary Ann Evans)
(b. 1819)
Andre Gide (b. 1869)
Featured Website/Blog:
http://www.sparknotes.com/writing/style

SELF-PROMPTS:

NOVEMBER 22
PLOT LINES: Realization and Recognition

Characters are more than creatures of action and automatons that move plot. They walk into a story with the sum of their lives, experiences, ways of doing things and viewpoints. Once inside the story, they change, realize new things, recognize old or new ways, and grow as the book evolves. Their realizations and recognitions happen at important times. Their self-awareness usually serves the theme, and works toward the resolution of the central conflict(s).

Look at your story, creative non-fiction piece or essay. What will your characters or subjects realize or recognize? Write a scene in which one character *realizes* something that can change his/her course of action in the story. Have that character discuss with another, and *recognize* elements of self, or the outside world, that fed that realization. Then see how you can apply it to your story.

"The suspense of the novel is not only in the reader, but in the novelist, who is intensely curious about what will happen to the hero."

— Mary McCarthy, author, *The Group*

NOVEMBER 23
BRAIDED NARRATIVE

Good writers and journalists weave bits of historical information into their stories, giving the piece color, perspective and richness of detail. I call this technique "braided narrative," because when past, present and future are woven together masterfully, the story reads and feels like a taut, well-braided rope of various colors.

Let's write some braided narrative. Think of a news issue (local to international) that affects you today. Write it down. Think of several historical facts about that issue. Write those down. Ponder three possible outcomes of the issue; more specifically, how it will impact your life. Jot 'em down.

Take your items and weave a few pages together. Open with an anecdote that shows its impact on you today. Go into the issue's history; write a paragraph tracing the issue from then to now. Finish your essay by showing the possible future outcomes. Practice this technique; it leads to quality non-fiction that readers and editors love.

Signs:
Sagittarius • Owl • Reed
Featured Website/Blog:
http://www.sparknotes.com/writing/style

"I like to braid together bits of languages from different traditions. I pull from ancient sources and bring back into the contemporary. I work to make sure we deeply recognize our past."

— Arthur Sze, poet, author, *The Redshifting Web*

NOVEMBER 24
STUFFING THE TURKEY

We live in a society where emotion and drama are celebrated, but our *readers* will best remember the stories and books we write that challenge their minds, prod them to see things in a new way, create thought and growth.

Let's enrich our prose. Write about a topic that interests you, or one in which you are involved. In your home library, look for a book on the subject. Try to resist Googling, at least for this exercise. Research your topic, and find four or five things you didn't know about the subject. Write your research into the prose in a way that evokes more thought; choose your facts carefully

Feed your readers the most delicious literary candy they can imagine, but make it as nutritious as megavitamins soaked in bee pollen.

"I am looking for the novelists whose writing is an extension of their intellect rather than an extension of their neuroses."
— Tom Robbins, author, *Fierce Invalids Home from Hot Climates*

Signs:
Sagittarius • Owl • Reed
Birthdays:
Arundhati Roy (b. 1961)
Featured Website/Blog:
http://www.thoughts.com

NOVEMBER 25
PLOT LINES: Spicy Sub-Plots

Tangents or spin-offs, complications or issues in the plot contain their own motives, conflicts and dramatic climaxes. They can stand as short stories away from the large plot while remaining interdependent to the overall story. It's almost impossible *not* to write spin-offs in first draft, when the creative mind jets in all directions. The trick is to decide which of these sub-plots can work in your story, and which need to be trimmed.

Use a spin-off to create a sub-plot. Birth the situation from a point in your story. Take the character in this other direction, either through narrative or dialogue. When this spin-off reaches its resolution or climax, return the character to center stage or walk him or her off-stage. Notice how the sub-plot enriches your story.

"If writing is thinking and discovery and selection and order and meaning, it is also awe and reverence and mystery and magic."
— Toni Morrison, author, *Beloved*

Signs:
Sagittarius • Owl • Elder
Featured Website/Blog:
http://www.thoughts.com

NOVEMBER 26
RECIPES

New pieces of writing can be daunting. We have lavish ideas, we know where we want to start, and our creative mind surges with energy ... then what? How do we corral everything that is possible into our next story, essay or book?

One approach comes from the cookbook—literally. Plan out your next piece of writing as though it were a recipe. Write down the "ingredients" — characters, setting, plot/action, known twists. Feel how they will work together in your creative mind. Then write out a 100-word recipe for the story that shows how you're going to blend and cook these "ingredients" into a fine literary casserole or cake. Tweak your recipe until it gives you a direction that you can follow. Then cook your next masterpiece.

"The kitchen is a place that sharpens us. It's a place that wakes us up. Our sense of smell becomes keener. We taste with greater subtlety. We see with more clarity and our movements become quick and sure."
— Bettina Vitell, author, *A Taste of Heaven and Earth*

Signs:
Sagittarius • Owl • Elder
Birthdays:
Charles Schulz (b. 1922)
Featured Website/Blog:
http://www.thoughts.com

NOVEMBER 27
WRITING THE 'OTHER' SENSES: Warmth-Temperature

One of our most common figures of speech comes from the 1960s: "She's cool." But what does 'cool' mean? That she's got a low body temperature? That she's composed in all situations? Or that she's warm, engaging, friendly and a pleasure to hang out with?

The sense of warmth-temperature can be used to establish one's comfort level and reflect their natural emotional thermometer. To say a person is 'hot-blooded' can mean hot-headed and/or warm-skinned. When we refer to someone as cold, we think of them as emotionally aloof or distant. Call to mind your characters, featured non-fiction subjects, or someone you know. Do they run hot or cold? Do they react (hot) or respond (cool) to a confrontation or provocative remark? Do they put on or pull off a sweater when they walk into a 65-degree room? Does their spoken language contain more allusions to coolness, or to warmth? Are their eyes hot and focused, or cool and dreamy?

"I write to exorcise my demons. I write because it gives me focus. I write to create beauty...I write because writing is sexy. I write because writing is renewal. I write to find out who I am. I write because it is a positive force...I write to explore vicariously lives different from my own."
— Eudora Welty, author, *The Optimist's Daughter*

Signs:
Sagittarius • Owl • Elder
Birthdays:
James Agee (b. 1909)
Gail Sheehy (b. 1937)
Featured Website/Blog:
http://www.writersonlineworkshops.com

NOVEMBER 28
PLOT LINES: Climactic Moments

Each major complication in a novel or non-fiction story will have a peak moment—its own dramatic climax. After the characters set off to deal with the complication, the whole story builds to the resolution, the high point, the most intense scene. You know you've written an effective climactic moment when the main character in that scene learns something and changes forever in some way. Then, the story pivots off that point into a new, or enhanced, direction.

Write a climactic moment. Bring a character and his/her complication toward its peak. Use short, dramatic sentences. Put us in the character's body and senses. Express the climactic action, *as it would happen in real life.* Combine narrative and dialogue—and dramatic punctuation. Show how and why change was provoked in the character.

"When the plot flags, bring in a man with a gun."
— Raymond Chandler, author, *Farewell My Lovely*

Signs:
Sagittarius • Owl • Elder
Birthdays:
William Blake (b. 1757)
Featured Website/Blog:
http://www.writersonlineworkshops.com

NOVEMBER 29
THROW YOURSELF INTO THE FIRE

The more we sit back and wait for inspiration, the less inspiration we will receive. Conversely, the more we seize inspired moments with gusto, the more frequently inspiration will visit us. *Inspire* is an active verb. It returns as much energy as we give it.

When an inspiration, deep fear or strong feeling hits you, throw yourself into the fire. Grab pen and paper, and pour out everything that follows. Draw, sketch or write; whatever gets it out fastest. Treat every second as a precious commodity. When you're finished, set the piece aside, and let it percolate. Think about what you wrote, then slip in additional details.

Populate your writing with inspired and heightened moments.

"Write about what you're most afraid of."
— Donald Barthelme, poet-novelist, author, *The King*

Signs:
Sagittarius • Owl • Elder
Birthdays:
Louisa May Alcott (b. 1832)
C.S. Lewis (b. 1898)
Madeleine L'Engle (b. 1918)
Featured Website/Blog:
http://www.writersonlineworkshops.com

SELF-PROMPTS:

NOVEMBER 30
COMMAND (AND EXPAND) YOUR LANGUAGE

We may not deal with subjects that make it possible to re-create languages. However, we can always expand our language. We can find — or invent — words that speak to specific gestures, moments, voice inflections, and specks of circumstance.

Write a one-page vignette, journal entry, essay or story. Read your work, and identify words and phrases that aren't quite what your creative mind pictured. Highlight the words. Replace them with words and phrases that *feel and move through you,* words you extract from your life experience, words that resonate with their strength and ability to convey meaning. Work your phrases over and over, integrating the new words, until they form a richer, improved narrative.

Expand your written language, constantly.

"I go wherever it takes me. I try everything. I completely test it, jostle it, so I'm not locked in the rhetoric, or the order I wrote it in."
— Michael Ondaatje, author, *The Collected Works of Billy the Kid*

Signs:
Sagittarius • Owl • Elder
Birthdays:
Jonathan Swift (b. 1667)
Mark Twain (b. 1835)
M.T. Kelly (b. 1946)
Featured Website/Blog:
http://heartandcraft.blogspot.com

December

DECEMBER 1
PLOT LINES: Resolution

All complete stories arrive at resolution. We entered the story with the characters departing from an opening situation. We followed them as they made their way through their world (that you created), enjoying the motives, conflicts, twists, surprises, realizations, discoveries, complications and sub-plots along the way.

Now, we're ready for resolution. How will your story end? What resolution will the story and characters reach? What will happen?

Write a one-page ending to your story. Wrap up your loose ends with a solid, conclusive scene. The resolution can either be predictable, a bit of a surprise, or a shocking twist ending. Once the resolution feels right, use it as a compass to guide the rest of your story.

"I must feel that this story is well worth having lived and it is meaningful; that this life accomplished something; this life went through all the drama and against all of the obstacles and the stone walls…and emerged on the other side."

— Irving Stone, author,
Dear Theo: The Autobiography of Vincent Van Gogh

SELF-PROMPTS:

Signs:
Sagittarius • Owl • Elder
Birthdays:
Rex Stout (b. 1886)
Woody Allen (b. 1935)
Featured Website/Blog:
http://heartandcraft.blogspot.com

SELF-PROMPTS:

DECEMBER 2
QUILTING MEMORIES

Memories work in patterns. We remember one thing, and it leads to another. That triggers a thought of several experiences that affected us. We remember more. Before we know it, an entire pattern from our life has reappeared. What are your patterns? Sit down today, write down a core memory, and follow its offshoots. Write down one-sentence remembrances, then "quilt" them together and describe the pattern that forms. Address all new memories that spring up; add them to your mosaic.

"It's always good to remember where you come from and celebrate it. To remember where you come from is part of where you're going."
— Anthony Burgess, author, *A Clockwork Orange*

Signs:
Sagittarius • Owl • Elder
Birthdays:
T.C. Boyle (b. 1948)
Ann Patchett (b. 1963)
Featured Website/Blog:
http://heartandcraft.blogspot.com

SELF-PROMPTS:

DECEMBER 3
WHEN TRUTH IS THE HARDER CHOICE

To write well and connect with our readers, we must write authentically. To write authentically, we must write truthfully. To write truthfully, we often must exhume or explore places that are best left buried, or told in personal myths and fables, where the core truth is shrouded.

Sometimes, truth is the harder choice. Memoir writers know this well. What to do when the truth creates a deep hurt in a parent or sibling—but omitting it will result in a less authentic story? This is a question only you and your conscience can answer, but it's important to know *how* to write the truth when it's almost unbearably difficult.

Write the hard truth. Assimilate the words and their impact. Draw it out. When you feel yourself drifting toward distracting language, or switching subjects, then re-read your sentence, take a moment, and start writing again. Always circle back to that sentence, and write out the hard truth.

"A point of view can be a dangerous luxury when substituted for insight and understanding."
— Marshall McLuhan, author, *The Medium is the Massage*

Signs:
Sagittarius • Owl • Elder
Birthdays:
Joseph Conrad (b. 1857)
Featured Website/Blog:
http://www.writerstudio.com

DECEMBER 4
HANGING BY A THREAD: Suspend Your Reader

SELF-PROMPTS:

"I can't wait to read what happens next!"

Nothing builds the reader-writer partnership more than a book so full of suspense, mystery, intrigue and anticipation that it becomes painful to *stop* reading it. Think that's an exaggeration? Ask *Harry Potter* fans.

Write a short-short story or essay that creates a state of suspense. Build up to the suspense with crisp-moving prose or dialogue. Stop the paragraph or passage before resolving the matter, and switch quickly to the next paragraph. Make your suspense *breathless*. Close by resolving the situation or mystery and tying up any loose ends.

"What is a suspense novel? People in doubt, people mystified, people groping on their way from one situation to another, from childhood to middle age, from joy to sorrow."

— Daphne DuMaurier, author, *Rebecca*

Signs:
Sagittarius • Owl • Elder
Featured Website/Blog:
http://www.writerstudio.com

DECEMBER 5
WRITING THE 'OTHER' SENSES: Well-Being

SELF-PROMPTS:

We commonly think of Ego as a psychological term to describe how we see our place in the world, and among others. By writing it as a sense, we can *show* the person's feeling about himself or herself, and how the ego permeates everyday life.

Write a page in a character's or subject's point of view. Does he use a lot of personal pronouns to describe his observations? Or to extol his skills, talents and virtues? How opinionated or judgmental is he? Does she focus on what interests others in a crowded cocktail party? Or tug at her dress, cock her eyebrow, flick her hair and otherwise draw attention to herself? Does he give himself credit for ideas, intuitions and inspirations suddenly handed to him? Or does he give credit to a greater source — or the friend whose conversation sparked the idea?

Show your subject maneuvering the world with either a large or modest ego. The character can say it all without you ever writing, "He was an egomaniac," or "She was modest."

"I like the language of fiction to be very transparent, conventional even, so it reaches those gliding, slip-knot sequences of human interaction poetry can't easily get to."

— Tess Gallagher, author, *Moon Crossing Bridges*

Signs:
Sagittarius • Owl • Elder
Birthdays:
Rose Wilder Lane (b. 1886)
Calvin Trillin (b. 1935)
Featured Website/Blog:
http://www.writerstudio.com

DECEMBER 6
UNUSED BACK STORIES

SELF-PROMPTS:

If every author kept every draft or treatment of every manuscript he or she wrote, as well as every story he or she started and/or finished, the amount of material would dwarf actual published books, poems, essays, articles and stories. In fact, libraries, museums and universities across America are filled with many hundreds of such special collections.

Each character, incident and setting must have a developed back story. The setting of the book has a history, as do all businesses and homes. Many historical events conspired to arrive at the moment of Page One. Yet, for every 100 pages of back story notes we generate, we might use five to ten pages in the final draft. Maybe not even that much.

What to do with our unused back stories? Pore through old journal entries, manuscripts and notebooks. Locate back stories you wrote, but did not use. Cut and paste them into separate files or pages of a notebook. Take one of the pieces and rewrite it as a stand-alone story. Don't be surprised if it runs on its own legs.

Signs:
Sagittarius • Owl • Elder
Birthdays:
Cornelia Meigs (b. 1884)
Elizabeth Yates (b. 1905)
Featured Website/Blog:
http://www.literarymarketplace.com

"I always try to write on the principle of the iceberg, there is 90% underwater. If a writer omits something because he does not know it consciously, then there is a hole in the story."

— Ernest Hemingway, author, *The Sun Also Rises*

SELF-PROMPTS:

DECEMBER 7
PREGNANT PAUSES

Literature is full of pregnant pause moments that cause dramatic, suspenseful, excruciating, and agonizing delight for readers. They connote power on the part of the speaker, anxious anticipation on the part of the listener, and a brief, potent shot of the unknown to readers who can't wait to find out what happens next.

Write out a conversation between two people, or an essay in which you come upon something that frightens, alarms, worries or shocks. Write until you reach a dramatic climax. Instead of writing your next sentence … insert ellipses to create the pause. Then write the next scene, the next movement.

Create a dramatic moment … and show the aftermath in a succinct sentence or phrase after the ellipses. Make it habit-forming, and watch the *realistic* drama level of your work grow.

Signs:
Sagittarius • Owl • Elder
Featured Website/Blog:
http://www.literarymarketplace.com

"The pauses between the notes — ah, that is where the art resides!"

— Artur Schnabel, composer

DECEMBER 8
WRITTEN SUFFERING: Present Tense

One of the toughest writing tests is to bring personal suffering onto the page. For many, it's the last thing we want to explore. However, suffering creates and drives many great essays, memoirs and novels. Readers willingly journey to resolution with the author. No two writing subjects grab a reader's heart more than love and suffering, both of which add emotionally irresistible dimensions to your work.

Writing about suffering requires diving into the center of the struggle—where any and all negative energy, hurt, sorrow, grief and shame sits — and writing *from that place, outward, toward a place of realization, resolution and healing.* Suffering cannot be written externally. It is very much an inside job.

Think about something that recently (within the last month) caused suffering to you or a close friend or family member. Revisit the churning energy, and write until you can't squeeze out another word. Be as truthful and clear as possible. Paint a complete picture of the affliction or issue. Write your account in first person; write another's struggle as a fictional piece.

"Here I am, walking through my memories and all this grief comes through. To get in that space, you have to be strong. Part of writing these stories is getting in the middle, looking, and describing what's happening."
— Joe Loya, author, *The Man Who Outgrew His Prison Cell*

Signs:
Sagittarius • Owl • Elder
Birthdays:
James Thurber (b. 1894)
Bill Bryson (b. 1951)
Featured Website/Blog:
http://www.literarymarketplace.com

DECEMBER 9
WRITTEN SUFFERING: Past Tense

We all suffered in our past. We all became wiser for it. In writing about past suffering, we can put that acquired wisdom to work, along with the story of how we emerged from it. Enough time and distance has separated us from the suffering that we can convey the full feeling of the experience, without being submerged by the emotions.

Think of the biggest trauma or periods of suffering in your life. When did it happen? Were other people involved? How did it begin? What were your first choices once the suffering began? How did you proceed through it?

Write a piece about the growth, changes and lessons incurred during your period of greatest suffering. Provide time, setting, how you felt each stage along the way, what happened next, and the redemption: the healing and wisdom gained. Write as though someone in the world will use your words as a guiding hand to climb out of their situation.

"The reader recognizes that you're putting them in a place where you're suffering. They're suffering by witness."
— Joe Loya, author, *The Man Who Outgrew His Prison Cell*

Signs:
Sagittarius • Owl • Elder
Birthdays:
John Milton (b. 1608)
Laura Goodman Salverson (b. 1890)
Featured Website/Blog:
http://www.mattfacer.com/fridge

SELF-PROMPTS:

DECEMBER 10
WHEN OPPOSITES ATTRACT

Think of two real or imagined people who are polar opposites in beliefs, lifestyles, skills and just about everything else. Visualize or write down enough characteristics to form talking points for a conversation. Then cut them loose—two people in a room, bringing their opposing lives and views to the table. Write the dialogue to create points in common so they can find agreement. Make this exchange fun, spirited and snappy. Show the differences. Show points in common. Show the opposites attracting.

"What two people do in a room together seems to me the beginning of everything—everything familial, everything societal, everything political."
— Richard Ford, author, *Independence Day*

Signs:
Sagittarius • Owl • Elder
Birthdays:
Emily Dickinson (b. 1830)
Featured Website/Blog:
http://www.mattfacer.com/fridge

SELF-PROMPTS:

DECEMBER 11
WINTER'S FIRST BLAST

Winter's first blast serves notice — and sends us running for coats, shovels and hats. Whether a blizzard barrels into the Rockies or Great Plains, or a Gulf of Alaska monster storm buffets California with 20-foot waves and torrential rain, the first blast launches us into the forthcoming season. It heightens our senses.

Write about winter's first blast and how it impacts you. Create intimate relationships between you, the storm, and your surroundings—no separation if possible. Write images, similes or metaphors that link you to the immediate environment; i.e. "When the snow crusted on my face, I stood cold and concealed as arrowheads beneath the limestone bluff."

"I don't feel at home in the writing—I don't know where I am setting down my feet or where the characters are — unless I have this visual backdrop for them."

— Louise Erdrich, author, *Tales of Burning Love*

Signs:
Sagittarius • Owl • Elder
Birthdays:
Naguib Mafouz (b. 1911)
Aleksandr I. Solzhenitsyn (b. 1918) Grace Paley (b. 1922)
Featured Website/Blog:
http://www.mattfacer.com/fridge

DECEMBER 12
WRITING THE 'OTHER' SENSES: Well-Being

The sense of well-being wraps all 12 senses around a central question: How do you, or your subject, feel about your life and everyone and everything in it—right now?

Does your subject talk about lack, or abundance? Stand tall—or hunch? When confronted with a mistake, does his head remain straight—or does his chin fall to the chest? When she walks into a crowded room, do people gravitate to her? Or keep to themselves? How does he handle receiving sudden fortune—or losing it?

Show the answers to these questions in a descriptive character sketch or essay. *Show* the sense of well-being.

"The greatest revolution in our generation is that of human beings, who by changing the inner attitudes of their minds can change the outer aspects of their lives."

— Marilyn Ferguson, author, *The Aquarian Conspiracy*

SELF-PROMPTS:

Signs:
Sagittarius • Owl • Elder
Birthdays:
Gustave Flaubert (b. 1821)
Featured Website/Blog:
http://www.writeaway.co.uk

DECEMBER 13
SHOWER TALES

We love to dream, create and think while taking showers. Something about warm, pulsating water triggers our brains and opens our hearts. How many times have you felt shut down or uninspired, only to emerge from a shower ready to write for hours?

Next time you take a shower, keep track of everything you think about. After you towel off, write down your thoughts and ideas. See if they grow legs and voice, or just swirl down the drain. Perhaps they are missing pieces to a work-in-progress; if so, add them immediately. Later, try to further develop one or more of these ideas into a story— and don't hesitate to place a future character or subject in the shower.

"It all came together between the hand and the page."
— Samuel Beckett, author, *Waiting for Godot*

SELF-PROMPTS:

Signs:
Sagittarius • Owl • Elder
Featured Website/Blog:
http://www.writeaway.co.uk

DECEMBER 14
12 DAYS: What Moves You?

Today begins "The Twelve Days of Christmas" for those who celebrate the holiday. Regardless of which holiday we observe—Christmas, Hanukkah, Kwanzaa, or Eid—let's use these next Twelve Days to write stories, poems, essays and vignettes based upon our experiences this season, and memories of seasons past. Let's create our own stories to commemorate the holiday tradition with family and friends.

Today, answer the question, "What Moves Me This Holiday Season?" Is it the spirit of the season? The snow now beginning to fall outside? Friends or relatives who have been most significant in your life? Helping others? Hanging out with your friends and telling stories or singing songs? Write what moves you—and start a collection of writings for the season.

"Most of the books that I have written have been questions that I couldn't answer."

— Toni Morrison, author, *The Bluest Eye*

SELF-PROMPTS:

Signs:
Sagittarius • Owl • Elder
Birthdays:
Shirley Jackson (b. 1916)
Featured Website/Blog:
http://www.writeaway.co.uk

DECEMBER 15
12 DAYS: Gift of People

What event, person or circumstance stirs you and reminds you of the most important values and virtues of the season? Think of everything about the person or circumstance that embodies the spirit of giving and receiving, and commemorate them in an essay or story that includes the way that they have impacted you.

"The secret of artistic unity is to create for one person; anyone else who comes to it will sense this focus in the book."

— Kurt Vonnegut, author, *Player Piano*

SELF-PROMPTS:

Signs:
Sagittarius • Owl • Elder
Featured Website/Blog:
http://www.blogstreet.com

DECEMBER 16
12 DAYS: Stories of the Elders

SELF-PROMPTS:

Ask an older relative about the first holiday that he or she remembers — and create a short story around that setting. Research the time period to pin down scenic details, develop a character or two (either real or imagined), and write from the eyes of your older relative after listening to their story. Take yourself deeply into their first holiday, and show us both the thrill and the world of that time.

"I'm trying to write good books, make people laugh, make them cry, provoke them, make them angry, make them think if possible."
— Edward Abbey, author, *Down The River*

Signs:
Sagittarius • Owl • Elder
Birthdays:
Jane Austen (b. 1775)
Penelope Fitzgerald (b. 1916)
Arthur C. Clarke (b. 1917)
Featured Website/Blog:
http://www.blogstreet.com

DECEMBER 17
12 DAYS: Then and Now

SELF-PROMPTS:

Take your older relative's memoir-story and compare it with today's celebration. Note the differences in time, types of gifts given, foods cooked, parts of the holiday that the relative emphasizes. Also note the similarities — the way in which gifts are given, traditions honored (for how long?), decorations still used, and how the spirit of the holiday spreads throughout family and friends for days or weeks afterward. Create a "then and now" montage.

"The trick is leaving everything out but the essential."
— David Mamet, author, *Glengarry Glen Ross*

Signs:
Sagittarius • Owl • Elder
Birthdays:
Erskine Caldwell (b. 1903)
Featured Website/Blog:
http://www.blogstreet.com

SELF-PROMPTS:

DECEMBER 18
12 DAYS: Surprise!

Nearly 20 years ago, I received a harmonium for Christmas — an Indian keyboard for playing sacred bhajans, or chants. That single gift led to learning keyboards, harmonica, guitar, and writing music. Music is now a major part of my creative process—which includes writing lyrically. The present was a complete surprise, and it allowed me to tap a part of my creativity that I had left behind after fourth grade.

What is the most surprising present you've ever received? Who gave it to you, and why? How did it change your day, week, year—or life? Was it something for which you wished? What about it honored you as a person?

When you write this piece, use the gift as your departure point, and show how it took on a life of its own to influence and change your life.

Signs:
Sagittarius • Owl • Elder
Featured Website/Blog:
http://www.librarything.com

"I like to think of what happens to characters in good novels and stories as knots — things keep knotting up. And by the end of the story — readers see an 'unknotting' of sorts, a reproduction of believable emotional experiences."
— Terry McMillan, author, *How Stella Got Her Groove Back*

SELF-PROMPTS:

DECEMBER 19
12 DAYS: Wild Party

Fifteen minutes before the New Year, I stood inside a Twin Falls, Idaho home. The owner, a regionally known poet, was shooting spit wads at his friend, a Mayan archaeologist, with a 10-foot-long Amazon blow dart gun. In the background, partiers reveled as Gene Autry's voice crackled from a 1915 recording. On the wall sat a photograph of the same poet, and his son, bouncing off side boulders in their kayaks — *after* being pitched down a waterfall. I'll never forget it. *Craaaazy…*

Who is the craziest (in a positive way) person you've ever seen at a holiday party? What made the person seem crazy to you? What were their antics? How did they enliven the party? How did they embody the spirit of the day? Characterize them as they interacted with you. See if you can write a short story that puts your readers in the middle of both the party and the interaction. Read the story aloud, and refresh it until it captures the emotional charge on the night and the person.

Signs:
Sagittarius • Owl • Elder
Featured Website/Blog:
http://www.librarything.com

"Art is for entertainment, and if a book doesn't entertain, it's useless. Everything else must derive from that."
— T.C. Boyle, author, *The Road to Wellville*

DECEMBER 20
12 DAYS: Christmas Fantasy

Let's consider Christmas Day in the childlike spirit of two traditional favorites: *The Night Before Christmas* and *Rudolph the Red-Nosed Reindeer*. First, try to transport yourself into an excited child's mind frame. What was (is) your favorite Christmas dream or fantasy? Hanging on the North Pole with Santa? Building toys? Riding on the train that encircles the Christmas tree? Being buried in a White Christmas? Hijacking the reindeer?

From the eyes of a child, spend some time writing a story that places you in the Christmas setting you have always coveted or about which you've dreamed.

"One has the play side, the gift when it is mere gift, the unapplied gift; and the gift when it is serious, getting to business. And one relieves the other.
— Virginia Woolf, author, *To The Lighthouse*

SELF-PROMPTS:

Signs:
Sagittarius • Owl • Elder
Birthdays:
Richard Atwater (b. 1892)
M.B. Goffstein (b. 1940)
Sandra Cisneros (b. 1954)
Featured Website/Blog:
http://www.librarything.com

DECEMBER 21
12 DAYS: Chapbook of Images

Spend the next week capturing specific images of this holiday season in your journal — settings, faces, moods, storms, twinkling lights. Even if you only have a minute or two of free time, jot down a quick image, feeling or observation. Write several little vignettes or poems. String them together into a commemorative chapbook of your holiday season. See if you can assemble an 8- to 12-page chapbook, full of your impressions of this season.

"If you remove personal pronouns, let the images do the confessing."
— Timothy Liu, poet, author, *Say Goodnight*

SELF-PROMPTS:

Signs:
Sagittarius • Owl • Elder
Featured Website/Blog:
http://www.greatwriting.co.uk

SELF-PROMPTS:

Signs:
Capricorn • Goose • Elder
Birthdays:
William O. Steele (b. 1917)
Featured Website/Blog:
http://www.greatwriting.co.uk

DECEMBER 22
12 DAYS: Favorite Setting

Where is the coolest place you've spent the holiday season? Deep in a snowbound New Hampshire forest? Rubbing your toes in Hawaiian sand? Lighting a Menorah among four generations of relatives, with the exquisite smell of beef brisket permeating the air? Singing Christmas carols door-to-door in a small Midwestern town?

Take yourself to your favorite setting, and write a holiday travelogue. Show why you are completely enamored by the location. Remember to include the people with whom you spent that particular holiday.

"It is easy to fall in love with the things we've walked past so many times, because we realize that the world is offering itself to us like a lover longing for our embrace and recognition."

— Adriana Diaz, author, *Freeing the Creative Spirit*

SELF-PROMPTS:

Signs:
Capricorn • Goose • Birch
Birthdays:
Robert Bly (b. 1926)
Featured Website/Blog:
http://www.greatwriting.co.uk

DECEMBER 23
12 DAYS: Helping Hands

We all seek to extend helping hands to the less fortunate during this season. Remember the person who needed your help the most—and received it? What was his or her story? Did the person tell you, or did his or her eyes, gestures and appearance convey the story?

Recount the story, with your interaction as the plot line. Show the dance of giving and receiving in its most important form. Fictionalize the person's circumstances, if necessary, but capture the feeling and the meaning of your gesture—or an act of generosity that you witnessed.

"If the artist is touched by some social condition, what the artist creates will reflect that, but you can't force it."

— Susan Sontag, author, *The Volcano Lover*

DECEMBER 24
12 DAYS: Holiday Romance

During which holiday season were you immersed in the deepest love of your life? This season? Or another?

Take your spouse, partner or lover by the hand (literally or in words), walk to a fireplace, sit with each other, and write as if you're staring into your lover's eyes and every word beats from your heart. Go deep. Feel all. Embrace the love.

"Human beings are actually created for the transcendent, for the sublime, for the beautiful, for the truthful."

— Archbishop Desmond Tutu

SELF-PROMPTS:

Signs:
Capricorn • Goose • Birch
Birthdays:
Feodor Rojankovsky (b. 1891)
Noel Streatfield (b. 1920)
Stephenie Meyer (b. 1973)
Featured Website/Blog:
http://www.writehisanswer.com

DECEMBER 25
Christmas Day
12 DAYS: The Gift of Story

For our final holiday exercise, dig into your stocking of ideas. Pore through your journals of the past year, plus other sources that inspire you. Pull out five ideas that resonate with you today, and treat yourself to the special gift of storying out these ideas, either entirely or in preparation for a fast start to the next year.

"Science can explain us, but it can't save us ... story can."
— Mary K. Sandford, anthropologist

SELF-PROMPTS:

Signs:
Capricorn • Goose • Birch
Birthdays:
Charles J. Finger (b. 1869)
Johnny Gruelle (b. 1880)
Rod Serling (b. 1924)
Featured Website/Blog:
http://www.writehisanswer.com

SELF-PROMPTS:

DECEMBER 26
FINAL PAGE: Everything In?

You've worked for weeks or months—or more—on a first draft. Finally, the day arrives: When you stop writing today, you've done it! Off to the publisher and editor your manuscript goes!

Well … not exactly. The process of polishing and editing the book now begins. For the next four days, let's practice by running our work against a checklist of editing questions and steps.

Find a manuscript you wrote this year but haven't yet submitted for publication. First question: Is everything in? Does your piece contain all the stories, facts, dialogue exchanges or quotes, anecdotes and plot points that ran through your mind while writing? Identify areas where material is missing or needs further development, and jot notes in the margins of your printed manuscript.

"Just get it down on paper, and then we'll see what to do about it."
— Maxwell Perkins, editor to Ernest Hemingway and F. Scott Fitzgerald

SELF-PROMPTS:

DECEMBER 27
FINAL PAGE: First Edit

The goal of the first edit is to include everything essential to the story—and identify and remove the non-essential material. Most often, this involves rewriting the piece entirely. At the least, deep revision is required. This can be a gruesome process; Joyce Carol Oates shrank her epic novel, *Blonde,* from a 1,200-page draft manuscript to 752 pages.

Remove all non-essential material from your manuscript, any writing that does not advance the plot, relate to or deepen the characters. Sometimes, this will mean a single line; sometimes, a paragraph, page or more. Work in the material you added in your review, and revise or rewrite your piece by sticking to the essentials. Make sure the story makes sense, flows, and has a well-defined beginning, middle and ending.

"I'm certainly aware of the tension between speech and silence. After all, the act of writing is the transformation of the world into language."
— Scott Russell Sanders, author, *Hunting for Hope*

DECEMBER 28
FINAL PAGE: Revisions

Now that you've survived the cutting of your manuscript, let's dive into the fun. Revise your manuscript so that every element of your story is in proper sequence, and works with the elements before and after:

- The Beginning: Does your lead sentence and lead paragraph grab the reader?
- First Five Pages: Can we feel your narrative tone and voice, and understand the direction your story takes? Paint a picture into which the reader will leap. Waste no words.
- Is the action and narrative movement crisp and consistent?
- Are your characters unique? Are their motives and purposes for being in the story clear? Do they have distinct voices that we will know without you writing, "Susan said"?
- Are your paragraphs and sentences in the right order, or sequence? Cut your manuscript into pieces and rearrange, if necessary. I've done it several times; it works great.
- Is your point-of-view consistent and obvious in every scene?

"Read and revise, reread and revise, keep reading and revising until your text seems adequate to your thought."

— Jacques Barzun, author, *The House of Intellect*

Signs:
Capricorn • Goose • Birch
Featured Website/Blog:
http://www.getpublishedgetpaid.com

DECEMBER 29
FINAL PAGE: Polishing Act

Become as precise as a diamond jeweler. Polish your manuscript with this checklist:

- Are your verbs carefully chosen? Powerful? Do they drive the narrative? Make the vast majority of your verbs active, unless you're writing a scientific or academic paper.
- Do your nouns paint powerful, concrete pictures and images that enable the reader to easily imagine and visualize the story?
- Does *every* sentence advance the story? Did you use just enough words to convey the thought or action? Do your sentences sparkle?
- Have you read the dialogue or quotes aloud? Does it sound *perfect* to your ear and to your depiction of the characters?
- Are *all* grammatical, punctuation and spelling errors corrected? Have you spell-checked your piece on the computer? Did you proof it *after* you spell-checked it?

"You never have to change anything you got up in the middle of the night to write."

— Saul Bellow, author, *Herzog*

Signs:
Capricorn • Goose • Birch
Birthdays:
William Gaddis (b. 1922)
Featured Website/Blog:
http://www.getpublishedgetpaid.com

DECEMBER 30
WHAT A YEAR!

SELF-PROMPTS:

Signs:
Capricorn • Goose • Birch
Birthdays:
Rudyard Kipling (b. 1856)
Mary Higgins Clark (b. 1927)
Mercer Mayer (b. 1943)
Featured Website/Blog:
http://www.authorstart.com

Write down everything you remember from the most incredible or memorable year of your life. If an item sparks a cluster of memories, write them down. Keep writing until you can't remember anything else. Put the list away—then come back to it another day. See if the material sparks additional memories.

"A writer owes a debt of authenticity to his readers. Because of his profession he may go to the fountains of knowledge and drink as deeply as he wishes."
— Louis L'Amour, author, *Education of a Wandering Man*

DECEMBER 31
LAST DAY OF THE YEAR

SELF-PROMPTS:

Signs:
Capricorn • Goose • Birch
Birthdays:
Pamela Bianco (b. 1906)
Nicholas Sparks (b. 1965)
Featured Website/Blog:
http://www.authorstart.com

What did I write this year? Were my publishing goals met—or exceeded? Did I write as much in my journal, or pen as many letters, as I'd intended? What new forms or techniques did I try out—and then integrate into what I already know? What new authors did I read, or meet, or enjoy at a reading? What new types of scenes did I write with reckless abandon and major risk-taking—love scenes? Crime scenes? Horror scenes?

What did I confront through letters, essays, stories or characters? What new words did I learn? What writers did I read for the first time? What did I learn from a little child? Someone one or two generations older than me? Whose eyes captivated me the most? In what ways do I hope to grow as a writer and person next year?

"When I am ready to write a book, I write the ending first."
—Marcia Davenport, author, *Mozart*

Your Birthday

BONUS

TODAY IS YOUR BIRTHDAY: Honoring Thyself

As artists and creative beings, we owe it to ourselves to hold one day particularly sacred — our birthday. This is not about broadcasting your birthday to the world so you can receive accolades or gifts. Nor is it about trying to forget your day, or admitting your age (if you hide it). Today is the anniversary of the day you first appeared and breathed on this earth, the day the miracle of you left the womb.

Spend an hour or two in your journal, celebrating this most sacred of days. Journal your wishes, dreams, goals and coming adventures for the next year. Then find some friends or loved ones, go out for a nice dinner, blow out a candle — and celebrate!

"To love is to be part of the living world. To be loved is the most beautiful of dreams."

— Judith Chernaik, author, *Love's Children*

SELF-PROMPTS:

Featured Website/Blog:
http://www.authorstart.com

ALPHABETICAL INDEX OF EXERCISES

ACKNOWLEDGEMENTS

My deepest thanks to the writer's conferences, retreats, churches, libraries, colleges and universities, high schools, bookstores and other venues that have given me a place to teach and share what I love for the past twenty years. Most of all, thanks to the thousands of writers who have attended my workshops and classes. You were the first to try these exercises; this book bears your signature in many ways.

A special thanks to the author-teachers who have given me much of their time and energy, allowed me to visit and/or guest teach in their facilities or classes, and provided otherwise wise counsel: Regina Merrick, Stephen B. Gladish, Harvey Stanbrough, Sheila Bender, Meg Files, Dr. Terra Pressler, Missy Feller, Dr. Jayashree Alvarez, Carol Gray, and Andres Torres. Also, to the conference directors who have invited me in, time and again, wondering what the Energizer Bunny would come up with next: Michael S. Gregory and Wes Albers/Southern California Writers Conference; the late Ingrid Reti/San Luis Obispo Writers Conference; Penny Porter and Barbara Stahura/Society of Southwestern Authors; Quang Bao/Asian-American Writers Workshop; and Tony and Lillian Todaro/Greater Los Angeles Writers Society.

Many thanks to the magazines, book publishers, websites, newspapers, documentary producers, ad agency executives, and others who have published my works. I am celebrating my 40th anniversary as a professional writer in 2016; it never would have happened without you.

I'll be forever grateful to my teachers and librarians, who let an obnoxious creative firestorm erupt in their classes time and again, seeing what might be possible: Kenneth Youngdale, Roger Maioroff, Bobbie Hoder, Gerry Spangler, Dr. Bev Bosak, Tom Robertson, Steve Scholfield, Bill Missett, George Salvador, Jim Kempton, and Dr. Don Eulert. A very deep thanks to my most recent mentor, Gary Snyder, a Beat writing icon, one of the greatest poets alive, and winner of the 1974 Pulitzer Prize for *Turtle Island* — a book I bought 35 years before we became next-door neighbors and friends.

Now to the man who believes so much in *The Write Time* that he's bringing it out in this very special second edition, Paul Burt of Open Books Press. Paul and I first met in 2007, and found our mutual passion for writing matched by our passion for education. After all, isn't the whole point of school to kindle a lifelong love of learning that we carry through to deep, fulfilling lives? Paul, his wife Dee, and I share this vision. I hope you see it reflected in each of these pages.

To my collaborator in *The Write Time,* Melissa Jenkins, much gratitude for your hard work, and in continued admiration of your writing ability.

Finally, to my family, friends and clients, thank you for believing in me as a writer, editor, and teacher. And to my writing students at Ananda College: Yes, I really am crazy enough to bring out 366 exercises! I hope everyone who uses this book and sees the "Writing the River" excerpt has as much fun as you did.

PHOTO CREDITS
Cover Design - Min Gates
Introduction - Joyce Thomas
Facing Page - Robert Yehling
January-May, July-August, October-December - Robert Yehling
September - Theresa Jenkins
June - Paul Burt
Bonus Exercise - Stephen B. Gladish
The Write Time Live! - Cynthia Wang
About the Author - Wayne Millikan; Joyce Thomas

ABOUT *THE WRITE TIME*

Whether you're a long-time professional seeking to hone your skills, an aspiring professional writer, one who writes for fun and personal satisfaction or a student writer in middle school, high school or college, *The Write Time* serves as your hub of your interactive, ongoing 21st century writing experience:

Companion Websites and Blogs: *The Write Time* reaches across the Internet through a pair of dedicated websites. *The Write Time* Companion (www.thewritetimecompanion.com) will offer information on contests, workshops, book festivals, readings, conferences and other events. The site also contains a list of recommended books for writers, a sit-down interview with the author and publisher, a website directory for the authors quoted in *The Write Time,* as well as their latest books and links to You Tube interviews. *The Write Time* Companion also houses the official blog for *The Write Time* discussions, 366writing.wordpress.com.

For those interested in trying additional exercises, new material will be available beginning in Fall 2009 at www.thewritetimeexercises.com.

You can also find updated information on the publishing site, www.penandpublish.com, and the author's site, www.wordjourneys.com.

Workshops: The author will present *The Write Time* and teach writing, editing and book marketing workshops nationwide to professional writers' conferences and organizations, working writers' groups, libraries, colleges and universities, high schools and middle schools, bookstores, writing and retreat centers. Contact info@penandpublish.com or bob@wordjourneys.com if you're interested in presenting *The Write Time* for your organization, business, group or school.

Contests: Beginning in Fall 2009, we will sponsor seasonal contests pertaining to exercises and themes found in *The Write Time*. Prizes will vary from cash prizes and scholarships to the opportunity to be published in *The Write Time Anthology,* a collection of the best writings inspired by the exercises. Check in with www.penandpublish.com for further details, rules and deadlines.

Bulk Orders: Need *The Write Time* for your school, group or organization? Contact Pen & Publish at 866-326-7768 or info@penandpublish.com for details on our bulk purchase program and discounts.

COMING MAY 2016

The Long-Awaited Return of the Companion to *The Write Time*

Writes of Life: Using Personal Experiences in Everything You Write
Winner of the Independent Publisher Book Award

How do you transform your life experiences, relationships, dreams, adventures, discoveries, and memories into wonderful stories of all lengths?

How do you utilize them in novels, essays, songs, poems, memoir, journalism, self-help, teaching and educational materials, short articles, and most forms of business writing?

How can writing your life experiences change and transform *your* life?

In *Writes of Life*, author Robert Yehling draws on all 40 years of professional writing experience to deliver a tight, 120-page narrative, complete with thought-provoking questions, exercises, and more than 50 suggestions to expand your writing reach with the material you know best—your own experiences. He combines dozens of examples woven into published works, with techniques that can be utilized today.

Available from Open Books Press and everywhere books are sold on May 31, 2016

For $3 off of *Writes of Life*, visit:
www.openbookspress.com/books/writes-of-life.php
and use coupon code **WOL2016**.

PRACTICE PRESENCE

One day, noted naturalist and author Joseph Cornell issued an assistant to a classroom of Navajo students in Northern Arizona: "Draw a picture of yourself." The protégé of the great John Muir expected to see what he might observe in a typical American classroom: a stack of stick figures, exaggerated portraits, and other depictions that showed a child's one-pointed relationship to self.

That's not what happened in one portrait. The student was a small figure in the middle of canyons, cornfields, fluffy cotton clouds, a bolt of lightning and family members. His self-portrait completely connected with his surrounding environment. In the boy's view, the high Arizona desert and everything in it was as much a part of his body as his nose and mouth.

When I first heard this story, I shuddered inside. It spoke of the reverence Native Americans have given nature for thousands of years. They derive their spirituality, cosmology, medicine, sustenance, lodging and relationship from nature; the natural world *is* their life, individually and collectively. "For us, there is not just this world, there's also a layering of others. Everything has presence and meaning within this landscape of timelessness," Muskogee author and poet Joy Harjo wrote.

Moreover, the boy's drawing illustrates the power of presence—how being *present,* right now, encompasses the world that feeds, nurtures and inspires us. It also is the one and only place in mind and spirit from which to write effectively and persuasively.

A saying I learned long ago: "The point of power is in the present." Focus, attention, concentration, creativity and potential join forces at this point. Only through presence can we enter the Creative Dream. Only through presence can we truly observe something, derive a relationship between it and our lives – or our subjects or characters' lives – and write something fresh and new.

The little Navajo boy encompassed everything that fed him, and everything to which his mind and spirit attached: "Center everywhere, circumference nowhere," Indian poet Rabindranath Tagore wrote. Presence is *not* worrying about tomorrow's errands or yesterday's parent-teacher conference, nor is it daydreaming about your weekend plans or the incredible nature hike you took last month. When you write, direct your focus on your story as it rolls through your fingertips *right now.*

A quick exercise: For the next 3-5 minutes, write down everything you are thinking, feeling, observing, desiring. Don't lift your pen off the paper, and don't go back to correct a sentence or even change a word. Just write. When you're finished, read your piece and see how much of your mind is focused on the present moment. Are your verbs in present tense? Are you writing about the here-and-now, the been-and-gone, or the not-here-yet?

ABOUT THE AUTHOR

ROBERT YEHLING began reading when he was four; writing came two years later. A native of Carlsbad, Calif., became a newspaper journalist at age 16 in 1976. In the years since, he has written or co-written 17 books, edited numerous magazines, taught high school and college writing, and presented at writing events and conferences. message: 'The easiest way to write is to pick up the pen write what you see in front of you. Every sentence can carry the entirety of your life experience within it; start from there and expand your world a little more.'

Yehling's books cross multiple genres (as do the exercises in *The Write Time*), but typically speak to that which inspires, informs, and enlightens. They include *Just Water*, the highly acclaimed biography of autistic surfing great Clay Marzo (2015: Houghton Mifflin Harcourt); *The Champion's Way* (2012: SwymFit Publications); and *When We Were The Boys* (2014: Taylor Trade), written with guitarist-singer-songwriter Stevie Salas, the former Smithsonian Institution music advisor. Yehling has written five collections of poetry and essays, most recently *Backroad Melodies* (2013: Tuscany Publishing). The predecessor to *The Write Time, Writes of Life,* won the 2007 Independent Publishers Book Award; the second edition will be released in Winter 2015-16 by Open Books Press. Yehling also co-edited *Freedom of Vision,* an anthology written by inmates; and wrote *Poetry Through The Ages,* an interactive journey through 5,500 years of western poetry (www.webexhibits.com/poetry, produced by the Institute for Dynamic Educational Advancement. He has worked on major projects with LucasFilm, NASA, *American Idol, Mr. Holland's Opus* star Richard Dreyfuss, and members of the Rock & Roll Hall of Fame. He is editor of *The Hummingbird Review* literary anthology.

In addition to writing, editing, mentoring and consulting, Yehling is a four-time Boston Marathoner and successful high school track and cross-country coach.

ABOUT THE COMPILER

MELISSA JENKINS was born in Oceanside, Calif. She moved to Kentucky at a young age, becoming enthralled with reading and writing as a student. After editing and writing for the Crittenden County (KY) High School newspaper, she began her professional career at Faircount International, working on magazines for the British Film Institute, Rolls-Royce, and late golf champion Payne Stewart. She has also been a contributor and assistant editor to the *Freedom of Vision* and *The Hummingbird Review* anthologies.

Melissa assembled and ordered all of the materials in *The Write Time,* often writing out the exercises to better determine location. The mother of three, she now works, writes, and lives in Portland, Ore.

CPSIA information can be obtained
at www.ICGtesting.com
Printed in the USA
BVHW062150120620
581226BV00003B/91